A Sense of Sexuality

for
JAMES R. ZULLO
colleague and friend

Books by the Whiteheads

A SENSE OF SEXUALITY

THE EMERGING LAITY

SEASONS OF STRENGTH

COMMUNITY OF FAITH

MARRYING WELL

METHOD IN MINISTRY

CHRISTIAN LIFE PATTERNS

A Sense of Sexuality

CHRISTIAN LOVE AND INTIMACY

Evelyn Eaton Whitehead
and James D. Whitehead

Doubleday

NEW YORK   LONDON   TORONTO   SYDNEY   AUCKLAND

Published by DOUBLEDAY, a division of Bantam Doubleday Dell Publishing Group, Inc., 666 Fifth Avenue, New York, New York 10103

DOUBLEDAY and the portrayal of an anchor with a dolphin are trademarks of Doubleday, a division of Bantam Doubleday Dell Publishing Group, Inc.

Library of Congress Cataloging-in-Publication Data
Whitehead, Evelyn Eaton
 A sense of sexuality: Christian love and intimacy
 Evelyn Eaton Whitehead and James D. Whitehead
    p. cm.
 Bibliography: p.
 Includes index.
 1. Sex—Religious aspects—Christianity.
I. Whitehead, James D. II. Title.
BT708.W44 1989   88-15675
241'.66—dc19   CIP

ISBN 0-385-23614-X

CONTENTS

Acknowledgments

Many people helped us write this book. Much of its content we developed in the good company of James Zullo. Jim is a psychologist, teacher, therapist, religious brother, colleague and friend. In all these ways he has deepened our understanding of the themes we treat here. With appreciation and affection, we dedicate this book to him.

Dee Ready edited the manuscript at several stages, showing us practical ways to uncomplicate our prose and simplify our sentences. Her criticism was always on target, her courtesy without fail. We are greatly in her debt. Several colleagues reviewed particular chapters, improving our work by their comments and suggestions. We thank especially Catherine Lacugna, Vern Arceneau, Josephine Caratelli, Michael Cowan, Ray Flachbart, Mercedes Iannone, Joseph Iannone, Alicia Lee, Judy and Ed Logue, and Kate Scholl.

Mary Ulrich, John Sinnwell, and Gene Ulrich took active interest in the book, sharing insights and resources from their own study and ministry. Gordon Myers has been a companion throughout the project. His professional work continues to instruct us in the dynamics of personal and social grieving; his friendship continues to show us the shape of faithfulness, compassion, and grace.

For all this, we are grateful.

June 1, 1988
E.E.W. and J.D.W.

Part One
The Possibilities

We are the body of Christ. What are the erotic possibilities of the body Christian? What sense do we make of our sexuality? In Part One we attempt to give voice to the wisdom of Christian experience in its testimony that sex is good, sex is mysterious, and sex makes promises.

The Christian vision expands the scope of love. The gospel brings good news for the body, rescuing sexuality from narrow understandings that limit eros to genital activity. The robust virtue of intimacy equips us for the wider challenges of love and work.

Part One concludes with a meditation on caritas—Christian charity. Here we trace the transformation of affection and passion into those durable charities of justice, reconciliation, and care.

1.

Making Sense of Sexuality

Christians have a sense of sexuality. It is a communal wisdom, rooted in the graciousness of God's creation and shaped by the witness of Jesus' life. For two thousand years Christians have struggled to believe the good news of the gospels—that God is among us, within us. Gifts of a loving Creator, our bodies are not barriers to grace. If we could truly accept this, then we would know God even in the ambiguous delights of our sexuality.

After Jesus died and was raised, his friends sensed that he was still present in their gatherings. "Now you together are the body of Christ" (I Corinthians 12:27), Paul proclaimed. As the body of Christ, the Christian community carries a shared wisdom about sex and love, a wisdom born of our efforts to have God's word shape our sexuality. This communal sense, which recognizes that we are accountable to one another and to the gospel, is not limited to formal pronouncements and received doctrines. Rooted in the daily practical decisions through which we try to love well, this fragile wisdom emerges from our frequent failures and our continuing hopes.

In this book we attempt to give voice to the wisdom of the body. We begin this chapter with four stories of sexual Christians. Then we name the yearning heard in these stories. Finally, we will look again at the image of the body of Christ. We view this metaphor in terms of an emerging wisdom of the body Christian, a seasoned sense of sexuality to which contemporary believers bear witness in their lives.

Christians and Their Sexuality: Four Portraits

Julie and I were married nineteen years ago yesterday. It seems more like ten years, but our three teenagers remind us that it is almost twenty. The weekend retreat announced in the parish bulletin last month looked like an opportunity to catch our breath and relax. We thought the time away would be a good chance for us to unwind. We thought that until we heard the question from the leader couple: "What was the biggest crisis in your marriage?"

We both knew the answer to this question but were reluctant to return to "the scene of the crime." It wasn't a dramatic crisis like alcoholism or sexual infidelity, but it was still very painful. Five years ago, on a very snowy night, we finally admitted that we had lost touch with each other. Our absorption in two jobs and three children had aided this gradual separation and had also disguised it. We admitted that we hardly talked; we got angry with each other for no apparent reason. We didn't share much of anything; we didn't even make love anymore. To outsiders we may have looked like a wonderful family, but underneath our marriage was dying.

We started seeing a good marriage counselor and began slowly to find our way back together. Old and stubborn habits, especially Julie's sarcasm and my tendency to withdraw, needed to be broken. We began to learn again how to talk about our feelings and fears, without punishing each other. We began to remember to thank each other for little things, to take the time to express affection. As we got to know each other again, we were surprised how much we had changed in fourteen years. We hadn't noticed each other changing, hadn't allowed for it. With the counselor we began to discover what fidelity means for us: to stay in touch, to nurture the commitment we have—not just for our children but for us as partners.

Some wounds remain from that crisis five years ago. But today we enjoy being together. We still have arguments but they are aboveboard and direct, and we find our way through them without much damage. We even look forward to the days ahead when our three children have flown the coop and we are on our own again. The weekend retreat was no picnic, but it was very good for us. It wasn't relaxing, but it was energizing. We are grateful for the crisis; it got our attention and started us on the task of rebuilding our love.

· · ·

I joined a religious community of sisters twenty-six years ago because I wanted to be a teacher and to become holy. In our early training program we were instructed not to form special friendships. As vowed religious, we were to love everyone, but not to show any particular affection for another individual. In the years that followed this early training (I entered the novitiate at seventeen), I learned to be very restrained in my emotions. I was seeking a deep relationship with Jesus Christ, and I saw the love of others as a hindrance to this goal. Celibacy protected me on this solitary journey.

For two decades I seemed to "forget" my body and my emotions. I don't think I hated my body; I just ignored it and the emotions that resided within it. When I fell in love at age thirty-eight, this well-constructed world disintegrated. Something both terrible and wonderful was happening: I was losing the control that had become the cornerstone of my religious life. I was being introduced to a very different God—a livelier, more affectionate, (dare I say it?) more feminine God.

With the crash of my well-protected lifestyle, I thought that my religious and celibate vocation was over. In time I found that it was not ending, but only changing. Now I have three very close friends with whom I delight in sharing my heart. With my dearest friend I have been learning—with some awkwardness—how to express affection in ways that respect my vow of celibacy. And I have, happily, become more a friend of my own body—this wonderful, lovely, neglected part of myself. I listen with less panic to its stirring, whether of anger or sexuality; I pay more attention to its hints about fatigue and loneliness. Celibacy is no longer just a way for me to hide from contact. I am aware in deeper ways how this commitment fits me, how my celibacy is a part of my own way of loving well. The affection of friends sustains me on days when I sorely miss being married and having children. In my teaching I feel fruitful. I will never be a parent, but I give thanks for the new life to which my ministry contributes. And I am most grateful for the affection that is such an exciting part of my life these days.

. . .

Dear Alice,

That was such a good talk on the phone last night. Your tough questions rattled me, but in a good way. When I woke this morning our conversation was continuing in my head. Here are some of my tentative responses.

I am able to say, for the first time, that I may not marry. I have been defensive about this until just recently; I think this was part of my curtness toward you last night. I had always assumed I would marry (don't all good girls?), even as I resisted my parents' growing pressure for me to "meet someone nice and settle down." I am becoming more comfortable with myself as unmarried. I like my life and feel that I can make a real contribution as I am. I really don't feel "incomplete."

What I miss most is any support for being single. At work I am seen as either a threat or someone to "hit on." Our parish does not seem much interested in anyone who is not married. It lavishes attention on the teenagers and is doing more for family life. Often I not only feel left out, but that I am, in some way, dangerous. Surely people don't think I am going to seduce someone's husband or some poor, defenseless youth! (Could they believe that I am really not all that interested?)

As a Catholic I find myself asking the question: What does it mean to be single and sexual? I have not chosen a celibate life. But I do not "sleep around." Is there any ground between these extremes of abstinence and promiscuity? Where can Catholics even have this conversation? Sex is such an all-or-nothing proposition for us. There may be some wisdom in this approach for teenagers (I'm not even sure that's true!) but what about mature adults?

It seems that as a relationship deepens, questions of sexual sharing arise as a natural part of this growth. In my experience this is neither irresponsible nor sinful. I suspect that many single Catholics have these experiences; my regret is that no one speaks about it. Will this ever change?

Thanks for listening to my ramblings. Call or write when you can. Love, Sue.

. . .

Last Christmas we received the worst possible surprise: our son Nicholas told us he is gay. Our response sounds funny now, but his mother and I tried to talk him out of it! Surely he was mistaken! Not our son! When Nick assured us that he had been aware of his sexual orientation since junior high school, we refused to believe him. There was a terrible scene and our anger drove him out. For a week a thick cloud hung over the house. The two of us spent all our energy avoiding the topic. Finally we couldn't stand it anymore. We went to our good friend at the parish, Sister Ann.

When we gave our embarrassing news, Ann was neither astonished nor alarmed. We were so relieved that we spent the next hour expressing all our feelings of dismay. When we had finished, Ann asked a simple question: "How is Nick different now that you know he is gay?" This confused us both: everything is different! But Ann pushed on: "Is Nick promiscuous?" No. "Is he selfish, immature, turned in on himself?" No. "Then what is different?" We weren't sure. This was all we could handle that day. As we left, we carried the odd realization that Nick was still the same lovable person—our son—even if he is this new and terrible thing called "homosexual."

The next week Sister Ann had another question for us: "What do you most regret about Nick being gay?" My wife regretted that her son was committing mortal sins. My regret was that he would not marry "a nice girl" and have a family. As we talked, we had to admit a third regret: we were ashamed of what our friends and neighbors would think. We would be looked down on by them because we had failed as parents.

At our third meeting Sister Ann asked another question: "What do you most want for Nick?" At last, an easy question! We both want him to be happy, to have a good life. It is hard to say, but we want him to know love. Beyond that Ann helped us name some other wants: that Nick would "make us proud," that he would give us grandchildren. It wasn't until then that we saw we want these things for ourselves more than for Nick.

All these questions and answers happened a year ago. This Christmas Nick introduced us to his friend, William. What are we to think? We love Nick so much but are still so confused about his life. How can we best love him?

The Yearning

In these stories of Christian lives we hear a yearning. These voices long for a more optimistic and generous view of our sexual lives. The longing takes shape in three hopes. First, we hope to recover the sense of our sexuality as a gift. As Christians, we believe that sexuality is a part of the original blessing of creation; for this we are grateful. We give thanks for our own lives—a gift from our parents' generous sexual love. We give thanks for the gift of those who share with us love's delights. We give thanks for the gift of fruitfulness (our children and our other "works of love") that comes to be through our passion. All these gifts surprise and humble us for we have not earned them, nor are they under our control.

But another powerful emotion often usurps the place of gratitude for sexuality. Guilt insinuates itself into our heart. We know guilt can be a valuable and necessary response, "the guardian of our goodness," as psychologist Willard Gaylin says. We know that genuine guilt arouses the heart, warning us of a wound for which we are responsible. We know this emotion can serve our sexuality—reaffirming our values, protecting our commitments, alerting us to the selfishness that can too easily infect our lives. But this powerful emotion often goes astray, crippling our ability to express affection and turning us away from the risks of sexual love. When this happens, guilt drives out gratitude. Obsessed with sexual temptations, we become absorbed in our own wretchedness. Hounded by guilt, we forget to be grateful for the gift of sexuality. Garrison Keillor's character in *Lake Wobegone Days* speaks for many Christians as he describes his religious upbringing with bitter humor:

> You have taught me to feel shame and disgust about my body, so that I am afraid to clear my throat or blow my nose . . . You taught me an indecent fear of sexuality. I'm not sure I have any left underneath this baked-on crust of shame and disgust . . . A year ago a friend offered to give me a backrub. I declined vociferously. You did this to me.

A genuinely Christian response to sexuality insists that gratitude precede guilt. But here a painful realization dawns: religious institutions have sometimes used guilt as a tool to manage the faithful. Through guilt, institutions exercise control: they tell us what is shameful, what is sinful, what merits punishment. So in our sexual lives—where control seems so important—these institutions, perhaps inevitably, stress guilt more strenuously than gratitude. Unfortunately such an approach produces a peculiar kind of Christian: one who avoids contact with other people, lest they become an occasion of sin; one who mistrusts pleasure because it threatens the loss of control.

The yearning among many Christians today is for a reversal of these religious sentiments: to recover the priority of gratitude in our sexual lives and to put genuine guilt into a secondary role.

The second hope is for a more incarnational attitude toward sexuality. The abstract word *Incarnation* has at its core a wonderfully concrete meaning: flesh. Christians hope for a spirituality of sexuality that is more comfortable with the flesh.

Christian teachings on sexuality have become abstract and idealistic. Official statements about marriage, for example, compare this relationship to the exalted union of Christ and the Church, but remain silent about the important daily dynamics of love and conflict. At times Christian spirituality was more than abstract; it was hostile to the body and sexuality. Spiritual guides in our religious tradition often suggested that holiness and sexuality were incompatible; sexual arousal was essentially selfish; the human body, an occasion of sin, was to be punished and subdued. It was not to be befriended but mastered. A dualism of body and soul, flesh and spirit, sapped the best convictions of our faith.

All this was heresy, of course. But it powerfully influenced centuries of Christian spirituality. What Christians hope for today is a return to the best belief of the Incarnation: in the flesh we meet God; in our bodies the power of God stirs; our sexuality is an ordinary medium through which God's love moves to touch, to create, to heal.

Christians have a third hope that springs from their longing. They want to appreciate the positive links between pleasure and commitment. Religious writers have often portrayed these two aspects of our sexual lives as antagonists. A virtuous life seemed

to demand an either/or choice: either we selfishly pursue pleasure or we settle down to a responsible, if arid, adult life. Commitment and duty appeared incompatible with pleasure and delight.

In such a standoff, both sides suffered. We came to understand
commitment as drab and unexciting; we understood physical
lovemaking as only *taking* pleasure, not sharing or giving delight.
To such a selfish act we gave the sinister name *concupiscence*. In
this view, heaven became the proper place for pleasure. Through
the centuries, the mystics delighted in describing union with
God in the most erotic imagery. This beautiful poetry was often
interpreted to mean that pleasure and delight have little place in
this world.

Christians today give witness to another wisdom: in lovemaking, couples learn to both give and receive pleasure. The erotic
life is about much more than "taking" pleasure—in its rapacious
and selfish meanings. Lovemaking invites us into a rhythm of
pleasuring and being pleasured—as does any lasting experience
of mutuality. This combination of activity and passivity, of control and letting go, requires a genuine discipline. As Catholic
philosopher Dick Westley observes, "The fact is that sexual activity, when it is truly love-making and the work of the spirit, is the
antithesis of self-indulgence. It is the height of asceticism." At
the core of sexual love, this discipline links pleasure to both
responsibility and fruitfulness.

A Bodily Wisdom

Today the body Christian wants to reclaim the original optimism
of creation—God's confidence in the body and its passionate
hopes. This book is part of that effort. In the chapters that
follow we explore the connections between the experience of
sexuality and the life of faith. In pursuit of a spirituality of sexuality, we give special attention to three sources: Christian tradi-

tion, the culture in which we live, and the experience of Christians today.

Most of us carry our religious heritage as a rich and dense storehouse; energizing values and lingering guilts abide there together. Images abound: God as a loving parent, God as an unforgiving judge, our bodies as temples of the Holy Spirit, our bodies as shameful and inherently sinful. Christian tradition holds an especially ambiguous set of images and values about sexuality. The complexity starts in the book of Genesis. Having created woman and man as sexual companions, God judges that this creation is good! This compelling account of a couple delighting in one another and in the presence of God moves all of us. It speaks of a promise and a hope—a hope realized in our own experience in those extraordinary moments of uncovering ourselves to one another in love. In such moments, however rare, we find a more than genital pleasure in the discovery of the goodness of life.

But in this same story, another view of sexuality insinuates itself. The failure of this couple—some terrible, original mistake that seems necessary to account for the deep and continuous ways men and women fail themselves and one another—appears to be connected in some way with sexuality. Although Genesis describes this original sin as disobedience, the original couple feel its results in their bodies. After their sin, the couple's punishment is alienation—from God (they are driven from the garden), from one another (they are suddenly aware of their nakedness), and from an easy delight in their bodies (man's work will be "by the sweat of his brow" and women will bear children "in anguish").

The complexity of religious attitudes toward sexuality is discovered again in early Christian tradition. The image of the Incarnation itself reveals a central ambiguity concerning the meaning and value of sex. God is made flesh, becomes embodied as a sexual person like us. In this event our bodies, too, are blessed and reaffirmed in their holiness. Yet this en-fleshing of God's son was interpreted in the early Christian centuries as having happened asexually. Growing suspicious of sexuality under the increasing influence of the Greek world, the early Church decreed that God became human but not through a genital act. For many Christians today, this interpretation drains the Incarnation of its promise.

The Christian tradition is more than a sacred and unchanging reservoir of revelation concerning sexuality. This heritage also includes all the misuses of history to which our fears and neglect have led. Our religious tradition is both holy and wounded— and some of its wounds are self-inflicted. The Christian understanding about sex is both grace-filled and desperately in need of purification. Our religious history combines God's gifts and our malpractice. The task today is, as it has always been, to discern amid this marvelous and conflicted history the revelation that still excites us to faithful and generous love.

A second source in our reflection is the culture in which we live. Living in America at the end of the twentieth century influences our perception of sexuality. Our religious heritage is complex and ambiguous; so, too, is our cultural inheritance. Pornography, consumerism, popular entertainment affect our understandings of sex and our judgments about fidelity and commitment. But culture also makes other, more valuable, contributions to our appreciation of sexuality. In this book we draw on information available in psychological research and therapeutic practice. This information concerns a range of issues that influence mature sexuality. We give particular attention to the growing body of research and theory that takes up the thorny issues of gender—similarities and differences between women and men.

A third important source in this reflection is the lived experience of Christians today—the wisdom of the body. A dialogue between theology and the social sciences remains sterile unless it is joined by the testimony of mature Christians in the variety of lifestyles that constitute the community of faith. A traditional theological category for this wisdom of the community is *the sense of the faithful.* This ancient but largely forgotten metaphor points to a *sense* or *intuition* that belongs to the body of believers. The metaphor comes close to our image of visceral wisdom. A century ago John Cardinal Newman described this sense of faith as "a sort of instinct . . . deep in the bosom of the mystical body." Not yet articulated in a clear statement of doctrine, this knowledge is more a sensual sureness, rooted in the body's mature belief. A maturing Christian community, then, can possess a "sense" or instinct of what Christian faith requires. Included in this larger sense of the faithful are the believing community's understandings of sex, pleasure, commitment, fidelity, and fruitful love.

In the Second Vatican Council the Church returned with some enthusiasm to this metaphor of the sense of the faithful. The Document on the Church, for example, says that this active intuition "clings without fail to the faith once delivered to the saints, penetrates it more deeply by accurate insights and applies it more thoroughly to life." In the 1980 Synod on Christian marriage, a number of participating bishops appealed to this practical wisdom that, abiding among married Catholics whose instincts about sexuality have been tested and refined over decades of faithful love, can teach the Church—especially its unmarried leaders.

In both the thought of Cardinal Newman and the documents of Vatican II, this instinct of faith is understood to be more than simply a passive reflection of what is currently expressed in formal religious teaching. Newman believed that the community of faith must sometimes safeguard aspects of genuine belief that are being overlooked or neglected by religious officials. This may be especially true in sexual matters.

For centuries the Church's official teaching portrayed marriage as "a remedy for concupiscence." This understanding, crafted by Augustine at the end of the fourth century, argues that marriage exists as a haven for the lustful. If one must use others for personal sexual pleasure (the definition of concupiscence), at least do so in marriage. Then the evil of promiscuity will not be added to that of lust, and responsibility can be taken for children—the fruit of one's passion. This definition of marriage became part of Church law and shaped Catholic teaching about marriage for almost sixteen hundred years. Finally, the reformulation of Church law in the 1970s officially dropped this demeaning definition of marriage.

But throughout these sixteen hundred years, deep in the body Christian, another religious conviction prevailed. Many married Catholics recognized a very different truth about marriage. From their experience they knew that sexual arousal is about more than lust, that sexual delight is not always selfish. In a wisdom often unspoken, these couples came to know and cherish the links between pleasure and generous love. The sexual relationship they shared made life richer and more religious.

This wisdom of married Catholics survived in private. Seldom did they question or directly challenge the "official position" of the Church. If Church teaching on some sexual question contradicted their experience, then they had to be wrong or, at least, they had to keep quiet about their differences. So, many lay Christians held on to their conscientious judgments and remained mute. But their public silence deprived the Christian community of important resources of faith. Instead of lively debate the Christian community often settled for dead formulas for sexual conduct.

But today the body speaks. Lay Christians seem more confident and determined to share their sense of sexuality. Dick Westley encourages married Christians to break their silence:

It is time for sexually active believers to proclaim in the Lord's name, and without fear, what they have learned in bed, confident

that it is, when communally funded, as authoritative as any episco-
pal letter or papal encyclical.

"Communally funded" means our experience as it is heard and
tested in the Christian community. An objective of this book is
to draw out and make public the sense of the faithful about
Christians and their sexuality.

Three Options Today

When we face the confusing relationship of sexuality and Christianity, we may be tempted to respond in one of three ways. We
may choose to interpret Christian tradition as a unified and
absolute revelation. To do this we need to ignore or deny the
seamier side of our religious history. In an effort to remain faithful to the Church in a time of enormous transition, some of us
may feel the need to affirm the tradition as it now stands, arguing
for its unchanging stability, clarity, and rightness.

Another way to respond is simply to reject the tradition. A
body of thought that contains so many negative attitudes toward
sexuality, a history of pastoral practice that has offered so much
harmful counsel, an institutional system that is punitive toward
so many of its members—women, those who are divorced and
remarried, persons who are homosexual—must be rejected, even
denounced! Many people, wounded by biases they feel they have
learned from the Church, now judge it to be bankrupt. The
murky heritage of Christian belief and behavior around sex offers them no enduring values.

Others respond by acknowledging this complex religious tradition as both *mixed* and *mine*. Since Vatican II many Catholics
have struggled with the institutional Church and arrived at a
deeper realization that they *are* Catholics—for better and for
worse. The Catholic faith is our heritage and home. It is not a
home that we choose to leave like angry children, but a home
where we belong and for which we must care. We begin to recog-

nize that the Church, in its history and practice, is not simply the "umblemished spouse of Christ" or the "perfect society." Incomplete and wounded, it is very much like ourselves. The marvel of Christ's promise—"to be with you all days, even until the end of the world"—is that it is *this* Church, this flawed, often shortsighted, and sometimes arrogant group—ourselves—with whom God has promised to stay.

As we are stripped of a childish fantasy of a perfect and sinless Church, we find that the conviction "we are the Church" takes on a new and more powerful meaning. The reality of the Church fits better with who we know ourselves to be. We can experience this as an invitation to a new level of participation in our religious faith. This third response can lead us to a more personal investment in our lovely but scarred heritage. We are called to help heal Christian prejudices against the body. And we are invited to recover the tradition's deepest convictions about the goodness of sexuality and the fruitfulness of love. In a lively dialogue among the Christian tradition, our culture, and our personal experience, we will be able to develop a spirituality of sexuality that is genuinely Christian, contemporary, and practical.

REFLECTIVE EXERCISE

We invite you, the reader, to participate in this reflection on the wisdom of the body Christian. Through the chapters of this book we include a variety of exercises for personal reflection. The first goal of these exercises is self-exploration—to come to a clearer and more confident awareness of your own convictions on a particular issue or theme. Beyond that, our hope is that these exercises may be part of a larger effort to give voice to the wisdom of the body. The exercises are designed so that they may be used alone, but their value is often greatly enhanced by sharing with a friend or in a small group. In these communal settings we may begin to see the links between the personal journey of faith and the emerging sense of the faithful.

In a time of quiet, recall the many images and convictions about sexuality that have come to you from the Christian tradition. These may be passages from Scripture, memories of prayer or preaching, the attitudes of religious people. Take time to let the memories come.

After a while, choose one of these memories that speaks to you positively about sexuality. Spend time with it. What is the central conviction about sexuality that this religious memory holds for you? What are the feelings that accompany this memory?

Then turn to a memory or an image that is more negative in its view of sexuality. What information comes to you here about sexuality? What feelings return with this image?

Finally, think of your life today. Which of these religious convictions about sexuality has more influence on you now? Why do you think this is so?

ADDITIONAL RESOURCES

The Vatican II document that reinstated the sense of the faithful as an element in theological process is *The Constitution on the Church (Lumen Gentium)*; see Paragraph 12 in *The Documents of Vatican II*, edited by Walter Abbott (America Press, 1966). Cardinal Newman's analysis of the sense of the faithful appears in his *On Consulting the Faithful in Matters of Doctrine* (Sheed & Ward, 1961). We have explored the contemporary potential of this religious dynamic in Chapter 12 of *Community of Faith* (Harper & Row, 1982) and Chapter 5 of *Seasons of Strength* (Image Books/Doubleday, 1986).

In *Between the Sexes: Foundations for a Christian Ethics of Sexuality* (Paulist Press, 1985) Lisa Sowle Cahill draws on scriptural research, Catholic moral tradition, and the findings of psychology for her discussion of the shape of Christian sexuality. Eugene Kennedy has long served the Christian community through his courageous and careful reflections on matters sexual and more. Of particular interest are his *Free to Be Human* (Image Books/Doubleday, 1987), *A Time for Love* (Image Books/Doubleday, 1987), and *Sexual Counseling: A Practical Guide for Non-Professional Counselors* (Continuum Books, 1980).

Dick Westley's call for married Christians to speak of sexuality out of their experience was made in an address delivered to a national gathering at Waterloo, Ontario, in June 1987; see also his excellent discussion of sexuality in *Beyond Morality* (Twenty-Third Publications, 1984) and in *A Theology of Presence* (Twenty-Third Publications, 1988).

2.

The Good News About Sex

> Let him kiss me with the kisses of his mouth.
> Your love is more delightful than wine . . .
> I shall praise your love above wine;
> How good it is to love you. (Song of Songs 1)

The good news about sex is that sex is good. The Catholic community's discussion of sex starts with this conviction, deeply rooted in the religious heritage we share as Jews and Christians. Part of the gift of creation, sexuality is good. In the community of faith today we eagerly affirm this ancient belief, true to our own experience as well.

Sex is good—a simple statement and yet one often disputed. Some see sex as evil, a source of shame to be avoided by those pursuing holiness. Others regard sex as an unpleasant, if necessary, part of the uneasy union of body and soul. Only in the institution of marriage can we cloak and control this embarrassing passion.

These negative evaluations of sex represent more than past history. Sex lies at the heart of the most vexing social problems of our own day: rape, incest, pornography, teenage pregnancy, abortion, AIDS. Sex perplexes our personal lives as well. We find ourselves both excited and confused by our bodies, with their desires and hesitancies. Some of our best moments in life—and some of our worst—involve sex. Our creativity finds expression in sex, as does our destructiveness. Genital arousal turns us outward in love and care; it can also turn us inward in self-absorption. In the face of this ambiguous evidence, the Christian conviction that "sex is good" comes as especially good news.

Christians believe that sex is good because our bodies are good and holy. "Your body is the temple of the Holy Spirit," Saint Paul wrote to his friends in Corinth. God inhabits our bodies; the Creator delights to be present in this fleshly dwelling. But this conviction, at the heart of Christianity, remains incredible even to many Christians. The doctrine of the trinity or the resurrection or the last judgment—these can be accepted on faith. But that God delights to dwell in *this* body—with its erections or menstruations or aching loneliness? Impossible! The contrary evidence seems too compelling: we use physical strength to strike out in violence; we misuse sex to abuse others and degrade ourselves. Too frequently our bodies are instruments of disorder, co-conspirators in our worst behavior.

Despite our negative experience, the Christian conviction stands: the body is holy; sex is good; God dwells here. The Incarnation, a conviction at the very core of Christian theology, reinforces this optimism. Being Hispanic may help one to recognize the word *flesh (carne)* in this abstract theological term. The fourth gospel tells us that "the Word was made flesh" (John 1:14). This is strong language: God becomes not a human being nor a moral agent nor a thinking person but *flesh*. God enters into a life like ours—bodily, sexual, emotional. The Incarnation is good news for the flesh.

Sex Is Good

> How Beautiful you are, my love,
> How beautiful you are!

> Your eyes, behind your veil, are doves . . .
> Your lips are a scarlet thread
> And your words enchanting . . .
> Your two breasts are two fawns . . .
> You are wholly beautiful, my love,
> And without blemish. (Song of Songs 4)

The Song of Songs, a lyrical poem about two lovers, helps us in the struggle to believe in the inherent goodness of sex. Neither a historical narrative nor a catalog of laws, this brief book seems out of place in sacred Scripture. To the surprise and even shock of many, the poem celebrates erotic love. In describing the arousal and passion of these lovers, the poem moves from explicit description to suggestive metaphor ("Let my beloved come into his garden; Let him taste its rarest fruits" 4:16).

This poetry has scandalized both Jews and Christians. What is this sexually provocative story doing in our Scriptures? Because this book was originally ascribed to King Solomon, no one dared remove it from the Scriptures. But how to explain it or blunt its erotic message? Two historical efforts to "save" this text stand out. One method of interpretation viewed the poem as a dialogue between a bride and her bridegroom. Seeing these lovers as married makes their passion more legitimate. A second method of interpretation, the favorite for more than two thousand years, regarded the entire book as an allegory about the love between God and the human soul. Thus a poem about human "profane love" was transformed into a story of pure (that is, nonsexual) devotion.

Recently scripture scholars have returned to the poem's most obvious meaning: the celebration of the goodness of sensual love. In this interpretation, the ancient poem can symbolize God's passionate love for us only because erotic love is, itself, good and holy. Christian morality has, of course, most often made sexuality's goodness dependent on fertility: making love is acceptable when a married couple intend to have a child. But this poem—part of Christian revelation—does not yet speak of children. Instead it lingers, with delight, on the essential goodness of sexual desire. In his discussion in *The Jerome Biblical Commentary*, Roland Murphy notes this special focus: "The course of events does not appear to be leading anywhere; the lover and beloved are simply enjoying each other's presence and affection."

The revelation here challenges Christians to reaffirm the goodness of sex. The poem itself concludes with a powerful assertion of the link between human passion and the flame of God's creation:

> For love is strong as death,
> Passion relentless as hell.
> The flash of it is a flash of fire,
> A flame of Yahweh's own self. (8:6)

In returning to the original meaning of this poem, scripture scholars reinforce the wisdom of the body Christian. More and more members of the community of faith—lay people, pastoral ministers, theologians—are urging the institutional Church toward a more wholehearted recognition that sex is good. These efforts are beginning to bear fruit. In preaching and pastoral counseling, in religious education programs and spiritual retreats, the good news about sex is becoming a lively part of Christian formation.

What is the truth that we, the Christian body, find in our sexual experience? We discover, first, the goodness of sexual arousal itself. This stirring in our bodies is one of the roots of our creativity; it draws us to others; it ignites the attraction that sustains the fruitful commitments of life—in friendship, in marriage, in devoted love. Second, we recognize that sexual love has more to do with fruitfulness than with fertility. Sex is, with its unexpected awakenings and unearned delights, an echo of creation. Third, we realize that in the touches and strokes of sexual sharing we are revealed to ourselves; we are brought to see a loveliness that we had been incapable of imagining on our own. And finally, we know that in our sexual lives we often find spiritual healing. Our physical embraces soothe old wounds and make forgiveness tangible. In the intimacy we share with a sexual partner, the reality of God's goodness and forgiveness finally becomes more than rhetoric. As lovers, we give thanks for this grace.

As Americans, we live in a society that complicates our attempts to tell the truth about sex. Even as we proclaim that sex is good, we know that it is not the only good. Sex participates in a community of human goods, an arena that includes generosity and justice and sacrifice. In adolescence, sex necessarily looms large; it can excite and even threaten us as nothing else can. Maturing into adult life, we gradually befriend sex—we learn to appreciate its power, to savor its delights, to see through some of its illusions. We make decisions that integrate sexual activity in our lives in ways that are consistent with our deepest values.

Cultural forces can stunt this integration. America's fascination with sex, for example, coaxes all of us to linger too long in adolescence. Our society exalts sex as the peak experience and primary focus of life. The industry of pornography feeds this fantasy, but it thrives in more "respectable" forms as well—in advertising, in the media, in entertainment. This national preoccupation takes sex out of context, separating pleasure from the accompanying dynamics of mutuality, responsibility, and commitment.

As Christians, we put sex in context by turning to the witness of Jesus in the gospels. A first fact that impresses the reader of the gospels is the relative absence of talk about sex. The gospels reveal a life that is overwhelmingly concerned with change and healing. Jesus heals the sick and the possessed; he invites sinners to change their lives; he urges others to leave all and follow him in a different way of life. Personal change, conversion, and a life lived with and for others—these, rather than a set of specific instructions about moral behavior, form the core of Jesus' message in the gospels.

As recorded in the gospels, Jesus' mission did not include marriage. Christians have seen this as a sign of his radical commitment to the service of God. In his life and lifestyle Jesus speaks to us of the relative unimportance of everything beyond love and justice and the healing that these virtues can effect. Good and holy as it is, sex is not the most important aspect of life. Sex is a significant part of life and, for most of us, a central dynamic in both maturity and spirituality. But Jesus' life witnesses that we are sexual and more. The gospel thus invites us to take sex both more and less seriously than otherwise we might.

The body of Christ knows that sex is good, but that it is not ultimate. Sex is not the meaning of life; sexual pleasure will not bear the weight of a life focused primarily on its pursuit. The life of Jesus challenges us all, married and unmarried, to a more than genital love, a larger than biological family, a fruitfulness that goes beyond biological fecundity. Some of us build lives of deep intimacy that do not include genital sharing. All of us learn the lessons of love that come only in seasons of abstinence—the death of a partner, the end of a friendship, the loss of consolation in prayer. In the midst of the challenges and invitations that surround our sexual lives, we proclaim our basic conviction: *sex is good.*

> In his longed-for shade I am seated
> And his fruit is sweet to my taste.
> He has taken me to his banquet hall,
> And the banner he raises over me is love. (2:3–4)

Sex Is Mysterious

Over the past hundred years, medical research has expanded our understanding of human reproduction. This explosion of knowledge has produced effective new procedures for treating a range of problems: sexual dysfunction, infertility, high-risk pregnancies, birth defects. It has also generated a host of complex ethical and legal questions related to reproduction—issues from birth control and abortion to in-vitro fertilization and surrogate parenting. During this same time, social scientists have been studying patterns of sexual behavior. These investigators— Sigmund Freud at the turn of the century, Alfred Kinsey and his associates in the 1940s and 1950s, William Masters and Virginia Johnson more recently, to cite only a few—have described the actual sexual behavior of women and men. Here again, the findings have been significant, inviting a reexamination of many previously accepted assumptions—about masturbation, homosexuality, sexual behavior in marriage, and the physical responsiveness of women and of men.

But there remains so much we still do not understand. Those most involved in the study of sex are the first to acknowledge our continuing ignorance. Physiologically and psychologically, much about the human experience of sex remains unclear. Part of the mystery of sex is rooted here, in the limits of our current understanding.

But what we do know about sex is hardly less mysterious. For instance, sexual reproduction links the human species with the rest of the animal kingdom. But the arena of sex is one in which humans differ most from other animals. For most animals, sex is seasonal. For a brief period of time at a biologically determined stage of development males and females are capable of mating. Outside such a mating season most animals display no sexual activity. The attraction and union of women and men, by contrast, does not depend on a mating season. Sexual activity among humans is less controlled by biological cues.

In most animals, sexual activity is narrowly focused on reproduction. For example, among the primates closest to humans in evolutionary development—the great apes—the female is receptive to the male's sexual approach only during estrus, a recurring but relatively brief period of biological fertility. Among humans, in contrast, sexual interest is not limited to reproductive periods. A woman can experience sexual arousal throughout the menstrual cycle, not just during the limited phase when conception is possible. Both women and men remain interested in and capable of genital behavior long after their biological fertility has come to an end. This would seem to confirm that for the human species sex is about more than reproduction.

The links between pleasure and genital behavior deepen the mystery of human sex. In many species, physical agitation marks sexual readiness, and sexual release reestablishes physiological calm. But there is little evidence that animals experience genital activity itself as pleasurable. In the human species, sex and pleasure are intimately linked. And the links seem to go beyond the commonsense explanation, that sexual pleasure is the decoy Nature uses to draw otherwise reluctant humans (especially the male of the species) into the onerous responsibilities of parenthood. Consider, for example, the role of the female clitoris. When appropriately stimulated by lovemaking, the clitoris is a significant source of pleasure for most women. Yet biological research has been unable to identify any reproductive purpose for this organ. Unlike the multipurpose male penis, the clitoris seems to function simply in the service of sexual delight. Even physiologically human sexuality is about more than reproduction.

We also recognize the mystery of human sexuality in the ambiguity of our personal experience. Sex is a source of our greatest delights and of our most painful confusions. In the experience of sex we can come to a profound awareness of our own goodness and worth. In sex we can also come face to face with the inner conflicts and compulsions that drive us. In sexual encounter we sometimes experience a communion so profound that it shatters the illusions of our isolation. We can also use sex to punish ourselves, to control other people, to diminish joy.

Sex is mysterious in its meanings. Sex is almost always about something more or something else. One of Sigmund Freud's most influential (and most controversial) contributions has been to show that much apparently nonsexual behavior is sexually motivated. Therapists today remind us that the reverse is also true: factors that have little to do with sex motivate a good deal of sexual behavior—from flirting to masturbation to intercourse. Rape is an extreme example. We find the roots of this violent act in aggression and hostility rather than in sexual passion.

Sex is symbolic. It escapes any simple definition. Consider the different answers that people give to the question of what sex means. Some people look at sex as recreational; they focus on pleasure, on sex as diversion and delight. Sex certainly does re-create us. But to view sex as primarily recreational leads to the moral stance of casual sex: among consenting adults, as long as no one is hurt, "anything goes." This partial view neglects the connections and consequences of our sexual actions; it fails to tell the whole truth about sex.

Other people appreciate sex as relational. Focusing on the quality of the relationship, they view sex as a gift to be exchanged between friends. This is true. But to view sex as simply relational leads to the moral stance of companionate sex. In this understanding, sex is appropriately shared in a relationship where there is genuine affection and concern for each other, even without expectations of continuity, exclusivity, or permanent commitment.

Many people regard sex as reproductive. Here the focus is biological, stressing sex as the means of human reproduction.

Clearly this, too, is true. When reproduction is seen as the dominant truth about sex, the moral stance focuses on the links between sex and marriage. Then sex is appropriate only within legally sanctioned marriage and only in the service of biological reproduction.

The body of Christ acknowledges the truth of each of these perspectives—and goes beyond. For Christians, sex is sacramental. This predominant truth is not so much antagonistic to these other perspectives as it is complementary. The recognition of sex as sacramental does not contradict the truth that sex is re-creative, relational, and reproductive. Rather it places these insights —each true, each partial—in a larger context of meaning.

Sex is sacramental. This is part of its mystery. Saint Paul described the uniting of a man and woman in marital love as "a great mystery" (Ephesians 5:32). When this phrase in Ephesians was translated into Latin and then English, the "mystery" of marriage became the "sacrament" of marriage. For Paul, marriage is a mystery in the same way that Christian community as the body of Christ is a mystery. Sex is sacramental because it is suggestive, reminding us not only of the mutual commitment of this couple but of our link with our Creator. Our passionate unions resonate with that covenant of affection and fidelity that God has made with humankind. This ability of our sexual lives to hint at God's presence among us makes sexuality mysterious and holy.

In its fierce privacy and its unavoidable socialness, sexual life symbolizes the life of faith. The covenant between us and God, resonating in the deepest recesses of our heart, affects all our public behavior. The Church has long cherished the image of marriage as a compelling metaphor of its own commitment and fidelity with God. Sex is mysterious because it is sacramental: it can remind us of God's passionate affection for us. For this reason, too, sex is very good.

Sex Makes Promises

"The last time we made love was sad, violent, filled with the awfulness of endings." This poignant sentence opens Sam Keen's account, in *The Passionate Life*, of an affair in which "good sex" gradually turns sour. Two persons had come together from very different lives, united more in flight than in pursuit.

> So we finally agreed to meet in exile, on the island of the flesh. When the heat was upon us, we came together, made love, had a meal together, and went our separate ways. We pretended the void between us was neutral space.

But the balm of sex did not work its reputed wonders. A mood of discontent interfered with delight; the relationship began to disintegrate. Having agreed that sex would make no promises, these lovers found that

> something in us did not respect our contract. Our agreement to sever sense from spirit violated our longing for the unconditional. The ghost of the bonds we would not acknowledge returned to haunt us, until we came to hate each other for all that was missing.

". . . for all that was missing . . ." Keen's moving lament recalls another conviction of the body Christian. Sex is not a neutral ingredient in our relationship; sex changes things. Sex generates more than passion; a sexual relationship arouses hopes and enkindles expectations. As sexual sharing continues, promises are made—sometimes explicitly, often in subtler ways. Recreational sex is bankrupt not because it focuses on pleasure but because it does not keep its promises.

Sex makes promises. This is part of the wisdom of the body Christian. The problem with casual sex is that keeping sex casual is difficult. A couple may come together determined simply to

have an enjoyable sexual relationship. "We like each other and
want to give each other pleasure," they avow, "but with 'no
strings attached.'" They agree on this limited arrangement, but
the experience develops differently. Beyond their plans, even
against their conscious ambitions, they confront the deeper issues of sexuality. They find that physical intimacy and psychological intimacy are connected. Sex play reveals more than their
bodies; it often uncovers hidden hurts and fragile hopes. In their
lovemaking, more than pleasure is aroused. Sex raises issues of
dependence and commitment, even when these matters have
been ruled out of bounds. Casual lovers come to admit, "We
started out with modest expectations of one another. At first, we
just depended on each other to be available when we had agreed
—in a good mood, if possible! But our expectations started to
expand; it's as though we couldn't help expecting more from
each other. We began to look for deeper ways to share our lives
with one another. We began to depend on one another for understanding and support, even more than for sex!"

Sex goes somewhere. That, in fact, is part of its fascination.
Sexual intimacy has intellectual and emotional ramifications that
extend beyond our immediate control. Sexual sharing can move
us beyond ourselves; it can lead us deeper into our relationship.
Sex and love are not the same thing. We learn, often from our
mistakes, how risky confusing the two can be. But if sex and love
are not identical, they are closely related in human experience.
At its best, sex is about making love. And love carries a future,
for it brings with it both shared hopes and mutual obligations.

The word *lovemaking* reminds us that sex is about more than
the experience of pleasure or the discharge of tension. Making
love generates new life—sometimes in the generation of children, more often in nurturing the deepening bonds of mutual
care.

Sexual love gives new life; this is part of the wisdom of the
body of Christ. If love is to endure, it must be creative beyond

itself. This is true of sexual love as much as of compassionate care. Sexual attraction often begins in a stage of mutual fascination. Enthralled with each other, lovers find everything about the other person engrossing. Little beyond their absorption with one another seems worthy of attention. The world tolerates this attitude in lovers—at least for a while. We know this shared obsession represents an early phase of romance; but soon infatuation passes. The relationship may mature into a deeper love, or it may die from lack of any further substance. But in either case the charmed circle of sexual fascination will be breeched. Soon the lovers will rejoin the rest of us—better, we trust, for the experience.

Sex points beyond itself. Sexual love, as it grows, moves beyond mutual absorption. We learn that being *for* one another does not require us to be indifferent to everyone else. Love enriches us, giving us more of what is best in each of us. We feel the impetus to move beyond ourselves, to share this blessing, to bring the power of our love to others.

Love that does not look beyond itself will die—Christian wisdom has long proclaimed this sometimes fleeing insight of our own experience. Moralists have sometimes expressed this truth in narrowly biological terms—that every genital act must be open to the conception of a child. Many Catholics today, especially married persons, find this statement of the connection between sex and generative love to be at odds with their own experience; it is too restrictive. Riveting attention on fertility makes of sex both too much and too little. This approach places too much emphasis on particular activities, but fails to recognize the broader contributions of sex to the full range of fruitful love. The Christian conviction remains: an essential connection exists between making love and giving love. But the wisdom of the body proclaims that this connection has more to do with fruitfulness than with fertility.

> On my bed at night I sought him
> Whom my heart loves.
> I sought but did not find him.
> So I will rise and go through the city,
> In the streets and the squares
> I will seek him whom my heart loves. (3:1–2)

While sex can be fun, experience teaches that it is not to be treated lightly. Recently a friend recounted a conversation she had shared with her young adult daughter, Mimi, who had enjoyed a casual friendship with Dan for several years. During their senior year in college, the friendship between Mimi and Dan began to deepen. As their affection grew more passionate, sex became part of their relationship. "Sex is really confusing," Mimi confided to her mother. "Dan and I agree that marriage is not what we want now, with both of us just beginning graduate school. We love each other a lot and are still really good friends, but things are different since we started sleeping together. I'm not even sure I can say exactly what the difference is. Lovemaking is great, but there's a lot more tension between us. Dan and I talk about it sometimes. We've decided maybe it's just that sex complicates a relationship."

Sex complicates a relationship. Mimi and Dan are not alone in this realization. "Sex stirs longings in us that are not easily stilled," psychologist Lillian Rubin confirms. For most people, even in this age that recommends "cool sex," sexual sharing changes a relationship—sometimes for the better, sometimes for the worse, often both. The cultural norms of an earlier generation suggested that psychological intimacy precedes sexual intimacy. Most of us now in midlife grew up with the expectation that sexual sharing would come only after a couple knew one another well. In the relationships of many young adults today this expectation is reversed: sexual intimacy precedes psychological depth or even emotional closeness. The sense seems to be "if we are good together sexually, we may be willing to face the riskier challenge of sharing our lives." In whatever direction the couple moves—from psychological to physical intimacy, or vice versa—experience still confirms the conviction: sex changes a relationship.

Sexual sharing opens new questions—of trust and vulnerability, of belonging and commitment, of autonomy and interdependence. These issues arise even for couples who, like Dan and Mimi, have decided ahead of time that sex does not imply anything beyond the here and now. While we may declare the bigger questions out of bounds, that simple declaration seldom succeeds. Questions of trust and commitment continue to arise. We find ourselves relying on one another more and more. Whatever our verbal agreements, our sexual embraces continue to promise more.

Sex is promising because it can hold us together in the midst of difficult changes. Early on, before we have found our rhythm of compromise and reconciliation, we can expect some rocky times. Often our sexual sharing soothes some of these confusions. Sex, of course, cannot of itself heal a relationship in trouble. But it can remind us of the delight of our mutual love and can promise that we will come through these difficulties.

The promises of sexual love are real but fragile. Passion hints at a union between us that goes beyond the joining of our bodies. But passion comes and goes. Our lovemaking confirms that "we fit together well," luring us to link our lives in other ways. But to forge these links we must depend on more than the spontaneous delights of sex. The promises sex makes are not well kept in casual encounter. These promises need a home, a protected place in which to grow.

The body Christian knows that sex finds its home in commitment. Commitment gives passion a place to flower and be fruitful. For many people, the form that this commitment takes is marriage. As a legal contract, marriage is the sanctioned shape of enduring sexual commitment. As a religious covenant, marriage is a sign and source of God's love. The commitments of marriage —communion, fidelity, permanence—provide a framework that can protect and purify the promises of sexual love.

But the supportive framework of marriage is not available to all. Homosexual partners find no social form to protect the promises that their love generates. Until recently, both American society and Christian ethics have denied the potential of such sexual intimacy. Convinced that these unions are unpromising, our society acts in ways that contribute to keeping these encounters casual and uncommitted. While social and religious pressures against homosexuality do not prevent sexual sharing, they do often defeat the promises of fidelity and duration. The rules of our society thus fulfill their own prophecies that these relationships will be unfruitful. Such social attitudes ignore the lives of gay and lesbian couples who *do* realize the promises of healthy interdependence and enduring commitment. These lives, if we would but welcome their testimony, have much to teach us about the promise of human love.

Marriage is not part of every life, and the commitments of marriage are not the only context that supports the promise of love. In the community of faith today, growing numbers of adults are not married—some have never married, others are divorced or widowed. All of us—single or married, gay or straight, celibate or sexually active—look to Jesus Christ as the paradoxical instructor in the good news about sex. The gospels give us no information of Jesus' sexual life, content with the assurance that he is "like us in all ways except sin." This unmarried and childless person shows us many ways to love. And from his life we learn the criteria of Christian love: mutual respect rather than coercion or selfishness; the deepening of commitment and fidelity; the healing of injuries; the quickening of courage.

The Word made Flesh is good news for the body. The revela-

tion of God that has been given in Jesus Christ has significance
for our sexual lives. From its outset Christianity has struggled,
not always successfully, to express this good news in ways that
illumine, purify, and liberate love. This effort continues today, as
the community of faith gives voice to its experience. Married
couples acknowledge the range of pleasures that make their life
together fruitful. Single adults speak out concerning the place of
sexuality in their lives. Mature Christians who are lesbian and
gay tell the Church—sometimes hesitantly, sometimes courageously—how sexuality and spirituality are part of their own
experience. As Christians learn to listen well to one another we
recognize that, in our sexuality as in so much else, we are more
alike than we are different. Across our different lifestyles, we
share similar concerns as we struggle to fashion faithful and generous ways to express our love. In these diverse experiences our
shared conviction is confirmed—*sex is good.*

REFLECTIVE EXERCISE

Draw on your own experience of the good news about sex. In a
prayerful mood, spend time with the convictions in this chapter.
Sex is good.

In what ways do you know sex to be good? How does your
own experience confirm this conviction?

Where does your experience lead you to challenge or question
this optimistic stance toward sex?

Where in Christian life today do you find this appreciation of
sex most authentically presented?

Sex is mysterious.

Consider the ways in which the mystery of sex is real for you.
How is sex surprising? How is sex confusing? How is sex profound?

What practical meaning is there, in your own experience, to
the phrase "sex is sacramental"?

Sex makes promises.

Recall your own life or the experiences of others you know well. What are the promises that sex makes—the hopes and expectations that accompany sexual sharing?

In your own awareness, what are the connections between sex and commitment? Between sex and fidelity? Between sex and fruitfulness?

ADDITIONAL RESOURCES

Roland Murphy provides a brief overview of the Song of Songs in *The Jerome Bible Commentary* (Prentice-Hall, 1968). Marvin Pope's exhaustive analysis in the Anchor Bible Series includes the traditional interpretations of this poem and summarizes more recent Catholic and Protestant interpretations: see his *Commentary on the Song of Songs* (Doubleday, 1977), especially pp. 199–210.

Morton Kelsey and Barbara Kelsey offer a wise and compassionate discussion of sexual behavior in *Sacrament of Sexuality: The Spirituality and Psychology of Sex* (Amity House, 1986). In *And They Felt No Shame: Christians Reclaim Their Sexuality* (Winston Press, 1984), Joan Ohanneson challenges morality and ministry to reflect more adequately the deeply Christian insight that spirituality and sexuality are inseparable. Andrew Greeley provides a valuable pastoral resource on sexuality in *Sexual Intimacy* (Thomas More Press, 1982).

Sam Keen explores the experience of love in *The Passionate Life* (Harper & Row, 1983). Lillian Rubin discusses the psychological dimensions of sex in *Intimate Strangers: Women and Men Together* (Harper & Row, 1983).

3.
Eros and Sexuality

The body gives gifts to the spirit. The lazy contentment of a summer day, an invigorating walk along the seashore, the warmth of a loving embrace, the pleasures of a meal shared with friends—these are benefits of our bodiliness. In our bodies we are stirred by beauty and moved by emotion. Our bodies want to be touched—held in affection, caressed by a lover, soothed by a comforting hand. The body delights in making contact.

Eros is the traditional name given to the body's desire and delight. In early Greek mythology Eros was the vital force active in every area of life. However, in contemporary usage *eros* has a considerably narrower meaning. The closest we get to *eros* is *erotic,* a word which suggests to many people a perverse preoccupation with sex. The erotic has vaguely pornographic connotations, calling up images of seedy adult bookstores and sleazy massage parlors.

Many theologians and psychologists today are appealing to the broader classical meaning of eros as the sensual face of love. Rooted in our bodies, our sensuality encompasses more than sex. Eros is our passionate drive for life and growth. This meaning of erotic experience includes much more than genital arousal. Eros moves in all our longings to make contact, to be—quite literally

—*in touch.* Arousal and affection, passion and response, intimacy and appreciation—these are all part of eros. In erotic experience we first feel the connections between presence and pleasure, between longing and new life.

The Importance of Touch

Silence shrouds the scene. Visitors move slowly along the wall of names. On this rainy day at the Vietnam War Memorial, no one is in a rush. Coming to the name he had been watching for, a man squints at the letters etched in marble. Then his hand reaches up to touch the imprint. Fingers edge slowly along the marks, spelling the name one more time.

Others repeat this poignant exercise of touching. Their fingers make contact with cold, wet stone. But watching their faces and tears, any observer can see they are touching much more than this wall. At this secular liturgy, repeated a hundred times daily, human touch performs its magic. Contact with mere stone is able to release memories and emotion. Pain and anger are summoned from some hidden spot; griefs are mourned again in a touch that both salutes and says good-bye.

Touch is a good example of the breadth and complexity of eros. In infancy, if we are fortunate, our parents hold and stroke and caress us. They wrap us in protective embraces that our memories still savor. Nursing, we taste the nourishing pleasures of touch. Soon our hands begin to explore the wonderful terrain of our own bodies—until we are instructed in the limits of this delight.

As children we experience the feel of cold sheets as we jump into bed on a winter night, the comforting texture of a familiar sweater, the delight of burying our face in a pet's luxurious hairy coat. But our memories of childhood may also include touch as a vehicle of punishment. Spankings and slaps or more violent reminders teach us that contact is not just about pleasure. Still our memories, unless they are so injured that they flee into amnesia, carry a rich history of our sensual contact with life.

In early adolescence the power of touch explodes in the experience of puberty. Suddenly our whole bodies become alert and eager for touching. Here, too, we are forced to taste the complexity of pleasure: our delight does not always guarantee someone else's pleasure; passion is not always mutual; touch can injure and humiliate as well as comfort.

Because we are so easily aroused by touch in adolescence, we may equate every touch with genital arousal. Dressing and bathing carry extra meaning; the casual touch of a friend excites us. Frightened by the links between touch and sex, we may avoid every kind of contact. In an effort to control the forbidden pleasures of touch, we keep to ourselves.

In time we may come to be "out of touch"—with friends, our own bodies, any tactile pleasure. We learn to abstain from reassuring hugs, relaxing backrubs, a friendly arm around the shoulder—touches that have echoes of genital arousal. We may conclude that whenever another person touches us, the contact and its pleasure have but one, genital meaning. This restricts the possibilities for intimacy in our life.

Maturing as sensual persons we learn that the pleasures of touch are many and different—not every touch is a genital signal; not every pleasurable contact is meant to initiate sexual sharing. In truth, the sensual can enrich our lives well beyond the pleasure of genital arousal. But often we need to recover this rich resource. Revisiting the Gospel of Mark and observing Jesus touching others may help us appreciate anew our own sensuality. In Mark's gospel we meet a very human Jesus, frequently in physical contact with other people. At dinner one evening a woman approaches and anoints Jesus' head with an expensive, fragrant oil. This sensual action startles and offends his companions. To deal with their discomfort about this unseemly intimacy, they argue about extravagance and waste. But Jesus responds, "Leave her alone!" He likes to be touched this way.

Throughout the good news recounted by Mark, those who are ill seek Jesus out. When they find him, Jesus often touches them in a way that changes their life. And Jesus seems to *need to touch them*. In the famous story of his healing a blind man, Jesus mixes some dirt with his own spit and presses the mud into the person's eyes; gradually the man regains his sight. In another story Jesus praises the simplicity of a group of children. "Then he put his arms around them, laid his hands on them and gave them his blessing" (10:16).

In one of the most compelling accounts of Jesus' contact with others, an ill woman approaches him with the conviction, "If I can touch even his clothes, I will be well again" (5:28). Jesus comes to a stop, aware that he has been touched in some special way. He asks who has touched him and his friends are surprised since they are jostling their way through a thick crowd. But Jesus tells them that he felt power going out of him. Like the hands on the war memorial wall, human touch made something happen. Touch has this mysterious power to heal—if we know how to use its sensual force.

Theologian Tom Driver gives us a wonderful example of touch as an element of healing. Driver describes how he awoke one summer morning after a late night of long conversations. Fatigued and foggy at that quiet morning hour, he felt both a complaint and a request arising from his body:

> Tired limbs and untoned muscle spoke to him. "Wash us," they said. There was a chorus of complaint in his body. "Take care of me. Treat me with love."

In this moment of leisure, his body made its plea for attention. It begged for sensual contact and healing. During a long and leisurely bath, Driver came in touch again with parts of his body that he had too long neglected. "He remembered that in forty-eight years and in spite of a deeply sensual nature he had never quite made peace with his body." In the course of this sensual meditation, Driver recognized that his body—in its stiffness—harbored some unforgiven hurts. Driver's long meditation brings the Christian theme of reconciliation to bear on our own bodiliness. Our bodies long for the wholeness and salvation that our religious rhetoric preaches. They carry ancient memories of guilt and shame that need healing; they do not want so much to be forgiven as to be loved. Here, as in the gospel, the needed healing is often communicated in the sensual experience of touch.

The Language of Sexuality

This man caressing his body in a bath provides a good example of the ambiguity of eros. Many of us have found only a genital meaning in sensual exploration. Driver reminds us that our bodies give us more than the gift of genital delight. But as we recognize the wider scope of sensuality, we are brought to the question of interpretation. We learn to assign certain meanings to our bodily stirrings. These interpretations take us into the realm of sexuality. Sexuality expresses our attempts—as a people and as individual persons—to make sense of and manage erotic life. Sexuality, then, is what we make of sex. We begin our consideration of sexuality with a look at vocabulary.

Sex, sexuality, intimacy—in ordinary speech these words seem interchangeable. But even when we see the terms as synonyms, we do not consider them as equally respectable. The word *sex* seems too blunt to be used in polite company. The word *sexuality* is more acceptable, for the added syllables somehow soften the impact. But most preferable is the term *intimacy*—a genteel code word to cover any necessary or unavoidable references to genital activity.

But if these three words are used interchangeably in casual speech, they are recognized as different by most careful observers. Sex, sexuality, intimacy—each refers to a particular realm of adult experience. These experiences are related and often overlap, but they are not the same. We can picture their relationship in three concentric circles. In this image, the smallest circle is the realm of sex. Sexuality, the next larger circle, holds within it the experience of sex but includes more. The largest circle, intimacy, takes in the realms of sex and sexuality but goes beyond to include other kinds of closeness. We will examine intimacy in Chapter 4; here we want to explore differences between sex and sexuality.

THE REALM OF SEX

The word *sex* carries two related meanings. First, sex refers to the reproductive organs. It points to the biological systems of the adult male and female that are involved in human reproduction and in the experience of genital pleasure. In this meaning, sex is rooted in the *x* and *y* chromosomes of genetic inheritance and depends on prenatal and postnatal hormonal activity for proper development. Here sex concerns the biological aspect of *who we are.*

The word *sex* is also used to refer to genital behavior. Here sex is about *what we do.* Included here are all those activities that are part of genital arousal and that can lead to orgasm—from sexual feelings and fantasies to masturbation, love play, and intercourse.

THE SCOPE OF SEXUALITY

The word *sexuality* ushers us into a more complex reality. Our sexuality includes the realm of sex—that is, our reproductive organs and our genital behavior—but encompasses much more of who we are. What our body means to us, how we understand ourself as a woman or as a man, the ways we feel comfortable in expressing affection—these are part of our sexuality.

Theologian James Nelson reminds us that sexuality "involves

much more than what we *do* with our genitals." The more has to
do with meaning. Sexuality moves us beyond biology toward the
social expectations and cultural ideals that influence us. Sexuality reflects the human effort—in language, in art, in moral reflection—to give meaning to sex. In this broadest sense, sexuality is
how we make sex significant.

Our society teaches us what sex signifies: romance and "sexi-
ness" are products of culture, not of biology. Our Christian heritage, too, assigns meaning and value to sexual behavior: chastity
and celibacy, for example, reflect religious interpretations of sex.
Culture and religious faith guide us, for better and for worse, in
making sense of sex.

Our sexuality is rooted in a particular consciousness we have
about ourselves. This self-understanding comes in part from our
own experience, but it is influenced by the messages we receive
from our family, our school and our church, and from the values
and biases of our culture. Our parents' easy display of their affection for one another teaches us to be comfortable with physical
closeness. A high school counselor's reassurance as we struggle
with masturbation helps us accept some of the confusions of the
adolescent experience of sex. Hollywood's romanticized version
of beauty leaves us self-conscious about our physical appearance
and envious of others who come closer to the "ideal body."
These awarenesses—these understandings of ourself—are the
building blocks of our sexuality.

BEING EMBODIED

Three elements of this self-awareness are crucial. The first is a
sense of embodiment—what having a body, being a "body-ed"
self means. We use different images to express the relationship
between self and body. Sometimes the experience is one of integration—body and self are one. Athletes experience this when
they are able to perform complicated physical tasks with both
ease and skill. This is part of the high that comes in sports, for

player and spectator alike. In viewing the film *Chariots of Fire*, even the nonathletes among us could sense this integration as the champion runner declared: "When I run I feel God's pleasure." Something similar often occurs in lovemaking, when the barrier of separateness is momentarily transcended and lovers experience a communion that goes beyond the joining of bodies.

But our experiences of embodiment are not always so positive. At times—in illness, perhaps, or "the morning after the night before"—self and body seem disconnected, linked only in an uneasy truce. We may know periods of even greater antagonism, when an unwilling body cages our spirit or when the unruly demands of the flesh defy the soul. This was the agony that Saint Paul experienced: "My body follows a different law that battles against the law which my reason dictates . . . What a wretched man I am! Who will rescue me from this body doomed to death?" (Romans 7:23–24). Now our body seems to become the enemy.

These images of embodiment capture the changing sense of what being a body/self means. Some images may be fleeting: after breaking a leg, we experience our body as a cumbersome burden. But the cast is soon removed and we quickly feel strong and agile again. Other images linger, becoming part of the characteristic way we see ourself—our body is clumsy or sickly or fat-and-ugly. These images of our embodiment become a significant part of our sexuality.

BEING "GENDERED"

A second aspect of our sexuality is gender—what being a woman or a man means. This awareness comes in part from our sex, that is, from the fact that our reproductive system is female or male. But our sense of ourself as a man or a woman involves much more than a check of reproductive organs. Gender goes beyond biology to social expectations. If sex is about male and female, gender is about masculine and feminine. Gender says less about how we are equipped than about how we should act.

Each culture forms its own roles and rules of gender. By determining what is appropriate for women and for men, the social group establishes its working categories of feminine and masculine. These definitions may differ from culture to culture, but every society develops gender expectations. Our society's expectations about what is masculine and feminine play an important role in our growing sense of what being a woman or a man means.

Our awareness that we are a woman (or a man) is central to our sexuality. Initially we come to this sense through the messages we receive from others, especially from our parents. From them we learn that "since you are a girl, you shouldn't fight back" or that "our little girl can be anything she wants to be." As we participate in school and Church and neighborhood, we learn broader expectations of femininity—what is necessary to be accepted as a girl/woman. In our community and in the media, we find role models who show us what being a woman means. We discover both the benefits and the burdens of our gender.

Being a woman means to locate ourself in the picture of femininity that our culture paints. This is the process of gender identification. We come to identify ourselves as women, to hold ourselves accountable to the norms of femininity that prevail in the group that is important to us. But the match is seldom perfect. As we compare ourself to the culture's image of a woman, we find both similarities and differences. Critical to our sexuality is what we do about the differences.

A cultural image of either masculinity or femininity is always close to a stereotype, because this image disregards the remarkable range of individual differences. Every woman, for example, has feelings and talents and hopes that do not fit the culture's description of what a woman is or should be. The parts of themselves that do not fit, that are not "feminine," embarrass many women. We may be more assertive than a "good woman," or too tall and too athletic to be really "feminine," or "unnaturally" more interested in living out a dream of personal accomplishment than in having children. Men who confront the "unmasculine" parts of themselves—tenderness or nurturance or the desire to be held—experience a similar dichotomy between what they are and how their culture defines them.

Mature sexuality challenges us to gradually come to greater confidence and comfort with the way that we are women (or men). In doing this we acknowledge the ways that our experience fits the social norm, and we accept the parts of ourself that contradict the culture's expectations.

Gender differences influence our stance toward relationships as well as our self-awareness. Both men and women recognize the benefits of drawing close to others—a sense of belonging, an awareness of inclusion, the possibilities of love. Both women and men know that close relationships make demands for give-and-take, for accommodating to the needs of other people, for generosity. Both men and women recognize the dangers that may accompany close relationships—domination, control, betrayal. But growing evidence reveals fundamental differences between women and men in their emotional response to close relationships.

Each of us carries images or assumptions about how life works. These internal models help us make sense of what happens to us. They also predict what to expect from our actions in the world. In her influential study of moral development among women, Carol Gilligan has shown that women and men often carry different internal models of their experience. As they approach relationships, for example, men and women have different interpretations of what is actually going on.

Relationships create bonds between people. A woman is likely to feel good about these connections. In her mental imagery, she views the links of relationships as a supportive net that holds her up and protects her from harm. Relationships provide a source of security for her. Thus, emotionally, women are positively disposed. A woman brings to her relationships a sense that "something good will happen here." Although the situation may be more complex and conflicted for a woman who has experienced emotional or physical violence from persons close to her, women characteristically approach close relationships with positive expectations.

Men have different internal models. In the imagery of many men, bonds mean bondage. They experience close relationships as emotionally threatening. The net created by close connections feels more like a trap than a safety net. In this image, the links of relationships confine rather than sustain. Characteristically, then, men approach close relationships with caution.

Rooted in these two different images, men and women have different fears about relationships. For men, as psychologist Ruthellen Josselson notes in *Finding Herself*, "the fear is that others will get too close, that they will be caught and diminished. For women, wishing to be at the center of connection, the dominant fear is of being stranded, far out on the end and isolated from others." We will return to these gender differences in relationships again in later chapters.

EXPRESSING AFFECTION

A third critical part of our sexuality concerns the movement of our affections, the feelings that we have toward persons of the same and of the opposite sex. Here again culture is critical, telling us what are appropriate feelings to have toward women and toward men. In this way the culture defines the categories of heterosexual and homosexual experience. Each of us, then, must come to terms with the movements of our own affectional life. As men, for example, we learn that our culture permits us to be sexually attracted to women and to show them physical affection.

We also learn that the display of physical affection between men is discouraged. Our culture views with suspicion a man who is emotionally drawn toward other men. With this cultural backdrop, each of us has to sort out and accept our own experiences of physical and emotional attraction.

Most of us, both women and men, find that our own feelings do not fit neatly into the culture's narrowest definitions of acceptable heterosexuality. We are drawn, to different degrees and with different intensity, toward both men and women. Some of us find that our strongest emotional orientation is toward persons of the same sex. This level of self-awareness—the ways we are moved emotionally by women and by men, the sense we have of ourself as primarily lesbian, gay, or heterosexual—is part of our sexuality.

Sexuality and the Sensual

Taking us beyond genital activity, sexuality includes a sense of embodiment, an awareness of gender, the movements of affection. This last aspect reminds us of the intimate links between sexuality and our emotional life. Emotions are the feelings that *move* us. Anger stirs us; compassion arouses us; sorrow and guilt cast us down. Our emotions, like our sexuality, are part of our embodiment. This does not mean that our emotional experiences are "really" genital, but that our ability to respond—in anger or sympathy or delight—is an aspect of our sexuality.

Our life constricts when we respond to others only in physical arousal and when we express closeness only in genital ways. Attraction and responsiveness remain aspects of sexuality even when they have little to do with genital sex. To be attracted by another's goodness, to be drawn to beauty in nature, to be moved by music and art—these emotional responses often stir us physically and enrich our lives.

Evidence from our own lives and from psychological research indicates that these emotional responses are part of the broader experience of sexuality. Hostility toward our body and fear of our emotions is often linked. If we are confused about our masculinity, we may find that reaching out to other people in genuine ways is difficult. If we are afraid of the ways in which our affections are stirred, we may retreat into a stance of no response at all. Soon the experiences of joy and beauty become as alien to us as the unwanted sexual stimulation.

The sensual is another name for the many ways that we are bodily moved, excited, and refreshed. This is the broader meaning of eros and sexuality. Let us listen to the impressive range of our sensual stirrings . . .

A long and exhausting week of work has finally ended, and I am driving home past a large lake. For once I notice what I usually ignore: the lapping of the gentle waves. Attracted by this sight, I park my car and sit for a time facing the water. Waves rhythmically massage the shoreline. Soon they do the same to some hardened interior coastline. Something in me lets go its grip; my body begins to relax a bit. A very gentle but clear arousal is taking place within me. If I pay attention, I can feel the sensual delight . . .

On a rainy Saturday afternoon I decide to listen to some music. The children are away. I turn off the telephone and settle down to this favorite relaxation. Before long the mood of the music insinuates itself into my body. Distraction and dissipation give way to a more peaceful mood. The music engenders a harmony, a feeling of being connected again with the universe (not with my children or household tasks, but with the universe!). This sensual arousal is not genital; it is part of the erotic possibilities of the body . . .

As a graduate student I am taking a course from an extraordinary professor. This person is able to tie together all kinds of historical events until I see, often with a sudden and startling clarity, their meaning. The other students and I talk about how stimulating the course is. Often I am thrilled by a particular lecture. This teacher excites my mind. But my body takes special notice for it sometimes trembles in sympathy with the excitement. Even in matters as cerebral as a history class, my embodied spirit is aroused . . .

These emotional and sensual stirrings are part of our sexuality. When we are in love, we notice nature and music in a new way. When we are lonely, a drabness darkens the landscape and robs us of the delights that usually refresh us. But if we are frightened by the surprising stirrings of our body, we may avoid *all* sensual arousals lest they lead to a loss of control.

Sexuality is, then, a more inclusive category than sex. Sexuality includes genital behavior and embraces much more that is of consequence. James Nelson, in *Embodiment*, captures the scope of sexuality when he says, "While our sexuality does not determine all our feelings, thoughts, and actions, in ways both obvious and covert it permeates and affects them all."

The Movement of Sexual Maturity

Sex and sexuality are not the same, but they are interrelated. Real connections exist between genetics (a determining factor in sex) and gender (a critical part of sexuality). Our emotional responsiveness and our comfort in being close to other people are linked. In fact, the erotic excitement of romance can lead to the broader commitments of mutual love. The way that we experience these connections is significant, especially to our sexual maturity.

Our experience of sex, our awareness of sexuality, our attitude toward close relationships—these all shape our sense of self. Sexual maturity is not a state that is achieved once and for all. Rather it is an ongoing process. To mature sexually is to become more confident and more comfortable with the ways that sex, sexuality, and intimacy are part of our own life. We express this maturity in many different lifestyles. The issue here is not married or single, gay or straight, celibate or sexually active. Each of these can be a gratifying and generous way to live. However, sexual maturity challenges us to develop a *pattern of life* that is rooted in the wisdom of our own experience and that is responsive to the values and commitments that give our life meaning.

In his insightful article "Reuniting Sexuality and Spirituality," James Nelson explores the connections between holiness and sexual maturing. Sanctification, he reminds us, means both wholeness and holiness. Christians today are especially eager to grow holy *in and through* their sexuality. Nelson gives some hints of the direction of this religious maturing:

> Sexual sanctification can mean growth in bodily self-acceptance, in the capacity for sensuousness, in the capacity for play, in the diffusion of the erotic throughout the body (rather than in its genitalization) . . .

Holiness—and wholeness—does not mean a flight from the sexual. It demands a befriending of this frightening but attractive force called *eros*. It requires that we become more profoundly erotic.

REFLECTIVE EXERCISE

Use the phrases below to explore your own experience of the range of sexuality. Complete the sentence begun by each phrase. There is no need to force an answer, just respond with what comes to mind at the time. For some phrases you may have several responses; others may call up little for you right now. Take advantage of the opportunity to share this exercise with a friend or in a small group setting.

When I think of myself as a sexual person, I . . .

For me, sexuality is . . .

These days, my body . . .

As a woman (or man), what I like most about being feminine (or masculine) is . . .

As a man (or woman), what I find most constraining about being masculine (or feminine) is . . .

For me, closeness with someone of the same sex is . . .

When I wonder whether others are attracted to me sexually, I . . .

For me, sexuality and spirituality . . .

ADDITIONAL RESOURCES

James Nelson continues to make a significant contribution to the Christian reflection on sexuality; see his *Embodiment: An Approach to Sexuality and Christian Theology* (Augsburg Press, 1978), *Between Two Gardens: Reflections on Sexuality and Religious Experience* (Pilgrim Press, 1983), and *The Intimate Connection: Male Sexuality and Masculine Spirituality* (Westminster, 1988). The quotation at the end of this chapter is from his article "Reuniting Sexuality and Spirituality," which appeared in *Christian Century*, February 25, 1987.

In *Sexuality* (Westminster Press, 1984) Letha Dawson Scanzoni provides a brief and readable overview of themes of sexuality in women's lives; this is an excellent pastoral resource. Tom Driver's meditation is part of his chapter "Speaking from the Body," in *Theology and the Body*, edited by John Fenton (Westminster Press, 1974).

Carol Gilligan provides a theory of moral development based explicitly on the experience of women in *In a Different Voice: Psychological Theory and Women's Development* (Harvard University Press, 1982). Ruthellen Josselson reports the findings of her study of identity formation in young adult women in *Finding Herself: Pathways to Identity Development in Women* (Jossey-Bass, 1987). Anthropologist Ashley Montague explores "the human significance of the skin" in his evocative essay *Touching* (Harper & Row, 1978).

Carol Tavris and Carole Wade review the findings of current research into male/female differences in *The Longest War: Sex Differences in Perspective* (Harcourt Brace Jovanovich, 1984). John Nicholson continues this discussion in *Men and Woman: How Different Are They?* (Oxford University Press, 1984). Anne Fausto-Sterling examines current biological theories about women and men in *Myths of Gender* (Basic Books, 1985).

For a comprehensive analysis of sexuality as a product of human culture, see Jeffrey Weeks, *Sexuality and Its Discontents* (Routledge & Kegan Paul, 1985). Social historian Peter G. Filene considers the development of gender roles in America in *Him/Her/ Self* (John Hopkins University Press, 1986). Ivan Illich offers a wide-ranging exploration of the cultural context of sexuality in *Gender* (Pantheon, 1982).

4.

Intimacy and Commitment

Ruth and I have worked in the same office now for six years. Yesterday she told me she would be leaving at the end of the month. I've known for a while that she's been thinking about this change, but it still came as a shock. I have been distracted all day, recalling the ups and downs of our time together.

When we first began to work together, I was suspicious of her. Ruth was older than I was but less experienced in our company. Which one of us would really be in charge? My suspicion quickly gave way to irritation. We had such different working styles: her quickness looked impulsive to me. I soon learned that my careful reflection seemed like foot-dragging to her!

But after about six months we began to mesh. In two years' time we had become a terrific team—able to depend on each other without a doubt or second thought. I respect her energy in approaching a problem; I've even started to show more enthusiasm myself! I know she's come to appreciate my deliberation and patience. We've learned a lot from working so closely together and had some good fun in the process. We still often disagree but our arguments feel clean; we don't need to punish or manipulate each other. Surprisingly, we spend almost no time together apart

from the office. Only now do I realize how close we have become.
What will I do without her?

This is not a tale of romance, but it is a story of intimacy. Intimacy is about engagement—the many ways we hold one another.
In some relationships we embrace one another as lovers. But the
engagements of adult life go beyond passion and romance. As
friends, we hold one another in affection; as colleagues, we hold
one another accountable in our work. More painfully, we often
engage one another in the confusing embrace of conflict.

In this chapter we will explore the wider experience of intimacy. Sometimes the phrase "an intimate relationship" is used
in a way that really means sexual sharing. But intimacy is more
than a polite synonym for genital behavior. Intimacy encompasses more than sex. Intimacy brings us close. An intimate relationship draws us close enough to one another that we are
changed in the process.

The relationship of friendship brings us close. We share ourself with friends, and they open themselves to us in return.
Friendship makes us intimates—emotional ties develop; our lives
overlap. This proximity, while offering comfort and support, also
makes friends our most knowledgeable critics. And dismissing
the criticism of a trusted confidant is not easy. Friendship confirms our sense of self (our friend knows us well and loves us
still!). Friendship also tests that identity, challenging us with new
information and influencing the way we understand ourself.

But intimacy is not limited to emotional closeness. Collaboration brings us close. Working together puts people regularly in
close contact. We see each other's strength and resilience; we
learn about each other's limitations and blind spots. Even without becoming friends, we can become genuinely involved in one
another's lives. This involvement is what intimacy is about.

In close relationships, however, we hold one another in conflict as often as in compassion and care. This more ambiguous embrace may be part of intimacy as well. Two friends, for example, struggle to resolve a painful misunderstanding. As the conflict develops, they feel distant from one another and dangerously exposed: "I am vulnerable here; I may be hurt." But often, as the struggle is resolved, they sense that they have grown closer. In the midst of—perhaps *because of*—the conflict, their relationship deepens. If this seems paradoxical at first, it makes sense. When we are in conflict, we are engaged with one another. This genuine engagement, more than warm feelings, makes for intimacy.

Friendship, love, collaboration, negotiation, compromise, conflict—these are the arenas of intimacy. Our embraces range from the erotic to the competitive, from the friendly to the antagonistic. These differing experiences raise the questions: Are we sure enough of our self to risk drawing close to someone else? Are we open to the new information that may arise as we come together? In these questions we face what frightens us most about intimacy —not what we learn about others, but what we learn about ourself.

A surprising lesson of intimacy is the ambivalence we feel. Being close to other people brings both delight and annoyance. And often these two feelings exist side by side. A friend's genuine concern consoles me, yet sometimes her interest seems meddlesome. The colleague with whom we work most effectively also makes us the most impatient.

Our ambivalence puts us in touch with the practical demands of intimacy. Drawing close, we enjoy each other's company; we bring out the best in one another; we love each other well. But being close, we also offend one another and make unrealistic demands. We misinterpret each other's motives; we get in each other's way. Maturing in intimacy means learning to live with both the exhilaration and the strain that come with being close.

Personal Strengths for Intimacy

Intimacy, then, carries costs. If its rewards are great, so are its requirements. To meet these demands requires a robust range of personal resources—strengths that we develop in the give-and-take of the relationships of our life.

What does being close to people require of us? In his classic studies in adult maturity, psychologist Erik Erikson has looked for answers. He uses the term *intimacy* to name an expectable cluster of personal strengths that support our efforts to draw close to one another. What are these resources? Following Erikson's lead, we will start with a working definition and then go on to explore its elements.

As a strength of adult maturity, intimacy is the capacity

- to commit ourself to particular people
- in relationships that last over time
- and to meet the accompanying demands for change
- in ways that do not compromise personal integrity.

THE CAPACITY FOR COMMITMENT

How is life to be lived well? Most of us are intrigued by the question. We recognize that our lives are likely to hold some dark times, periods of confusion or loss or pain. But we search for ways of living that, over a lifetime, will be both satisfying and effective. Satisfying: so that our life makes sense to us personally, bringing us joy and meaning and peace. And effective: so that our life makes sense beyond just ourselves. We want to make a contribution, to help other people, to give ourself to the larger world. To live this way means to link ourself to people and to values. We do this by developing a capacity for commitment.

Philosopher Hannah Arendt captures the importance of this capacity when she says, "The remedy for unpredictability, for the chaotic uncertainty of the future, is contained in the faculty to make and keep promises." Commitments rescue life from being a series of random encounters interrupting our isolation. We link our lives to people and to values in the hope that we may learn to be fruitful in consistent ways.

Personal commitment is the core strength in intimacy. In our commitments we pledge ourselves *for the future*—beyond both our vision and our control. This risk is necessary, for without commitment we limit our loyalties to the present. But this risk is also serious because we do not control the future. We cannot be certain that our present feelings will last. In a commitment, we summon our will in an effort to shape the future. We hold ourselves open to whatever is necessary so that the bond between us may endure.

As we move through life, we come to recognize two kinds of important commitments. One is the ability to commit ourself to ideals and values; without this, our life remains unfocussed. The other is the ability to commit ourself to persons; without this, we remain alone.

This difference is most easily seen in the following example: at sixteen, Eileen is approaching those initial decisions about personal values that will shape her early adult years. She is an idealistic young woman, already determined to pursue a career through which she can use her talent for humankind. She wants to be either a research chemist in pursuit of a cure for cancer or an agricultural specialist in drought-stricken Africa. Eileen's idealism is appealing; it also gives evidence of her growing ability to commit herself to values—one of the two essential commitments of adulthood.

But as we learn more, we see that all is not well in her life these days. Eileen, who yearns to give her life for humanity, is having a hard time dealing with people. To begin with, her relations with her parents are strained. Eileen thinks that they make impossible demands on her; their ideas are outmoded; they still treat her like a child. She also finds most of her teachers deficient: they are boring in class and generally "out of it." She is critical of her social world as well: none of the girls she has as friends are very popular; none of the really attractive guys are interested in her.

Learning these details of Eileen's interpersonal life can depress us. This young woman loves humanity but does not like people. In Eileen's case we may console ourselves by recalling that she is, after all, only a teenager. To love abstract humanity but to dislike most of the particular people we meet on an everyday basis— that is not a bad way to be sixteen. But it is an awkward way to be thirty-six!

In the move beyond adolescence, committing ourself to *particular* people becomes increasingly important. In the friendships and work that fill our twenties we begin to realize that "humanity" does not exist. All that is out there are people. If we are going to link our life in any meaningful way, the connection must come through commitment to people. But people come only in the particular; each is a lovely, if limited, instance of humanity-in-general. If life is not to be lived alone, we must be able to commit ourself to these real people, limited and flawed as they may be.

This commitment "in the particular" makes demands in all close relationships. In marriage, for example, we marry both an individual and an ideal. Our partner is "perfect" for us; he has all the attributes for which we have been searching. Gradually we discover that we have not wed the ideal husband. We have married this person who has not only wonderful gifts, but also fears and doubts that surprise both of us. Love matures as we commit ourself not to the idealized person whom we married a decade ago but to *this person* right now.

A similar purification can be part of our commitment to a group—a profession, a religious congregation, a working team. We may begin with an idealized sense of the members, but soon we learn the truth. This group is composed of "just people." Like ourself, they are both capable and flawed, wounded and blessed. Unless we can link our life with people like that, intimacy will be hard to come by.

In Relationships That Last over Time

Most of us can recall a dear friend we had in college or in the old neighborhood as we were growing up. As close as we were then, we are no longer in touch. We all know of marriages that, even though they seemed so well begun, have ended. These experiences raise questions: How long should a relationship last? How long, we wonder, does intimacy endure?

The issue of duration challenges us all. For some of us, the question is, Can I give my heart here, if it may not be forever? The question arises often these days, as the mobility of our lives complicates our relationships. In our first job, for example, we make new friends with gusto. When a job change moves us away, we feel the pain of losing these friends but we gamely set out to make new ones. After a few more moves, we become more hesitant: How long will we be here? Is getting involved really necessary? Is getting involved worthwhile?

With experiences like this, we want to strike a bargain: "Give me a relationship that is guaranteed to last and I will be open to the demands of intimacy. But anything short of that kind of guarantee is just not worth the risk." Of course, at the start of a relationship no such guarantee exists. Relationships do not come like appliances, with factory warranties. Even relationships once thought of as stable and permanent are now seen differently. We recognize more readily today that indissolubility is a graced achievement of a marriage over a lifetime, rather than an assurance at the start. In other relationships, too, loyalty and longevity are gifts of the relationship more than guarantees.

Others of us, suspicious of guarantees, try to strike a different bargain: "I am able to be present to you now but don't ask me to say 'tomorrow.' Tomorrow is too unknown. How can I pledge my future based only on what I know now? I may change, you may change, the situation between us may be different." Duration becomes the enemy here, as we draw back from establishing the links that will make a claim on our future. But without these kinds of links, we doom our life to loneliness.

Relationships cost. And some of the costs cannot be predicted or circumscribed ahead of time. To deal with the demands of duration as these emerge in our relationships, we must draw upon our resources for intimacy.

To Meet the Demands for Personal Change

Intimacy is not static. People change and relationships develop over time. Reminiscing with an old friend, we recall that when we first met we didn't even like each other! But over the years we have grown closer. Through lots of affection and not a little conflict, our friendship has blossomed in ways neither one of us could have predicted.

Sometimes we experience the developments in relationships positively, but often enough the changes have a more negative feel. A friendship begun with such vigor turns sour; the openness we used to enjoy has been replaced by defensiveness. We cry, "What has happened to us? You've changed and it's not fair!" These confusions can be part of our marriage: "You are not the woman I thought I married; things are not turning out the way I had hoped." Here change comes as disappointment, even betrayal. Promises have not been kept; someone is to blame.

Intimacy is not static. This seems true even of our relationship with God. We had thought that at least God does not change. God is dependable, eternal, immutable. But as we grow and learn more about the mystery of living, we see the childishness of much of our religious faith. We feel our faith maturing and deepening; we recognize our relationship with God is changing as well. In Psalm 77 we meet the lament that accompanies this realization: "This is the cause of my grief: that the ways of the Most High have changed!"

Relationships that last, change. We have been together awhile; now we sense our relationship becoming different. We may feel that our friend has changed or that we are now different or that the circumstances around us have altered. These changes make demands—for accommodation, for understanding, for tolerance, for forgiveness. In these demands the costs of intimacy become clear. If this relationship is to continue, a price must be paid. The price is tendered in the coin of personal change.

If this relationship is to continue, we must be different. For this marriage to continue, we must set aside some of our earlier expectations and struggle toward a new understanding of who we are for one another. For a friendship to grow, we must be open to the demands that loyalty makes. If we are to become real colleagues, we will have to let our co-workers see our weaknesses as well as our strengths. Close relationships involve an overlapping of space, a willingness to be influenced, an openness to the possibility of change. To weigh and meet these demands, we must draw on our resources for intimacy.

Intimacy invites us beyond ourself. But we can accept the invitation only if we have a strong and flexible sense of self. Without some flexibility we will find the demands of intimacy too difficult. If our sense of self is not strong, intimacy will appear not only difficult, but dangerous. We then fear closeness, because the other person may overwhelm us. Or, because we have no clear sense of who we are, we may try to become what the other wants us to be, or what we *think* this person wants us to be.

If our capacity for closeness is not rooted in some sense of our adequacy on our own, the intimacy that results will lead not to mutuality but to symbiosis. Mature intimacy, which is more than an impulse for merger, includes a sense of autonomy and an awareness of our continuing responsibility for ourself. The tension between closeness and autonomy is part of the ambivalence of intimacy. Maturity does not do away with the struggle but brings with it the resources that help us tolerate the strain.

WITHOUT COMPROMISING OUR INTEGRITY

Intimacy often demands compromise—a willingness to come to agreement through changes on both sides. But to the purist, compromise sounds like surrender, giving in without a fight, failing to stand up for what we believe. In close relationships many of us come to see compromise in quite another light. We learn that sometimes compromise is the best way to say "I love you."

But when and how to compromise? When is compromise a gesture of generosity and when is it a failure to meet an important challenge? How do we stay open to significant change without selling ourself out?

Sometimes the challenge is clear. We need to apologize, to admit we were wrong; we need to ask forgiveness. We make the first move toward reconciliation, even though we know that our friend shares some of the blame. We may feel awkward and embarrassed, but when we move toward the other person in this way we sense growth. Compromise puts us in touch with what is best in us.

But we have all had other experiences with compromise. We have recognized that for a relationship—a marriage, a working team, a friendship—to continue, we will have to change. This concession, however, does not lead to growth. The accommodation asked is that we give up ourself—let go of something that is crucial to who we are or who we might be at our best. In short, for this relationship to continue we must sell out.

Many forces may incline us to make such a compromise: we don't want to disappoint others; we want to do what appears virtuous. But beneath these voices we hear the call of conscience: the price of this compromise is our integrity.

The suggestion here is not that, if we were mature, personal change would always be easy. Nor is it that, if we were mature, we could easily tell the difference between the demands for change that lead to life and those that put us at risk of losing what is best in us. What we are suggesting is that maturity brings the ability to hang in there—to tolerate the ambiguity of the situation as we try to discern what is being asked of us and where these demands will lead.

Intimacy and Integrity: A Challenge for Women and for Men

Intimacy leads us beyond individualism but not beyond integrity. In close relationships we work out the connections between intimacy and integrity. We ask ourselves how we can share deeply with others, in ways that respect and replenish who we really are. This question confronts each of us. But as feminist psychologists are showing us today, the challenge posed by the question is often different for women than for men. The difficulty for many men involves the word *connection*. Men ask, "How can we draw close to other people, in ways that do not threaten our sense of self as independent?" Women more often feel the strain of the word *separation*. They ask, "How can we nourish a sense of personal autonomy, in ways that do not diminish the important connections we have with other people?"

Psychologist Nancy Chodorow has examined childrearing practices to help us understand the roots of this fundamental difference. In many cultures—ours included—mothers are the primary, sometimes the exclusive, caretakers of young children of either sex. Most often, the first emotionally close relationship that an infant experiences is with the mother. As this primary experience of love develops, a girl child comes gradually to recognize that mother is "not me," even though, as a woman, she is "like me." Her early awareness of self is as *like* mother, as connected with the loved one. The boy child grows into the realization that mother is "not me" but also "not like me." His awareness of self depends on a more profound sense of separation from the loved one.

This early developmental history influences us as adults. For many women, the sense of "who I am" comes from *connections* with other people. Relationships are thus central to a woman's identity. Closeness to other people confirms her sense of self. For many men, the sense of "who I am" comes from *separateness* from other people. For a man, emotional closeness creates tension because it challenges this separateness. Relationships, then, can be experienced as a risk to identity.

Reaffirming what all of us know from our own lives is important here. Both men and women appreciate the benefits of emotional closeness; women and men alike value the resources of personal autonomy. But in building a lifestyle that nurtures both intimacy and integrity, women and men are likely to experience different strains.

Most women find close relationships both essential and satisfying. For a woman, being close to other people confirms her womanhood (that's what women are supposed to do well) and reinforces a positive sense of herself. Acting independently—that is, relying on her own resources—is desirable in many ways but is a more ambiguous achievement than connecting with others. To succeed in this autonomous stance may leave her feeling less "feminine." (Men—not women—are supposed to be good at standing apart and acting on their own!)

Succeeding in independence may threaten a woman at a more basic level. For many women the earliest sense of self is developed by "drawing close," first to mother and then with others. As an adult, a woman's identity continues to be rooted in similarity and connection. Self-reliance suggests separation; this goes against the feminine sense of self as essentially connected with other people. Autonomy is then risky, for it demands differentiation, setting herself apart from others.

A comparable dynamic complicates things for men. For a man,

acting independently confirms masculinity (that's what men are supposed to do well) and helps him feel good about himself. Behaving in ways that bring him close to other people adds a good deal to his life, but these benefits are not without a price. Wanting close relationships calls his manhood into question (a "real man" is able to go it alone); being successful at drawing close to others may even undermine rather than support his self-esteem. (After all, women—not men—are supposed to be good at that sort of thing!)

At a more basic level, drawing close to people may be threatening to men whose initial sense of self is developed by moving away, by separating self from mother. This awareness of self is subsequently defended by developing a strong sense of the boundaries between himself and other people. Close relationships threaten these boundaries. The response of some men can be panic. Without being fully conscious of the cause of his distress, he senses that if he lets this person become close he risks more than personal preferences or his daily schedule. His very being is at stake, his sense of separate selfhood, his confident grasp of who he is as a man.

As we saw in Chapter 3, a woman usually interprets relationships as a source of security. She experiences bonds as links of love. Emotional connections form a nurturing network for her, a safety net that serves her survival and growth. She knows that healthy relationships include both union and separateness. Still, separateness seems risky. Her inner boundaries between self and others remain somewhat flexible, enabling her to more easily incorporate other people into the world of her awareness and concern. In her relationships, then, she wants to overcome the distance between herself and her partners. She strengthens her ties with other people; she accommodates her wishes to those of others, compromises for the sake of harmony, even acquiesces if necessary.

For most women, relationships develop wholistically, sometimes cutting across the clear distinctions (boss/worker; professional/client) that preserve separateness. A woman often wants to add emotional dimensions—affection, care, mutual concern—to those otherwise "cool" relationships, so that she feels more connected.

For most men, emotional security comes from a sense of separateness. They frequently interpret bonds established by relationships as bondage. Connections appear risky; relationships need boundaries and structures to make them safe. Close relationships, with their emotional dimensions and demands, threaten them the most. Some men deal with this risk by avoidance; they do not let themselves get close to other people. Others use control to lessen the risks; they reinforce power differences (dating only much younger women; working exclusively with junior colleagues) or insist on clear roles and rules for what goes on in the relationship. Others hold back essential parts of themselves—feelings, hopes, dreams, vulnerability, emotions—to protect a sense of separateness from their partners.

As women and as men, then, we develop—often without full awareness—characteristic responses to the demands for personal accommodation that are part of close relationships. When change is required in a relationship, some of us flee. Our underlying attitude is that we are open to relationships so long as they don't make demands, at least not at any serious level. As soon as there is a hint that we will have to change if this relationship is to continue, we leave. Even if we stay around physically, we withdraw psychologically. We remove ourself from relationships that make demands.

For others of us, the temptation is different. Faced with a demand that we change so that a relationship may continue, we give in. Many women report that this is a tendency to which they feel particularly vulnerable. Having learned early the importance of relationships to a sense of personal well-being, a woman may feel that she cannot risk losing a relationship—any relationship.

When she realizes that she must change in some way if the relationship is to continue, she is inclined to acquiesce easily, without weighing the cost to her integrity or self-esteem.

Maturity moves us beyond these automatic responses. Our intimacy resources enable us to experience the demand for change without always running away or immediately giving in. As we struggle with our partner toward a solution that is mutually respectful and mutually satisfying, we are able to tolerate the strain.

Sex and Intimacy

Sex is not the whole of intimacy, but for many of us sex has been part of our maturing in love. We have experienced the power of sexual sharing: it can open us to a larger communion. Risking closeness in sex play, we have learned to let down our defenses in other ways as well. Our nakedness has taught us that showing another person who we really are is safe—our lover will not mock us; our beloved will not desert us. In lovemaking we share a delight that helps appease the tensions that arise—inevitably and expectably—in our continuing close contact.

Personal experience affirms the links between sex and love. This connection has made sexual love a model and metaphor of intimacy. The rituals of lovemaking highlight, in dramatic fashion, features common to other experiences of intimacy as well—the impulse to share ourself with another, the anxious moment of self-revelation, the affirmation of being accepted, the delight in the give-and-take of the activities we share. Love play is a vivid example of the "mutual regulation of complicated patterns" that characterizes intimacy, whatever its shape. The birth of a child is a profound sign, reminding us of the vitality and fruitfulness of every expression of genuine love.

REFLECTIVE EXERCISE

What are the personal strengths that make intimacy possible? We have explored this question in the chapter. Now consider your own experience.

Begin by recalling the people who are your "intimates," those close to you in love or work or friendship. Take time to savor the presence of these special people in your life.

Select one of these significant relationships. Recall some of the details: the way you met, the ups and downs of your history together, what each of you brings to the relationship, how things are between you these days. Then respond to these questions:

As you reflect on this relationship, what does it tell you about your strengths for intimacy, about the resources you bring to being close to others?

Have you learned anything here about your limits regarding intimacy, about the frustrations and hesitancies you feel when you come close to others?

Are there ways this relationship has helped you get better at intimacy, more confident or more comfortable in drawing close to other people?

ADDITIONAL RESOURCES

Erik Erikson discusses intimacy as a strength of adult maturity in Chapter 7 of his *Childhood and Society* (Norton, 1963) and Chapter 4 in *Insight and Responsibility* (Norton, 1964). In *Vital Involvement in Old Age* (Norton, 1986), colleagues Joan Erikson and Helen Kivnick join him in an analysis of the effect in later life of the successful—and unsuccessful—development of these resources that make love and commitment possible.

Ethicist Margaret Farley examines the dynamics of commitment in *Personal Commitment: Beginning, Keeping, Changing*

(Harper & Row, 1986). In *Caring and Commitment* (Harper & Row, 1987), Lewis Smedes addresses the challenges and rewards that accompany the effort to keep faith through our commitments. Nancy Chodorow's influential analysis of the impact on gender of childrearing patterns is found in *The Reproduction of Mothering: Psychoanalysis and the Sociology of Gender* (University of California Press, 1978).

Mary G. Durkin explores themes of sexuality and intimacy in the religious perspective: see her *Guidelines for Contemporary Catholics: Sexuality* (Thomas More Press, 1987) and *Feast of Love: Pope John Paul II on Human Intimacy* (Loyola University Press, 1985). James J. Young speaks with honesty and compassion to the crises of intimacy experienced by those who are separated or divorced; see his *Divorcing, Believing, Belonging* (Paulist Press, 1984). We discuss the developmental characteristics of intimacy in *Christian Life Patterns* (Image Books/Doubleday, 1982) and *Marrying Well* (Image Books/Doubleday, 1983).

5.
Caritas—Love Realized and Transformed

No one has ever seen God, but as long as we love
one another God will live in us and God's
love will be complete in us. (I John 4:12)

Sex, sexuality, intimacy—in each of these we meet the human
ambition for love. Rooted in our bodies—in the delights and
needs that draw us toward one another—love leads us beyond
ourselves. Love can even lead us to God. Christians celebrate
love as the beginning and end of our religious tradition. Creation itself is a gift of God's affection. The Creator "so loved the
world" that Jesus was sent among us. Love becomes the great
commandment for Jews and Christians: "You must love the
Lord, your God, with all your heart, with all your soul, with all
your strength, and with all your mind, and your neighbor as
yourself" (Luke 10:27; Jesus is quoting Deuteronomy 6:5). Love
is to be the identifying characteristic of those who follow the way
of Jesus: "By this love you have for one another, everyone will
know that you are my disciples" (John 13:35).

The love that Jesus lived and taught has long been described by Christians as *caritas*—charity. Those who attempt to follow Jesus today, aware that love is central, recognize that religious rhetoric often robs the word *charity* of much of its force. Charity then degenerates into a sentimental "feeling kindly toward others," a bland virtue exercised in the facile enjoinder to "have a nice day." The robust challenges of *caritas*—urging us to effective action in social and political areas and compelling us to love strangers and enemies as our own—are lost in a piety that asks too little of us.

"Our love is not to be just words or mere talk, but something real and active" (I John 3:18). Genuine love moves beyond rhetoric and sentiment. Charity must carry through from arousal to action. *Caritas* shapes the affections of eros into generous care. As a virtue, charity becomes habitual—a resident strength that guides our love into consistent and effective behavior. Charity gives love endurance and sustains our hope to be faithful and fruitful. Among Christians, charity encompasses not only the affection we feel for our closest friends but also the actions by which we support the well-being of those who are not "our kind."

As we search for this hardier virtue of charity, we need to track the maturing of love. Love often begins in romance and erotic arousal. Strong feelings of affection accompany the attraction we feel for one another. We rejoice in the physical delights of love.

Eros, which begins in the body, becomes the enemy of *caritas* only when it stops there. Eros fails us when it leads us to equate loveliness with physical beauty or sexual prowess alone. When the body is love's only abode, change becomes an enemy. Fidelity is foolish; commitment a trap.

As love matures, eros moves toward a more profound and enduring bond. Erotic love expands beyond a narrow sexual focus to thrive on broader expression—the intimate exchanges of affection and concern that only time together can teach. This love sustains a relationship through a long period of absence or illness. Despite the loss of genital expression or even a lack of accustomed mutuality, the bond survives and affection flourishes. We see this strength today: a spouse succumbs to Altzeimer's disease; a lover is stricken with AIDS. Erotic excitement subsides but love endures. The partner continues the daily deeds of love—presence, patience, faithful care—not from guilt but from affection. Such intimacy is, most emphatically, not romantic. The emotion that sustains intimacy here is not sexual passion but the deeper bond of devotion.

Not all intimate relationships require this kind of commitment. Nor is such dramatic devotion always possible. But when we witness such fidelity, we are—all of us—reminded of the possibilities of love. Eros, begun in physical arousal and expressed in sexual delight, has been transformed in love. Devotion develops not by repudiating eros but by expanding its expression and deepening its bonds.

Charity accompanies friendship and delight, as part of our affection for one another. But *caritas* carries us beyond mutuality, enabling us to love the unfamiliar face of the stranger and the battered body of the wounded. This love, neither rooted in sexual arousal nor fulfilled in genital sharing, is both natural and more than natural: to love these others as our sisters and brothers is to be truly human, and yet the ability to do so makes us most exceptional.

Christian love is not a wholly different love. We are not called to love in a wholly unique fashion but to exercise the extraordinary capacity for love that we find within ourselves. The vision and values that excite us to such love stamp this maturation as Christian. Stories of the generous love of saints and prophets, missionaries and martyrs, fill our rich religious tradition. These models show us that courageous love is possible and strengthen us to act this way ourselves.

What does it mean to call this vision Christian? That life has a purpose that goes beyond ourselves alone, that "others" are more like us than different, that commitment and fidelity are possible—this vision illuminates several religious traditions. These are *Christian* insights because, for us, God has revealed these possibilities through the life of Jesus Christ. His way of living changes us, making us see life differently.

The Christian gospels confront us with the witness of Jesus. His behavior argues that personal commitment and vulnerability are worth the risk. His life challenges the cultural biases that make self-preservation and "getting my fair share" our central goals. Giving our life for other people, learning to forgive and to accept forgiveness, using our resources to make the future better —we begin to see these as possible and worthy goals.

This way of seeing marks the beginning of religious faith. Christianity carries a special vision of the world, revealing to us who we are and who we might be. But this vision sometimes seems evanescent. Its insights come and go; they do not always seem defensible. On certain days the evidence against this vision overwhelms us. We lose the point of our own life, or we are injured by someone we love, or confused by the senseless violence in the world. We become painfully aware that we are not the source of the vision; it comes instead as a gift. And when the vision comes, it arouses us to live differently. The vision of *caritas* invites the transformation of eros. Christians have traditionally called this vision-as-gift by the name of faith. Faith comes as a gift with strings attached, for the vision compels us to act in new ways. Like charity, faith is not a private sentiment, but a commitment to action. Our religious faith becomes practical in our effort to live, in a daily and concrete fashion, what we have received.

Christianity celebrates a deeper meaning of love that is easily lost or obscured in the hectic pace of life. Our religious heritage carries an insight, a vision into what is ordinarily invisible—the power and presence all around us of God's redeeming love for the world. *Caritas* connects us to that graceful vision. In our own actions of mercy and love we participate in the transforming power of *caritas*. The transformation of our love, which finds expression in care and forgiveness, carries us beyond ourselves in kinship and concern for the future.

Care

> Love is always patient and kind; it is never jealous; love is never boastful or conceited; it is never rude or selfish; it does not take offense, and is not resentful. Love takes no pleasure in other people's sins but delights in truth. It is always ready to excuse, to trust, to hope, and to endure whatever comes. (I Corinthians 13:4–7)

Caritas expands in care, both fulfilling and transforming love. Care is an active concern for the well-being of those we love, not just as extensions of us but for themselves. The capacity to care includes both power and nurturance. In this expansion of love, some of us struggle to learn how to nurture others. Some men, socialized to see themselves solely as makers and doers in their own right, find nurturance difficult. Learning to care—to invest ourself in other people's lives in ways that respond to their genuine needs—comes as a challenge. Many men welcome the challenge, recognizing that it opens them to a new world of affection and mutual concern. But other men find nurturance too difficult or too threatening or just too time-consuming. However, without the expansion of self that comes from nurturing other people, this kind of man can approach midlife with an uneasy sense of stagnation or loss. An aggressive self-starter in his thirties, in his fifties he takes on the defended rigidity of the "self-made man."

For women the challenge can be different. Trained since childhood to discern and respond to the needs of others, many women find that nurturing comes easily. But personal power remains alien. One woman notes, "I have never really thought of myself as powerful. I don't feel particularly competent or independent or strong. In fact, I feel that I don't have much direct involvement in life. I can take care of people—my children, my husband—and I think I do that pretty well. But I have little sense that I make any direct contribution of my own to the world. Sometimes I feel like an empty shell."

For a woman, learning to care well can mean developing a richer sense of her personal power. Without this self-awareness, and the confidence that comes with it, the nurturing woman can feel unfocused, insubstantial, "like an empty shell." Her care can disintegrate into anxiety or harden into a meddling concern. The capacity to care is rooted in an awareness of personal power. It is this power that we use, we spend, we give away as we care for others. If we see ourself as having no power, our efforts to care are continually imperiled: either we burn out trying to please others or we keep others dependent on us, so that we can feel strong.

But this is not *caritas*. Charity nurtures life, not continued dependency. To care is to use our power to support another's growth. To love well is to know how to come close to other people in ways that give life. To love well may also mean to learn how to let go.

To learn to let go in love—this is the special discipline at the heart of *caritas*. Care is purified as it expands beyond control. When we cannot "have it our way," when our relationship no longer develops according to our plan, can we still love? Can we continue to invest ourself in the well-being of others, when their lives take a direction that goes beyond what we think is best for them? Love remains untested until we experience the demand to love others, not just for what they bring to our life, but for themselves. Surviving this test, love is transformed.

Love expands as we learn to care with less control. Care ushers us into the maturity of stewardship. As stewards we are responsible for others without "possessing" them. When we are tempted to hold on too tightly, caritas reminds us that all love comes to us as gift.

Forgiveness

If your brother does something wrong, reprove him and, if he is sorry, forgive him. And if he wrongs you seven times a day and seven times comes back to you and says, "I am sorry," you must forgive him. (Luke 17:3-4)

One of the actions most emphasized by Jesus and most enjoined upon his followers is forgiveness. Forgiveness expands love. In forgiving, we choose not to let the hurt we have experienced get in the way of this relationship continuing. Forgiveness enables us to start again, to come to a sense of a new beginning.

Forgiving involves a decision that is not completed in the moment of choice. As a process, forgiveness gradually allows the hurt to heal and the trust between us to be renewed. The process of forgiving does not bring us back to where we were. Nor does it allow us to go on as if nothing had happened. Something has happened, something profound. The fabric of our interwoven lives has been torn. We can neither forget this nor deny it. Yet we can choose not to be defined by this rupture. Instead we can incorporate it as part of an ongoing relationship. We hope that the hurt we have experienced will not become the pattern, but we sense its contribution of depth and substance to our interaction.

Neither extending nor receiving forgiveness is easy. In order to forgive we must experience our pain and face the offense that is its cause. We must be willing to test our hurt to determine if our feelings of anger are justified. If we submit our feelings to this kind of scrutiny, we may find that we are wrong. Perhaps we have misjudged another's motives or overreacted to an event. But rather than acknowledging this mistake, we may prefer to nurse the anger and refuse to consider forgiveness.

The self-examination that forgiveness requires shows us ways in which we have contributed to the hurt. In few situations is one party solely to blame; most interactions are conjoint, with each of us contributing to the problems that develop. But again, seeing ourself as the innocent victim may be more important to us than risking the self-knowledge that forgiveness demands.

Genuine forgiveness also robs us of our hurt. We can no longer harbor it for later use against the other person. We must surrender the wound or injustice that may have become a cherished, if bitter, possession. Letting go of this vengeful possession, we lose a painful advantage we have been savoring, but we regain the personal energy that has been dissipated as we nourished this hurt. In a sense, forgiveness evens the score, for it undercuts the sense that we have something to hold over the other person. In forgiving, we start out anew, perhaps humbled (we know how fragile a relationship can be) but hopeful too.

Forgiveness is both hard to give and difficult to receive. To accept forgiveness we must revisit the pain we have caused. We have to acknowledge our responsibility; we may even have to admit that we were wrong. Here again, we may find that denying all this is easier than reaching out in love. To need forgiveness is humbling. As long as we are in the right, we have no such need. To accept forgiveness is to acknowledge our guilt—not only to ourself but to the other person as well.

But while difficult, forgiveness is often the only path to peace. At times we cannot talk enough or explain enough or regret enough to bring the two of us back together. The harm has been too heavy; the distance between us is now too great to bridge. In these situations we relearn that forgiveness is more than a personal achievement; it is a gift and a grace that, spent by our anger, we must await in hope.

The promise of forgiveness is one of the most startling of Christian hopes. We discover that we have the power to change the past! After a severe injury, our hearts tend to harden. Or after a failure of love, we stoically shrug and say, "It happened; nothing can be done." The gospels reveal another way. We can forgive—even ancient wounds and absent others. *Caritas* prompts us to expect the extraordinary even from ourselves. In the strength of love, we contradict the power of the past and the force of its failures. We can forgive what has been done to us—by parents, by adversaries, by institutions.

In Jesus' life forgiveness takes on an importance that even his followers found difficult to accept. Overturning the religious wisdom of his day, Jesus insisted that virtue is found less in an upright observance of the law than in forgiving one another. A woman caught in adultery is brought into a public square to be shamed and even stoned. Jesus seems uninterested in punishment. His care for the woman suggests the three elements of reconciliation: acknowledging the wrong, letting it go, and changing our life to turn away from future wrongdoing. Jesus did not invent forgiveness, but he refined the shape of this power and announced that it was available to all. And Jesus made this virtue an identifying characteristic of those who would follow him. We, too, must be willing to forgive—our enemies, our friends, even ourselves.

Forgiveness is a face of charity. This virtue alters the nature of Christian community, inviting us to see ourselves as a gathering of the wounded and sinful, not just the virtuous or chosen. Such a community carries an extraordinary resource—the power to forgive. The Christian community thus becomes a place of reconciliation.

Kinship

Lord, when did we see you hungry and feed you; or thirsty and give you drink? When did we see you a stranger and make you welcome, naked and clothe you or in prison and go to see you? And the king will answer, "I tell you solemnly, in so far as you did

this to one of the least of these siblings of mine, you did it to me."
(Matthew 25:39)

Caritas impels a third transformation of love. Intimacy expands
when we glimpse the hidden kinship among us. Jesus, echoing
the prophets before him, repeatedly calls us to this vision: the
poor, the orphan, the outcast are not just outsiders to be pitied
or ignored. They belong to our family; they are one of us. Influenced by this vision, Christians begin to see others not as aliens
and strangers but as our sisters and brothers. The walls that
defend family and neighborhood and faith from "those others"
begin to fall away. With the eyes of faith, we see that the stranger
is the neighbor and the neighbor is Christ. We see that even the
enemy is "our kind."

In this privileged moment, as we are given insight into human
community, love expands. We belong to one another; we have a
stake in each other's lives. *Caritas* calls us to this conviction. The
"others" who make up the world—whether these are the home-
less or the handicapped, undocumented workers or political ref-
ugees—are more like us than they are different. Putting aside the
defenses that protect us from those of a different color or custom
or economic class, we see their similarity to us. This peculiar and
surprising insight, which flies in the face of much of our socializa-
tion, invites us to respond to those others with love and justice.

Basic to the Christian vision is the conviction that we are for
more than ourselves. The call of Jesus reinforces this invitation
to generous love. "If a person who was rich in this world's goods
saw that one of his brothers was in need, but closed his heart to
him, how could the love of God be living in him?" (I John 3:17).
Christianity expands the boundaries of our concern. Our care
includes whoever is in need. Charity presses against the walls
that protect our private property. We find that we belong to a
larger family. Our resources are not just our "possessions"; they

are the means through which we contribute to a world that is more just.

The issues of justice and social action that we face in our own lives are complex. In many questions, the "right answer" does not emerge quickly or without doubt; persons of goodwill and wisdom come to different conclusions about what should be done. When the issues at stake touch directly on our own lives or our family's welfare—as in questions of job security or tax reform or national defense—determining the just response is even more difficult.

In these situations Christian awareness gives no easy answers but it does give us a starting point. We are not for ourselves alone. "Others" are not strangers but siblings. As Pope Paul VI proclaimed, action for justice and the transformation of the world is at the heart of our response to the gospel. The gospel challenges us to share the burdens of humankind and to participate in its liberation. The ways in which we participate in this mission of Jesus will differ among us. But we can expect that our own maturing as Christians will include this larger mission of *caritas*, to which the words and witness of Jesus call us.

Fruitfulness for the Future

> As a branch cannot bear fruit all by itself, but must remain part of the vine, neither can you unless you remain in me. I am the vine and you are the branches. (John 15:4)

Love that does not serve life will die: *caritas* calls us to this truth. Real mutuality is fruitful. The desire to create something together is close to the heart of intimacy—whether expressed in genital love or in collaborative work. A relationship that does not nurture this impulse is at risk. An unfruitful love will not thrive.

Psychologists are aware of the significance of this creative impulse. They warn that when we do not move beyond ourselves, we imperil a love relationship. A "pseudo-intimacy" can result, turning the partners in upon themselves in a way that gradually impoverishes the relationship. The result of this failure to expand our concern is not an intimacy more protected and complete, but stagnation. Having failed to share our love beyond ourselves we soon find that we have little left to give each other.

Our religious tradition has always cherished this truth: love is not a private affair. *Caritas,* which moves us beyond ourselves, even beyond "our kind," opens us to the future. In love, we generate the future. Our children, whom we have created in our love, belong to the future more than they do to us. This is true in other creative activity as well. Our projects, our plans, our productive work contribute to a world that goes beyond our own lifespan. Our creativity links us to the future. But the future always escapes us, for it is necessarily beyond our control.

Love invites us to pour out our power in creativity and care. But the invitation entails considerable risk. To be creative we must be willing to give our power to the future. This concern for the future is a movement of self-transcendence. The impulse to go beyond ourself may be fragile; it may even fail under pressure. But this urge may also develop strength, becoming part of the way we understand our relationship to the world. Our power, our resources are for more than just ourselves. They are, in fact, for more than that broader circle of intimates who are our family. We can give ourself to the future, a future we cannot fully control, a future we may not even live long enough to share.

To invest ourself in a future that we may not live to see, we must believe that our self-giving will bear fruit beyond ourselves. For Christians, this conviction is deeply grounded in faith, faith that the future belongs to God.

Our model here, once again, is Jesus. His life offers us a paradox of fruitful love: childless, he generated all those of us who name ourselves Christians. Calling humankind to a new way of being with God and one another, he gathered around him in love a group of followers to whom he would entrust the future of his mission. His prayer over Jerusalem, uttered as his own life was coming—prematurely—to an end, displayed his frustration and concern: "How often have I longed to gather your children, as a hen gathers her chicks under her wings, and you refused!" (Matthew 23:37). In the garden of olives Jesus struggled to understand the unexpected direction his life was taking; he labored to accept a more mysterious design for his contribution to those he loved. He rebeled against the loss of his own dreams and ambitions and begged for a different future: " 'Father,' he said, 'if you are willing, take this cup away from me' " (Luke 22:42). Surely now was not the time to let go of his own power and plan. His mission had barely begun, his followers were scarcely ready to carry on without him. Only in great turmoil and the anguish of a bloody sweat did Jesus come to accept this letting go of his life as part of his generative love.

As Christians, we are a people who struggle to let Jesus' life shape our own. So we, following him, give ourselves to the future in the faith that God will see it through, blessing and healing what we have generated in our love and what we must soon relinquish.

REFLECTIVE EXERCISE

The gospels abound in the stories and parables of Jesus. These images, deep in our consciousness, express most powerfully the convictions and hopes we hold for our own lives. Return to a gospel image that is important to you. What parable or event or saying comes to you as an image of the love that Jesus proclaims? Let the memories come as they will: there is no need to "force" a response. Wait for an image that holds power for you now.

When an image arises, spend time with it. Be attentive—let it disclose its meaning to you. After some time, consider these questions:

In what way does this gospel image strengthen and support your understanding of *caritas?*

How does this gospel image challenge your understanding of *caritas?*

What practical response does this gospel vision of love ask of you these days?

ADDITIONAL RESOURCES

Biblical scholar Pheme Perkins examines the words and witness of Jesus in *Love Commands in the New Testament* (Paulist Press, 1982). John Haughey draws together a collection of important essays examining Christian sources of action for social transformation in *The Faith That Does Justice* (Paulist Press, 1977); see, especially, his discussion of "Jesus as the Justice of God" in the final chapter. In *The Holy Use of Money* (Doubleday, 1986) Haughey considers the practical implications of Jesus' religious vision. Religious psychologist Jack Dominian explores the dynamics of charity in spiritual growth in *The Capacity to Love* (Paulist Press, 1985) and *Marriage, Faith and Love* (Crossroad Books, 1982).

In *Putting Forgiveness into Practice* (Abingdon, 1986) Doris Donnelly gives graceful assistance to the tasks of personal and social reconciliation. Today theologians, liturgists and pastoral ministers alike are involved in efforts to link more effectively the sacrament of reconciliation with the experience of forgiveness; see *Reconciliation* (Liturgical Press, 1987), edited by Peter E. Fink and *Repentence and Reconciliation in the Church* (Liturgical Press, 1987), edited by Michael Henchal.

Erik Erikson's discussions of generative care have become a classic in the psychology of adulthood. For a comprehensive statement of the place of generativity in adult development, see his *The Life Cycle Completed: A Review* (Norton, 1982). Drawing on his perspective, we discuss religious generativity in Chapter 5 in *Christian Life Patterns* (Image Books/Doubleday, 1982) and stewardship in Chapter 4 of *Seasons of Strength* (Image Books/Doubleday, 1986).

Part Two

Pleasure and Passion

To recover the good news about sexuality, we must reexamine pleasure and passion. How did sexual pleasure get such a bad reputation among Christians? How does erotic life become holy and healthy, moving us beyond the constraints and fears that wound our passion?

Part Two begins by turning to our religious heritage to explore the place of sexual pleasure in the Song of Songs and in Saint Augustine's life experience. To fathom our own passions, we explore God's arousals as these are revealed in the Scriptures. We then turn to a test case for pleasure: the vexing question of genital arousal apart from sexual intercourse.

Part Two ends with a reflection on the discipline of eros: the endless effort to heal the split between the physical and the spiritual, as erotic passion matures into generous and fruitful love.

6.

Sexuality and Pleasure

Whatever happened to pleasure? This question haunts the complicated history of Christian spirituality. Why has pleasure, which is about enjoyment, satisfaction, and delight, fallen into such disfavor?

Christianity has a curious relationship with pleasure. The fundamental Christian action is *eucharist*—thanksgiving. Giving thanks, we delight in the gifts of creation—gifts that include our bodies: we respond in sexual arousal; we act in devoted love; we become fruitful in generous care. In the religious feasts and rituals of our worship, we turn to song and dance and incense to pleasure our senses as we pray.

But a somber realization often mutes our celebration of the pleasure of creation. The staggering amount of suffering and destruction in life stuns us. Not only does death cut short our delight, but humanity has devised myriad other methods to spoil and pervert pleasure. How easily we come to use other people in pursuit of our private enjoyment; how easily we find satisfaction in actions that coerce or cause harm. In these perversions we see the seeds of the bad reputation that pleasure has earned.

A theology of sexuality depends heavily on the meaning we bring to the word *pleasure*. The dictionary assures us that pleasure is the "gratification of the senses or the mind." But we often use the word in a more limited sense, focusing only on sexual delight. As we have seen, Christians often suspected sexual delight. And when sex is suspect, pleasure becomes problematic.

To recover a more optimistic view of sexuality, we need to reexamine Christianity's historical understanding of pleasure. As Christians lost confidence in the goodness of sex, they took two approaches to pleasure. The first cloaked it in allegory; the second confused it with lust.

The Flight into Allegory

In the Hebrew Scriptures, the Song of Songs, as we saw in Chapter 2, paints a very positive picture of human love. The book celebrates the goodness of erotic pleasure. In graphic imagery, two lovers describe the longing and delight of their affection:

> His left hand is under my head
> And with his right hand he touches me. (2:6)

> His eyes like doves by waterducts . . .
> His loins smoothest ivory . . .
> His legs marble pillars . . .
> His mouth is sweet
> And all of him is desirable. (5:12, 14–16)

As Rosemary Ruether has observed in her *Sexism and God-Talk*, this is "a maverick book" in the Old Testament. Lacking the usual patriarchal tone of the other books, the poem shows us a couple who enjoy a striking mutuality. Often the woman initiates their lovemaking; seven times she tells us she will bring this lover to "her mother's home."

This poem is also maverick because it does not stress offspring as the goal and necessary fruit of making love. It simply and forcefully proclaims the goodness of sexual passion and erotic pleasure.

The Song of Songs celebrates the realm of sexual pleasure as a gift of creation. But to many Jews and Christians this was going too far. Their experience warned them of the danger of such pleasure. Scandalized by this book, they searched for an interpretation that could avoid its obvious erotic content. Their search led to allegory.

Nearly all Jewish and Christian interpreters have viewed this poem as an allegory, describing either God's love for the human soul or Christ's love for the Church. Its message, they argue, is about spiritual affection, *not* about human, erotic love! In his exhaustive commentary on the Song of Songs, Marvin Pope recounts the extremes to which this allegorical interpretation was pushed, in order to remove any scent of the erotic.

In Chapter 4, for example, the poem describes in rich sensual detail the physical attributes of the lover—her mouth and neck and breasts. Her neck is long and slender "like David's tower" (4:4). Pope notes that as recently as 1962 one interpreter saw in this description a reference to the woman's "inaccessibility, insurmountability, purity, virginity." This is the same "inaccessible lady" who, in Chapter 3, goes on a nocturnal prowl in search of her lover!

The opening verses of Chapter 3 provide one of the most moving passages of the poem:

> On my bed at night
> I sought him whom I love.
> I sought, but did not find him.
> I will rise and roam the city,
> In the streets and squares,
> I will seek him whom I love.

This is the portrait of a woman driven by her longing for the man she loves. A look at the influential commentary of Cardinal Bea, published in 1953, illustrates how the allegorical interpretation attempts to obscure any erotic meaning. Bea argues that the very passion in the poetry proves that it is not about human love. In the ancient Near East, he reasoned, a woman would never act this way! Other interpreters, commenting on this stirring passage, pushed the allegorical approach to its limit: as Pope observes, this nocturnal, erotic restlessness, "applied to the individual soul . . . was taken to indicate the impossibility of finding Christ while reclining in carnal pleasure and in the darkness of sin." Thus, the interpreters nullify the celebration of sexual pleasure as a gift of creation.

Only recently have scholars questioned this allegorical "apology" for the Song of Songs. In 1953 the biblical scholar Roland Murphy challenged Cardinal Bea's interpretation, suggesting that the text be taken at face value—not as an extravagant allegory but as a poem in praise of erotic love. Following Murphy's lead, Daniel Lys, Phyllis Trible, and other scholars are helping the Christian community recover this biblical perspective on sexual passion. This recovery encourages contemporary believers to trust their own convictions about the goodness of sexual pleasure.

Love and Lust

Having cloaked erotic pleasure in allegory, Christians proceeded to confuse sexual love with selfish lust. The chief architect of this pessimistic view of human sexuality was the influential North African bishop of the fourth century, Augustine of Hippo. This impressive figure personifies the Christian ambivalence toward sexuality.

Augustine was both married and not married (from his late teens until his baptism in his early thirties he lived with a woman in a common-law arrangement widely accepted in his day). He was convinced that marriage is good but that sex is bad. Augustine's painful resolution of the tension between faith and sexuality has had a profound influence on Christian history. His writings on this question became, for a very long time, the last word. He died in the year 430 as the Roman Empire was under final siege. For the next seven hundred years in Europe silence and stagnation replaced the energetic debates of Augustine's day. His convictions, unchallenged, became increasingly authoritative. They continue to influence Christian beliefs in our own day, almost sixteen hundred years after Augustine.

The Augustine of the *Confessions* is a compelling and very modern person. Writing his autobiography while in his early forties, just after he had become a bishop, Augustine gives us intimate glimpses into his life. His honesty and intensity dazzle us. He anxiously examines every corner of his life, questioning his motives and regretting his failures. His public self-examination invites our scrutiny, gives us a touching portrait of his strengths and wounds, and illumines for us the specific experiences upon which Augustine founded his theology of sexuality.

In the most famous passage in the *Confessions*, Augustine expresses his attitude toward life: "You have made us for yourself, and our heart is restless until it rests in you" (Book 1, Chap. 1). His autobiography reveals a person who is constantly restless and anxious. In Book 6, Augustine describes the distress of the years before his conversion: "I was toiling away, spurred on by my desires and dragging after me the load of my unhappiness . . . I was eaten up with anxieties."

Augustine remembers his youth as a season of obsession in which he hungered for respect and esteem (6:6). He clung compulsively to his friends (4:6); he was constantly swept away by the impulses of his sexual appetite. This restlessness came to special focus while he was living in Milan in his early thirties. Since his late teens, he had lived with a woman in a stable, common-law kind of relationship. (*Mistress* is not an accurate description since this word, today, suggests an extramarital and secretive affair. Augustine's relationship was public and quite acceptable in the society of the fourth century.) This fourteen-year relationship seems to have been an ambivalent one: while the couple remained faithful to each other during this considerable period (4:2), Augustine remembered it more as the satisfying of a sexual need rather than as a loving companionship.

Now, in his early thirties, Augustine has moved from North Africa to the metropolis of Milan and has garnered a civil service appointment as a teacher of oratory. His career is on the rise; the time to marry has come. Augustine's mother, ever present and persuasive, arranges an advantageous engagement with a wealthy family. Approaching this commitment, Augustine will now have to part with his common-law partner. He describes the pain of this decision: "The woman with whom I was wont to share my bed was torn from my side as an impediment to my marriage. My heart still clung to her: it was pierced and wounded within me and the wound drew blood from it" (6:5). Oddly—at least to the contemporary reader—this companion of more than a decade and the mother of his only child is never mentioned by name!

But Augustine's bride-to-be is too young to marry; his wedding must be delayed two years. Unable to face the prospect of such an enforced abstinence, Augustine chooses an interim mistress. With shame he admits his sinfulness: "In the meantime my sins were multiplied . . . I was not so much a lover of marriage as a slave of lust, so I procured another woman, but not, of course, as a wife" (6:16).

Finally, with God's grace, Augustine breaks free from his compulsive, anxious search for pleasure. Baptized as a Christian, he embraces a celibate life and returns to North Africa where he will serve the Church as priest and bishop for almost forty years.

SATISFYING THE INSATIABLE

Theologian Margaret Miles, in a most sympathetic study of Augustine, suggests that "we must accept Augustine's evaluation of himself as addicted to sex, from which, he tells us, no friendship was free." Christian readers of the *Confessions* have traditionally seen Augustine's self-recrimination as a saint's admissions of youthful foibles. But to do so, Miles reminds us, "is to ignore his feeling that sex dominated and *ordered* his life."

In addictive behavior a person attempts to satisfy an insatiable need. Augustine himself uses this phrase to describe his sexual distress: "The habit of satisfying an insatiable appetite grievously tormented me" (6:12). Usually we associate addiction with drugs and alcohol. But a similar compulsive and destructive behavior can infect our work patterns ("workaholics") or our interpersonal relationships.

Compulsiveness and unfruitful repetition characterize addiction. Augustine describes his own addiction to honors and esteem: he desperately wanted to win at childhood games (1:10); he hungered after honors and wealth as a young adult (6:6). This grasping and clinging also infected his personal relationships: compulsive and self-absorbed grieving pervaded his mourning for a dead friend (4:6). A possessive, clinging attachment wounded even his affection for his mother (5:8). Whatever he approached, Augustine tells us, he snatched and clung to. Even good fortune is something to be seized, though, he admits, "before I could grasp it, it had flown away" (6:6).

Conversion for Augustine—his very survival—would mean deliverance from this addictive behavior. He describes his conversion in two compelling sentences. In Book 9 his description is ornate and rhetorical: "Now was my mind free from the gnawing cares of favor-seeking, of striving for gain, of wallowing in the mire, and of scratching lust's itchy sore" (9:1). In Book 7, he gives a more pointed description that warms the heart of anyone who has experienced the pain of compulsiveness: "I let up on myself a little" (7:14).

This interpretation of Augustine as an addictive personality is not meant to tarnish the memory of this holy man, but to illumine his life. He repeatedly tells us that, *for him,* sexual desire was addictive. He experienced this arousal as compulsive and selfish. He felt driven to use others "to satisfy this insatiable appetite." In Book 2 of the *Confessions* he describes his confusion of love and lust:

> Clouds arose from the slimy desires of the flesh and from youth's seething spring. They clouded over and darkened my soul, so that I could not distinguish the calm light of chaste love from the fog of lust. Both kinds of affection burned confusedly within me and swept my feeble youth over the crags of desire and plunged me into a whirlpool of shameful deeds. (2:2)

As sexual love and selfish lust became confused in Augustine's life, all physical affection seemed to be lustful craving. Wounded by this addictive tendency, Augustine came to understand sexual desire as necessarily compulsive. Sexual attraction, for him, always seemed to be grasping and possessive. As for a person addicted to alcohol or drugs, abstinence was the route to Augustine's healing.

In Augustine's life, as he recounts it, selfish craving swallowed up erotic pleasure. Genital arousal always seemed to lead him to compulsively use others for his pleasure. For Augustine this was the meaning of concupiscence: "By concupiscence I mean that affection of the mind which aims at the enjoyment of oneself and one's neighbor without reference to God" (see Miles, p. 66). In his essay on *The Goods of Marriage,* Augustine insisted that even in marriage we bend concupiscence—our selfish lust—to the good purposes of procreation: "Marital intercourse makes something good out of the evil of lust" (Chap. 3).

In his seventies Augustine found himself in a bitter debate concerning sexuality and marriage. His protagonist, a bishop like himself, saw sexuality as a neutral power that could be used well or poorly. Bishop Julian, a married man like many other ecclesiastics at this time, argued that pleasure was a good and healthy part of a marriage. This argument incensed Augustine:

> Really, really: is that your experience? So you would not have married couples restrain that evil—I refer, of course, to your favorite good? So you would have them jump into bed whenever they like, whenever they feel tickled by desire? . . . If this is the sort of married life you led, don't drag up your experience in this debate! (see Brown, p. 391)

To Augustine all sexual pleasure looked like lust. Rooted in shameful arousals and the compulsion to take pleasure for oneself, these stirrings were more punishment than gift. While they might be forgiven in marriage, they could hardly be celebrated as delightful gifts of the Creator.

TAKING PLEASURE; SHARING PLEASURE

Whenever Augustine considers sexual pleasure, he speaks about *taking* pleasure. Missing from his many discussions is any mention of *giving* pleasure, of pleasuring one's partner. Nor does he refer to *receiving* pleasure, allowing oneself to accept the gift of bodily delight. The life of this holy and wounded man seems not to have included these privileged experiences. For Augustine, sexual excitation would always be felt as punishment—a reminder of his selfishness and a bitter fruit of original sin. He did not know sexual arousal and pleasure as a gift exchanged between lovers. But other Christians do. Many couples today understand the receiving of sexual delight as a gift. We experience pleasure as something shared rather than as something taken for oneself. We know the special joy that comes in pleasuring our partner. We learn the discipline of becoming attuned to the rhythm of another's arousal. And we find that careful attention to such shared pleasure enhances our life, rescues each of us from isolation, and makes all we do together richer and more fruitful. But this positive experience of sexual pleasure tends to remain hidden. It is a wisdom of the body Christian that is too rarely celebrated. Kept modestly private, it has yet to make itself felt in the Church's official view of sexuality.

Another conviction of Augustine must be examined. Repeatedly he tells us that genital arousal is indecent and shameful. In *The City of God* he refers to "the shameful motion of the organs of generation" (14:19, 21). Here we meet a theme that will become central in Christian theology: the masculine anxiety over control. Erections escape our control; they humiliate us by refusing to obey our will. Even in marriage, Augustine argued, Christians must attend to these shameful stirrings in private.

Missing in Augustine is an acknowledgment of the normal process of maturing by which our genital arousals are transformed from shame into delight. In our teens our sexuality confuses and embarrasses us. But when we fall in love, we are gifted with that surprising revelation that our partner loves our body. In a maturing sexual relationship, we learn that our arousals are neither indecent nor shameful. Partners salute each other's arousals and give thanks for them. These stirrings, in the context of our committed love, are not sordid, but praiseworthy. Without them, our love would not be complete and could not be fruitful.

In his *Confessions* Augustine shows us, with great honesty and candor, his woundedness. We should take him at his word. But we must not conclude that this wounded experience expresses all the possibilities of erotic love. If we authorize his painful experience as definitive for Christians, we do a severe injustice to sexuality and its fruitful pleasures. By a quirk of history, Augustine's judgments about sexuality had the last word for seven hundred years. Thomas Aquinas, in the thirteenth century, while respectful of Augustine's views, provided Christians with a much more positive portrait of sexuality and its pleasures. As we will see in Chapter 9, Aquinas' special gift was his understanding of habit and virtue. In Augustine, habit most often means a compulsive, sinful practice. For Aquinas, human habits can be either destructive or graceful. Graceful habits, or virtues, guide our erotic lives and purify our pleasures. For Aquinas, virtues are even meant to be enjoyable. But Augustine's pessimistic view of sexuality outlasted Aquinas' more sanguine approach and continues to powerfully influence Christian life today.

Two Kinds of Pleasure

Pleasure delights and distracts us. Pleasure refreshes our life. But, for the sake of pleasure we can turn selfish and even destructive. Pleasure can either make us mindful of God or forgetful of anything beyond ourselves.

In *The Four Loves,* C. S. Lewis provides us with a valuable distinction between two important kinds of delight: need-pleasures and pleasures of appreciation. Pleasures of need, Lewis suggests, are more urgent and instinctual. They impel us to a quick satisfaction. An example would be the thirst that we feel after working several hours in a hot sun. Suddenly we experience a sharp desire for water. We go inside and drink a large glass of cold water. As we quench this thirst, we feel a deep satisfaction. This experience of pleasure focuses on a very specific biological need. As we drink this glass of water, our need is quickly extinguished. Both the need and the pleasure are quickly over. This rapid satisfaction causes us to speak of this kind of pleasure in the past tense—"That was really good!"

In Lewis' analysis, such need-pleasures are complemented by pleasures of appreciation. These arousals, while less urgent and instinctual, point to another aspect of pleasure in human life. An example is the peculiar pleasure we feel when we come upon a field of wild flowers. Their color and profusion, their movement in the breeze arouse our delight. As we gaze at them, another kind of thirst stirs us. But this time we are not so quickly sated. No sharp biological need is relieved. We linger over our pleasure, savoring rather than quenching it. This pleasure is not as abruptly concluded as a quick drink of water. We tend to describe this kind of pleasure in the present tense: "How good it is to be here!"

The mood accompanying the pleasure of appreciation is not relief. It is more gratitude than gratification. Feeling pleasure, we are often taken out of ourselves. We have been depressed or sad, but in the presence of our pleasure we let this self-absorption go. Then a very different mood settles over us. We do not consume this kind of pleasure; instead we give ourselves to it.

In sexual attraction we experience a pleasure that links need with appreciation. To neglect this complexity in our sexuality imperils our pleasure. Sometimes we are tempted to focus on sexual arousal as if it were only a biological need: we treat it as an instinct that wants to be satisfied, an itch to be scratched. Our language is filled with instances of this approach: "I need a good (preferred obscenity)." Or, "I need a woman" (implying that any woman will do). The pleasure sought here is the relieving of an instinctual need. We don't need a partner or a lover; we want someone (anyone) that will meet this basic need. As with the drink of water, this genital need is quickly satisfied. Both the need and the pleasure quickly pass. We are left gratified rather than grateful.

When we isolate the need-pleasure aspect of our sexuality, we focus on taking pleasure rather than sharing it. Neglecting the mutuality of sexual partners, this attitude focuses on pleasure as my need, a need to be quickly gratified. Such an intensely selfish view of sexual pleasure is, indeed, the meaning of concupiscence. Pleasure's bad reputation is rooted in this narrowed meaning of sexual delight.

But the body Christian knows that sexual attraction combines the pleasure of need with the pleasure of appreciation. The sex drive is a profound biological reality, the basis of our survival as a species. But the pleasure of this intense need is joined, in our experience, to the pleasure of appreciation. A special delight stirs when we meet someone who is attractive to us. This person can absorb our attention. But we do not desire to consume this erotic delight, but to make it last. We feel a pleasure akin to wonder. This is not just someone with whom to have sex. The erotic pleasure of appreciation we experience makes us eager to explore, to touch, every part of this person—body, ideas, hopes.

As our appreciation grows, we feel the desire to *give* pleasure. We find that pleasuring this person—in body and in spirit—gives us great joy. Gradually we come to learn about the discipline of sexual delight. More than a biological need, it leads us into the complex world of partnership. We discover, sometimes painfully, the different rhythms and moods of sexual response between us. When we honor these differences, we find our shared pleasure deepening our life together. If we are fortunate, we also learn not just to give pleasure, but to allow ourself to receive pleasure. We become better able to let go of the full control of ourself and of the relationship. We can announce our needs instead of making the other person guess. We are able to surrender to the pleasure-giving initiative of our partner.

The appreciation of sexual pleasure invites us to linger in one another's presence. We dream not just of satisfying needs, but of sharing a life. This complex delight emboldens us to risk the commitment of marriage and to care for the new life that comes as a consequence of our love.

THE PERVERSION OF PLEASURE

Sexual excitement combines the pleasures of biological need and personal appreciation. When need and appreciation commingle in an energy that is both fierce and respectful, sexual pleasure finds its full potential. Desire consumes us and endures between us; it finds both gratification and gratitude. The perversion of sexual delight occurs when these two pleasures are divorced. Then each can provide only a partial answer to our fullest human desire.

A culture controlled by men and fascinated with youth is tempted to interpret sexual desire solely as a need-pleasure. The genital arousal of the young man appears so forceful, so in need of relief and gratification. In American society, entertainment and advertisement frequently idolize instant gratification and sex without consequences. Thus, society reinforces a vision of sex as essentially a biological need. The healthy instinct of sexual arousal, divorced from the pleasure of appreciation for another person, becomes a repetitive, unfruitful effort to quench a thirst that is seen as only biological. Recent research in sexual addiction, such as Patrick Carnes' *Out of the Shadows*, helps us understand the bitter fruit we produce when we divorce genital need from personal relationship.

If we can pervert sexual pleasure by reducing it to a bodily need, we can also wound it by exalting the pleasure of appreciation into romantic love. Romantic love often refers to the energetic ardor that fuels the early stage of a love relationship. But the phrase also refers to the tendency to idealize a relationship that thrives on *an absence of contact*. The courtly love celebrated in medieval literature romanticized sexual appreciation. A knight would praise a lovely woman whose charm was, in great measure, her unavailability. Concealed within a distant castle, her beauty grew the more it remained unseen. Contact—the everyday, mundane experience of a partner—would spoil romantic pleasure. Distance from the lover was essential to this particular kind of sexual fervor. In the heated imagination of the romantic, the lover's beauty remained forever spotless and unchanging. This is the definition of romance: affection without conflict, devotion without complication.

Longing sustains the sexual tension felt at a distance. Unlike a need-pleasure, romantic longing thrives on *not* being satisfied. To ensure that the distance between lovers will *not* be overcome, the denial of physical presence and physical contact must be enforced.

If secular cultures are tempted to reduce sexual pleasure to biological need, Christian piety is often tempted to reduce sexual pleasure to romantic love. Again, the ingredients are distance, lack of contact, and the emotion of longing. The exaltation of Mary, the mother of Jesus, into the Blessed Virgin bears some of these marks. This woman is placed on a pedestal, distant from other sexual women. The mother of Jesus becomes both virgin and immaculate—unstained by any carnal contact. A romantic Marian piety thrives on the distance between Mary and the needs and compromises of ordinary human life. Many Christians today seek a more robust devotion to Mary, rooted in an appreciation of her life as a model of our discipleship.

The religious gift of celibacy has, in Christian history, sometimes been entangled in this romantic separation of need and appreciation. The commitment of the celibate person has often been portrayed as an exclusive emotional attachment to God. Vowed religious have been encouraged to see themselves as "brides of Christ." The erotic imagery of the mystics describes spiritual union with God in terms of romantic longing. As we have seen, the Song of Songs was understood in a similar fashion. The language of sexual passion was used to describe the love between the soul and God. This dynamic is close to the heart of religion since our loving God is both present and absent, both tangible (in the people who surround us) and beyond contact. When celibacy and piety legitimize a withdrawal from the daily, loving contact with the community as the wounded body of Christ, this romanticism renders religious pleasure unreal.

Saint Augustine championed the religious emotion of longing. His own conversion lay in escaping a compulsive inclination toward sexual pleasure. Gradually he replaced his grasping after selfish pleasures with an intense longing for union with God. Throughout the *Confessions* and *The City of God,* he returns repeatedly to his yearning for God. A central image of *The City of God* is that of *peregrini,* "resident aliens." Augustine argues that we do not belong in this wounded, broken world. We are pilgrims on our way to another place, the city of God. As displaced persons in this foreign country, our proper emotion is longing.

After his conversion Augustine was still a driven man, but now his consuming ambition was to find satisfaction and rest in God alone. The powerful emotion of longing expressed the tension between his present lack of pleasure and his hope to find unending delight. Letting go the compulsiveness in his relationships, he sought "after pleasure that was free from disgust," and concluded that "it would be in none but you, Lord" (*Confessions,* 2:2). Rejection of sexual pleasure fueled Augustine's longing for God. To love God he felt he had to turn his back on human affection. This compromise by a wounded man worked for Augustine—he was able to live a long and fruitful life of service to the Church.

Christian wisdom today, especially the conviction of married Christians, tells another story. In the ordinary experience of our married lives, sexual delight links biological need and human appreciation. Our sexual instincts are not so brutish as to blind us to appreciation. Pleasuring one another, we enrich rather than dissipate our love. Often enough we fail one another, and sometimes sex is part of the failure. But that failure does not render our sexual love unholy. Christians have, from the beginning, been tempted to divorce a "fallen," fleshly world from a "superior," spiritual world. But this is romanticism and heresy. To hold this view is to compromise our best convictions about the goodness of creation. We find God in the contact of our bodies, not just in the longing of our souls. Longing is a genuine emotion, but so are sensual satisfaction and gratitude. Only by healing this divorce of biological need and personal appreciation will we come to understand responsible and fruitful pleasure.

REFLECTIVE EXERCISE

Revisit a relationship that is important to you. Take time to bring to mind this person who is close to you, to be aware of your presence to one another.

Now, recall the range of pleasure that is part of your love:

What is the special delight you feel with this person? How does enjoyment mark the relationship? What is the place of joy?

Can you point to instances of pleasure given, pleasure received, pleasure shared? How is this pleasure fruitful in your life?

ADDITIONAL RESOURCES

Rosemary Ruether's discussion of the Song of Songs is found in *Sexism and God-Talk* (Beacon Press, 1983); see p. 140. Marvin Pope's commentary on the Song of Songs is available in the Anchor Bible Series (Doubleday, 1977). For an excellent feminist analysis of this poem see Phyllis Trible's "Depatriarchalizing in Biblical Interpretation," *Journal of the American Academy of Religion* 41 (1973): 30–48.

Peter Brown provides a comprehensive portrait of Augustine's life and thought in *Augustine of Hippo* (University of California Press, 1967). For the text of Augustine's *Confessions,* we have followed the translation of John K. Ryan (Image Books/Doubleday, 1960). Margaret Miles' discussion of the addictive strains in Augustine's personality appears in Chapter 3 of her *Fullness of Life* (Westminster Press, 1981). John Noonan includes a useful reflection on Augustine's relationship to Manicheeism in his *Contraception* (enlarged edition, Harvard University Press, 1986).

C. S. Lewis contrasts need and appreciation as aspects of pleasure in *The Four Loves* (Harvest/HBJ, 1960). For a brief introduction to sexual addiction, see Patrick Carnes' *Out of the Shadows* (CompCare Publishers, 1983). Carl Schneider examines the connections among love, sex, and shame in *Shame, Exposure and Privacy* (Beacon Press, 1977). In *Leaving the Enchanted Forest* (Harper & Row, 1988), Stephanie Covington and Liana Beckett explore the addictive and destructive patterns that can be masked by the cultural images of romantic love.

7.

Graceful Passions

"Stir up your power, O Lord, and come!" In this ancient prayer, Christians recall that ours is a passionate God, One whose power can be aroused. In the life of Jesus we recognize the passion of God made tangible—in acts of healing and justice and compassion. But often in our own lives, passion puzzles us. How do we befriend this energy, to make it an ally—not an enemy—of our best hopes? How can our passions become graceful?

The Problem of Passion

Our trouble with passion begins in an ambivalence about arousal. We enjoy being excited, but we dislike feeling overwhelmed. We long to be stirred and touched and moved, but the threat of losing control embarrasses us. We know that a life without passion becomes, literally, apathetic. This reminds us of our continuing need to be aroused—stirred by the loveliness and needs of others, stimulated by values and ideals. We eagerly search out the excitations—sexual, compassionate, grateful—that will rescue us from our lonely safety and link us in fruitful associations. We yearn for the passions that will lift us out of our isolation.

In the midst of this hope, we remember being hurt by our

passions. In jealousy or rage we have injured loved ones. Giving in to a compulsion for success or an unhealthy guilt, we have wounded ourselves. But we know we can also harm ourselves by becoming too good at inhibiting the arousals that might move us. Passion may be hard to live with, but it is even more danger-ous to live without.

Some of our problems with passion are rooted in cultural bi-ases that we have learned. In the traditions of Western thought, for example, arousal has often been interpreted as a *private* expe-rience to be *passively* endured as an unnecessary and unwelcome *disturbance.*

ARE PASSIONS PASSIVE?

The word *passion* shares its roots with the word *passive.* This connection supports our sense that passions happen to us. Our language is rich with images of this passivity: we are *overcome* by remorse, *consumed* by lust, *swept away* by sexual desire.

From the early Greeks to modern medicine, we have struggled to understand the forces that ignite and overwhelm emotional life. Contemporary science points to genetic patterns and hor-monal influences that shape our moods, apart from our own volition. At the beginning of Western civilization, the ancient Greeks saw the artist and the hero as *driven* by energies beyond their personal understanding or control. Classical mythology named these interior forces daimons, furies, muses—personal forces that prompted people to act in both creative and destruc-tive ways. Such personification expressed the Greek view that our passions often seem beyond our control. This ancient con-viction survives in our language: an enraged person is described as *possessed,* a compulsive achiever seems *driven.* And many of us take refuge, only half-humorously, in the lament that "the devil made me do it."

Our passions are passive to the extent that they are reactions. With our emotions we respond to others—their anger or pain or beauty. Christians often acknowledge their emotions as gifts. God's grace plays a part in the stirrings of affection and compassion, and even of genuine guilt.

But another truth can be left buried under this initial passivity. In our response to others' influence on our life, we *choose* to act in love or anger or grief. These arousals elicit our response and responsibility. Aroused by emotions that can be felt as either gift or curse, we finally choose to express or deny our passions. By this responsible reaction we become the authors of our emotional lines. The most graphic example of this for Christians is the "passion" of Jesus Christ. He was more than the passive victim of these events. Faced with the consequence of his beliefs and actions, Jesus *chose* the fate that befell him.

ARE PASSIONS PRIVATE?

A second cultural bias sees our passions as private. This arousal of anger or sorrow that is stirring in our body belongs uniquely to us! What happens in the privacy of our heart is no one else's business! The individualism of American society encourages a privatizing of emotion. But this interpretation isolates us in our passions. Our passions of guilt or sexual arousal are not about us alone, but about us as spouses or friends or co-workers. Our passions link us with other persons—in grievance, in sorrow, in delight. These powerful forces are not private, but social. Their movements stir us out of our solitude and connect us to other people. Our emotions bind us tenaciously to our values and ideals.

If our passions are private, we might legitimately silence them with private remedies—we swallow a pill to calm our loneliness; we exercise to burn off our anger; we masturbate to relieve sexual tension. But our passions are meant to connect us to others. These stirrings are social signals, alerting us and prodding us to respond. We are more likely to react responsibly to our passions if we acknowledge that these personal arousals are not private.

Are Passions Disturbances?

A third bias views our passions as disturbances. Our emotional life is, often enough, disturbing: anger flairs up; envy eats away at us; love upsets our well-planned schedule. In the first centuries of the Christian era, stoic philosophers throughout the Roman world argued that such disturbances make us less than human. The stoics aspired to a calm and balanced life. The wise person, they felt, ought to pursue a life removed from the tumult and disorder of the emotions. The stoics embraced the ideal of a *dispassionate* life, undisturbed by the abrupt and unruly influence of our passions. The stoics, both pagan and Christian, saw human passions as unnecessary disturbances. These energies make us victims of our emotions and moods. Life was better off without such volatile forces.

This stoic view of passions soon began to influence Christianity's vision of God. The Hebrew Scriptures portray a most passionate God—fiercely aroused by both anger and affection. But Christian theology began to question this view: a God swayed by passion seemed scandalous. Greek philosophy had described a detached deity, an "unmoved mover" who reigned beyond all emotion and disturbance. Must not the Christian God be like this?

Under the influence of Roman stoicism, some Christian theologians developed a theory of *impassibility*—God's inability to be swayed by passion. God acts toward us in mercy and judgment, but He (and this is definitely a masculine God) is unmoved by us. This God creates us and loves us but does not need us. Such a God remains aloof from human affairs, beyond our influence. In Augustine's thought we see the struggle in early Christianity to harmonize the God of the Scriptures with the god of stoicism: "God himself, according to the Scriptures, becomes angry and yet he is *never disturbed* by any passions whatsoever" (*The City of God*, Book 9).

The perfection of such a God—so unlike the passionate God of the Hebrew Scriptures—lies in total control. This solitary God is detached from the demands of affection. In this theology, God is remade in the image of a powerful, masculine fantasy: the ability to influence others without being moved by them. Such a portrait of God suggested, in turn, a discipline for good Christians: to separate themselves from the influence of emotions (and those people who caused them) and to seek a peace beyond passion.

These three biases—seeing human passion as passive, private, and an unnecessary disturbance—have powerfully shaped the Christian understanding of sexual desire. We need very different convictions if we are to appreciate sexuality as a necessary disturbance and a sometime graceful passion. These convictions await us in the Hebrew and Christian Scriptures.

God's Arousals

The Bible opens with an account of creation: "Now the earth was a formless void, there was darkness over the deep, and God's Spirit hovered over the water" (Genesis 1:2). In an atmosphere of emptiness and darkness, God's power stirs. The unmoved mover is moved. All life traces its beginnings to this original passion. In this initial stirring of God's power all human passion is rooted. Our own erotic stirrings echo God's first desire. The delight we take in our children and the other fruit of our arousals repeats God's pleasure: "It is very good!"

The biblical story recounts other arousals in God. Over time the human family forgets its covenant with God; they break promises; they set aside allegiances. These failings provoke the frightening response of God's rage. This anger deepens into remorse. The wonderful story of Noah and the flood recalls the range of painful emotions in God. "Seeing the wickedness of humans . . . God regretted having made humans on the earth and God's heart grieved" (Genesis 6:7). Aroused by anger, overcome with regret, God determined to end the experiment. Only Noah's integrity convinces God to transform the threat of total annihilation into a corrective action meant to chastise and reform. Moved by compassion, God sends the purifying flood.

Anger and compassion: the Hebrew Scriptures repeatedly link these arousals in God. Throughout Israel's tumultuous history, God's holy anger is ignited again and again. As often, compassion moves God: "Yahweh is a God of tenderness and grace, slow to anger and abounding in compassion" (Exodus 33:19). Turning aside from a vengeful punishment of Israel, "God's bowels tremble with compassion and God decides not to give rein to the heat of anger" (Hosea 11:8). This stirring of compassion in God (the word in both Hebrew and Greek literally means "gut-wrenching") is a complex emotion of affection. It is an affection that is far from the uncomplicated delight of the first creation. In compassion, affection is tested and bruised; love struggles to survive injury and misunderstanding. Compassion is a profound disturbance, not a likely emotion for a God who is an unmoved mover.

JESUS' PASSIONS

The life of Jesus Christ in the New Testament continues this story of God's passionate involvement in human affairs. Luke's gospel explicitly connects Mary's pregnancy with the first arousal of creation: "The Holy Spirit will hover over you and the power of the Most High will overshadow you" (Luke 1:35). The Creator is moved again and the fruit of this passion is Jesus.

The gospels show us Jesus being moved by a range of people: the foreign woman whom he meets at the well; the man who climbs a tree to get sight of Jesus passing by; the woman publicly shamed by her adultery. And his affection is not always subject to his initiation and control. When a woman approaches him at a meal and anoints his head with an expensive, pungent perfume, he delights in the pleasure. Her act calls forth his passion.

Sorrow is another passion present in Jesus' life. Near the end of his ministry he looks over the city he loves and muses, "How often have I longed to gather your children, as a hen gathers her chicks under her wings, and you refused!" (Matthew 23:37). Often his sorrow is mixed with compassion: hearing of his friend Lazarus' death, he goes to his tomb. When he asks where to find the dead man, he speaks "in great distress, with a sigh that came straight from the heart" (John 11:33).

Anger also moved Jesus. His confrontations with others frequently aroused this troubling passion. He becomes angry with hypocrites and with those who make a show of their piety. He becomes so enraged at the merchants peddling within the temple that he lashes out and overturns their tables. Jesus' passions run the gamut, like ours, from the pleasure of a shared meal to the sorrow of broken friendships.

But in this family of emotion, one passion of Jesus has always stood out for believers. This is the powerful stirring that guided him through his passion to his death. Seeing that his beliefs were leading him to a confrontation with authorities that could mean his death, he hesitated. In the garden of olives he is severely disturbed—sweating, pacing back and forth, snapping at his friends when they nod off (Luke 22). It makes no sense to die so young. Why give in to this defeat and public humiliation? But in an emotional struggle with his fate, a new and mysterious courage enlivens him. He will neither flee nor renounce his mission. His passionate attachment to his Father allows him to face his death. He will not be simply a passive victim of these events. In a paradox that still fascinates us, Jesus chooses his passion.

AROUSAL IN THE NEW TESTAMENT

The New Testament is not a very sexy book, but it is a story filled with passion. A guide to arousal in the Christian Scriptures begins with the Greek word for this experience. *Egerein* means to arouse or stir up. The word appears often to describe the necessary disturbance and change of pace required for a religious life. Joseph dreams that others want to harm his newborn son; in his bed he hears the command: *"Arouse yourself* and go to Egypt!" (Matthew 2:13). Joseph is stirred out of his sleep to save a life.

Elsewhere in the gospels the nuance of this word shifts from awakening to healing. Frequently Jesus touches a person afflicted with some trouble. After touching them he says, *"Get up* and walk" (Matthew 8:15, 9:5). Illness has paralyzed these people. Jesus' healing touch stimulates them, and his word arouses them to action.

Arousal as healing takes on a very special meaning in the New Testament. A central meaning of *egerein* is resurrection—being raised up from death. Here the gospels continue the Psalms' theme of God's ability to enliven. In Mark's gospel Jesus is brought to a girl who appears to be dead. His touch and attention rouse her to life (5:41). In Matthew's gospel, when Jesus' life is threatened, he replies that if he is killed, he will *be raised* up by God (16:21). Jesus is telling his friends that God's power is stronger than death. Death cannot extinguish our best hopes and values. The Creator and Enlivener is more powerful than death. Our God will raise us up again.

In Saint Paul's letters another religious arousal is announced: the life-changing stirring of conversion. Paul encourages the Christians in Rome: "The time has come. *Arouse yourselves!* Your salvation is at hand" (Romans 13:11). In this very theological letter Paul is not referring to the physiological slumber of Joseph. He is pointing to the religious effort and discipline required to be a disciple of Christ. This is the arousal of personal conversion.

In the compelling account in the Acts of the Apostles of Paul's own conversion, we once again find the vocabulary of arousal. In this famous story, Paul journeys to Damascus to continue his persecution of the Christians. But in the midst of this self-assured trip, he suddenly stumbles and falls. This fall is not simply a slip, but a loss of his sureness and control. He collapses into a crisis. His rising from this fall is described with this same Greek verb, *egerein:* he is being raised up. This is the beginning of his conversion. After some days of blindness and distress, he begins a new and vigorous life of following the Risen Lord.

Conversion, the central arousal of Christian life, guides our journey between the initial passion of creation and the final stirring of resurrection. But this graceful arousal has also been a source of much confusion. Christians are tempted to believe that once converted and baptized, they are fully saved. They become members of the elect, the communion of saints, turning their backs forever on sin. But then we stumble upon the obvious— even the saved are sinners. We repeatedly undo our best intentions. Unholy passions excite our selfishness and violence. Painfully we learn that conversion must be a continual discipline. Repeatedly we need to be aroused out of our hurtful habits. But this graceful arousal of conversion is always available to us, to enliven and heal us.

The Dance of Control and Surrender

Jesus' passionate convictions and friendships climaxed in his own passion. In this crisis he was forced to face, as we are, the mysterious rhythm of control and surrender. In his many choices and commitments, he had shaped and controlled his destiny. Now something else seemed required—a letting go and a surrender to another dynamic.

The dance of control and surrender happens many places in our lives, but it appears most graphically in our sexual relationships. Psychologist John Wood invites us to see the experience of sexual intercourse as an analogy for all the arousals that combine control and surrender. With our lover, an initial excitement moves through foreplay toward climax. Throughout the sharing, we experience the interplay of arousal and control. Early on we must decide whether to allow the arousal to move toward genital sharing. But the questions go deeper: How much will we let go?

How much do we need to control the tempo, the positions, the outcome? How much do we hold back in an effort to do what is expected?

When we recall our deepest experiences of joy in sexual intercourse, did they not come from surrender? The best delight is not in the performance but in letting go, in giving ourselves over to a mutual arousal that has its own rhythms and surprises. Such an experience of surrender differs greatly from failure. Here the nuance of surrender is not defeat. We lose only our individual control and our separateness. This abandonment is rooted not in weakness but in the strength and courage to let go. As we mutually let go, we experience something better than control.

In recent years social critics have noted a cultural phenomenon that is relevant to this dance of control and arousal. With few exceptions, American films portray men as cool and detached in their lovemaking. Women are expected to show every sign of arousal, delight, and surrender. Rarely does the male partner display emotion or ecstasy. Men—the movies seem to be instructing us—should hold back, should show little emotion, should keep control. The cultural rules about control, revealed in this influential medium, force on men an unkind discipline. Quite naturally then, the male partner becomes concerned less with shared delight than with personal performance. Sexual intercourse becomes more a question of mastery than an experience of mutuality.

In other areas of life, as well, we confront the questions: How are we to balance control and arousal? How are we to be both accountable for our passions and capable of responsible surrender? These challenges are rooted in the ambiguity of control itself. On the one hand, maturity requires that we learn control: we walk and talk by exercising an exquisite control of hundreds of muscles; we resist destructive rage by controlling the impulses of anger; we develop courage by curbing the fear that would lead us to retreat from every possible risk; we assertively check the destructive emotions of envy and self-pity.

Control, then, is a good and necessary part of any maturing life. But the danger appears as we get too good at control. Then the healthy desire to influence our environment and our fate expands into a compulsion—a driven need to regulate and repress every stirring in our heart. The vocabulary of control is instructive: we wish to master our unruly passions; we foster the ambition to be "in control." This compulsion, Wood reminds us, "robs us of experiencing many of our emotions. It takes away spontaneity. It deprives us of many sensual pleasures. It steals away our orgasms and other peak experiences."

If we succeed in mastering our passions, a worse distress may follow. Perhaps we can no longer get angry. Even in a situation of conflict and disagreement, we carry a frozen smile. Again and again we swallow our arousal until an ulcer or headache protests the self-abuse inflicted on our body.

Or perhaps we can no longer weep. Even at our parent's funeral, we are dry-eyed and calm. We have successfully stifled our sorrow—not for us the loss of control, the "weepy, female behavior" that we have learned to despise. We appear strong to onlookers, but in our heart we recognize that we have banished an ally. We are unable to grieve.

This freezing of our emotional life happens in subtler ways as well. We may have found that hard work and a full schedule bring control. We surrender to sleep, now and then, but to nothing else. In such a life we naturally do not notice such things as beautiful sunsets or cozy fireplaces; they do not fit into our busy schedule. In such a life we also find few friends. Deep and lasting relationships just seem not to happen to us. Only rarely do we get a hint of our collusion in shaping this wasteland of control.

Maturity *does* involve an active control of our arousals. Instead of being swept away by our rage, we must learn to *use* our anger. But to use passion means giving ourselves to it for purposes of personal change and social challenge. With time and practice, we can befriend this frightening arousal, making it an ally and not an enemy in our life.

A similar dynamic of control and surrender guides a mature experience of guilt. When we have genuinely offended another or betrayed a personal value, this painful emotion is appropriate. Its energy is meant to guide us toward reconciliation and change. But we are also aware of how easily false accusations trigger this passion: we may be tempted to feel guilty about events for which we are not responsible. We control this emotion by refusing to entertain such stirrings of false guilt.

And our sexual lives mature by balancing control and surrender. We assertively turn away from sexual arousal that does not honor promises already made. But in a privileged and committed relationship we dare to surrender to shared passion. In all these instances, we become the authors rather than the victims of our emotional life.

A metaphor that may describe the rhythm of control and surrender is that of "seasoning." This image has two major ingredients: time and influence. The influence on our emotions is the life and values of Jesus Christ. Over many seasons we struggle to model our anger on the forceful but tempered anger of Jesus. Repeatedly, through the years, we allow our compassion to be shaped by the example of Jesus. Gradually our affections are shaped by his.

Christian maturing entails the seasoning of our instincts. In conscious and unconscious ways, Christian values slowly transform our arousals. The fruit of this long process of seasoning is that our passions become trustworthy. We can trust our anger and guilt and affection. Our instinctual responses never become infallible, but they become, in time, reliable. Shaped and seasoned by Christian values, our passions become dependable. This happens only in a community of mature believers. Here we see, concretely, the shape of just anger, genuine guilt, and Christian compassion. Here, through many seasons, we learn to live with passion.

A God of Control, A God of Desire

What do our passions have to do with God? Do these bodily stirrings link us with or alienate us from God? After a discussion with us of some of the themes of this chapter, a friend sent the following response:

EROS AND LOGOS

Jesus is God's desire in the flesh.
Not God's command or control,
God's embodied desire.

The Logos is God's Eros
A word of desire,
God's body language.

Jesus is God's arousal,
Efficacious echo of creation,
Fruit of Israel's longing.

In our arousals,
The beginning of our fruitfulness,
The end of God's desire.

In *The Inner Loneliness* theologian Sebastian Moore explores the connection between human passion and images of God. He recalls that Christian history recounts a largely masculine search for God. With men as its priests, teachers, and theologians, the Church understandably sponsored a masculine quest for God. Both Judaism and Christianity pictured God in man's image—as masculine, as father. (Intriguingly, when theologians speak of the tendency to anthropomorphize God, they usually refer to attrib-

uting emotions to God, but rarely to our making God masculine.)

This religious search, as a masculine venture, was tempted to
portray Yahweh as a God of control, rather than a God of desire.
Many early Christian theologians pictured God as beyond the
sway of passion. This God of control seemed to demand that we
be like "him" by being in control. Moore describes this patriarchal world with painful succinctness: "Man is the centre, woman
the hazard, and control the name of the game." Mastery is the
chief discipline in this world view, which calls men to dominate,
to gain control over their passions. If sexuality is their most
disruptive arousal, it is in things sexual that mastery is most
required. And this will mean controlling women who are able to
arouse this passion.

This patriarchal world is, as we well know, coming to an end.
The image of a God of control is giving way to the experience of
a God of desire. A God of desire calls for a very different discipline: in place of mastery and control, we are invited to befriend
the ambiguous passions that stir within us. Befriending, as a
discipline, demands intimacy instead of flight; it invites us to a
greater familiarity and trust of our passions. This discipline includes both control and surrender.

The Christian Church today finds itself in a confusing passage. Our inherited discipline of mastery has taught us little
about surrender; the theologians' God of control has said little
about letting go. We look again at the life of Jesus "who did not
cling to his equality with God, but emptied himself to assume the
condition of a servant" (Philippians 2:6–7). Following his passionate lead, we struggle to surrender the traditional masculine
quest for mastery and control. And we begin to learn about
befriending our desire.

REFLECTIVE EXERCISE

Consider your images of God. In your life of prayer these days—in worship, in personal devotion, in spiritual reading—what images of God are most compelling for you? Spend some time reflecting prayerfully on these ways that God is most real, most alive for you. Then turn to the following questions:

In these images, do you picture God as masculine, or feminine, or in some other way? Which passions are most at play in your images of God? Are there links for you between these passions of God and your experience of passion?

Then consider sexual passion. Are there ways your passion has become more trustworthy in recent years, more a friend? In what ways is sexual passion troublesome or confusing for you? What connections do you find between sexual passion and your life of faith?

ADDITIONAL RESOURCES

Philosopher Robert Solomon, in his book *The Passions* (Notre Dame Press, 1983), gives a refreshing examination of the passions as positive strategies of a responsible life. Psychologist Willard Gaylin explores the physiological and emotional aspects of passion in *Feelings: Our Vital Signs* (Ballantine, 1979); see also his *Rediscovering Love* (Viking, 1987).

Feminist theologians and ministers are helping the community of faith recover the rich heritage of images through which God is revealed; see, for example, Anne Carr, *Transforming Grace: Christian Tradition and Women's Experience* (Harper & Row, 1986), and Joann Wolski Conn, *Women's Spirituality: Resources for Christian Development* (Paulist Press, 1987).

John Wood reflects on control and surrender in Chapter 9 in

What Are You Afraid Of? (Prentice-Hall, 1976). Sebastian Moore discusses control and desire in *The Inner Loneliness* (Crossroad, 1982). For a fuller exploration of the seasoning of instincts, see our *Seasons of Strength* (Image Books/Doubleday, 1986).

8.

The Place of Pleasure

Dear Donnie,

  I am writing this letter with a lot of embarrassment. When you raised those questions about sexuality last weekend you caught me off-guard. I pretended to be too busy, packing for this trip, but I was really just embarrassed. The four hours on the plane yesterday gave me time to think. I apologize for how I acted Saturday.

  On the plane I was remembering that my parents never had anything to say to me about these difficult questions. (I was too shy—unlike you!—to ask.) There seemed to be an etiquette in our house: never talk about sex! I really regret that, and I am determined that things will be different with us. Please accept my stumbling efforts, in this long-distance letter, to say some honest things about sexuality. Most of all I want to share your mom's and my hopes for you.

  You especially asked about masturbation. Let me start with my own story. When I was fifteen, as you are now, I was often overwhelmed by sexual arousal. I would masturbate and then hate myself for it. I was ashamed that I could not control myself. The priest encouraged me to keep trying, but this did not seem to help much.

I had learned that this action was a mortal sin, that it would separate me from God. If I died after such a sin, before confession, I would go to hell. This puzzled and angered me. How could this insistent desire that I couldn't control damn me forever? How could it cancel out all the rest of my life? I didn't have a satisfying answer to these questions, but I was still convinced that what I was doing was a terrible sin.

In this confusing time I was surrounded mostly by silence. Both in high school and later in college my counselors were as mute as my parents. Perhaps I was the only one who sinned this way again and again! I felt isolated and defeated. In college I finally stopped confessing this "sin"—mainly because it didn't look like I would stop. It seemed stupid to keep going to confession. I suppose, too, that this action became less terrible to me as time went on. I suppose I blocked it out mostly, though I continued to feel ashamed that I had so little control in this part of my life.

Only when I met and married your mom did I begin to learn about the goodness of my own body. With her my sexual pleasure found exciting and meaningful fulfillment. We learned together what it meant to give and receive this wonderful pleasure. You know that you and then Danielle and Rachel are the fruit of our love.

From this ancient perch of forty-two years, what shall I say to my teenage son? What to say to him who knows so much and wants to know even more? About masturbation I would say it is normal; it happens, with confusion and force, to most male adolescents. Its confusion comes from your body wanting a partner at a time when you know it is too early to start a life together. Your body, in puberty, is suddenly ready for things that your mind and heart cannot handle yet. When you do experience this self-stimulation, you probably feel that it is not your finest hour. But know that it is not terrible; it does not remove you from God's loving presence. By itself, this action will not turn you into a selfish person.

Maybe my best counsel is patience. This intense arousal will gradually feel better in your life: not so out of control, not so isolating. Our worst fear, your mother's and mine, is that this confusing urge would lead you to hate your body and to mistrust it. Our best hope is that you find, in time and with patience, a partner to share pleasure and to help you make it fruitful in a life together.

When I get home next week I look forward to your reactions to this letter and to your other questions. Let's keep talking, even if it is difficult.

> I love you very much,
> Dad

This father's letter acknowledges a painful truth: the question of masturbation confuses the young and embarrasses their parents. Christians rarely discuss it. This uneasy silence is broken only by occasional reiterations of the official Church teaching—these sexual actions are always gravely sinful and shatter our relationship with God. But another wisdom—that these actions are not so horrendous or sinful—grows in the body of Christ. Coming to this wisdom from the experiences of their own sexual lives, Christians remain reluctant to enter a public debate over self-pleasuring. This is due in part to personal reticence and in part to a concern not to give the question more attention than it deserves.

Our colleagues in ministry—married and single, clergy and laity—insist that the time has come to talk about this confusing aspect of human sexuality. Many mature Christians remain burdened by guilt and shame about masturbation. A frank exploration of this activity may heal some of this distress and may also illumine other aspects of our religious maturing.

Genital self-stimulation is a common, even pervasive, human experience. The Kinsey Report in the 1940s suggested that 94 percent of men and more than 60 percent of women had engaged in masturbation. In *Human Sexuality*, James McCary notes his later finding that about 95 percent of men and between 50 and 90 percent of women report sexual self-stimulation. From the medical perspective, as Dr. Domeena Renshaw of the sexual ·dysfunction clinic of Loyola University in Chicago attests, the activity of masturbation is ordinary and normal; it is neither aberrant nor unnatural. Such a starting point differs considerably from the attitude that flowered in the nineteenth and the first half of this century. During this period many physicians, clergy, and educators shared the conviction that masturbation was bizarre, degenerate behavior that resulted in a variety of mental and physical disorders.

A Troubled Heritage

How did Christians come to so negative a view of self-stimulation? Three currents in the Church's moral thinking converged to shape its suspicion of masturbation.

The first aspect of Christian morality that profoundly influenced our interpretation of self-pleasuring was the unhappy wedding of sex and guilt. We have seen this before: all sexual behavior came to be understood as "grave matter"—potentially a mortal sin. The Church assigned enormous importance to every arousal, each sexual fantasy. In our youth, then, many of us raised in religious homes *learned* to feel guilty about these stirrings of pleasure. Little attention was given to the healthy connections between sexual arousal and the commitment of marriage. We often drowned the delight of sexual arousal in a sea of shame and guilt.

A second aspect of Christian morality that influenced our present discussion was a fascination with specific behaviors. As theologian Charles Curran has noted, there developed in Catholic moral theology a concentration on certain actions—such as divorce, contraception, and masturbation—to the neglect of much attention to the motives or circumstances that influence these actions. In such an approach, all divorces look the same, no matter the circumstances; the separation of an immature couple did not differ from the flight of a mother and children from a violent and abusive spouse. All contraceptive acts fall under the same judgment, whatever the motivation; the discipline of the couple concerned about caring for the children they already have is not distinguishable from the self-centered decision of another couple. In such a moral stance attention focuses narrowly on the act to the neglect of the larger context of psychological or social influences. This kind of concentration gives the biological act of self-pleasuring an exaggerated importance.

Third, Christian morality was until very recently an ethic developed exclusively by men. Theological reflection, thus dominated by men, became overconcerned with male sexuality. Thinkers of an earlier epoch, with little or faulty knowledge of human biology, attributed enormous importance to the male seed. The man's semen seemed to be the exclusive potent ingredient in human procreation. This seed needed the warm, nurturing confines of a woman's womb in order to grow and develop into a human being. But in this understanding, the woman had no substantive role in procreation. Her only contribution was to nourish and protect the male seed, which was thought to hold within itself all the necessary potential for life.

The great medieval theologian Thomas Aquinas summed up this prevailing view of sexual reproduction: "When the generation is completed, *the seed itself, unchanged and fulfilled,* is the offspring which is born" (our emphasis). So self-sufficient is the male's seed that the birth of a female child signals a flaw in the process—a woman being, in Aristotle's succinct phrase, "a misbegotten male."

The almost obsessive concern in Catholic morality about masturbation has yet another, more recent root. The discipline of moral theology developed to help priests in their ministry. Instead of being a public reflection on morality (as it is today), moral theology was an "in-house" discussion—a pastoral discipline aimed at the education of seminarians and priests. These ministers would, in turn, use this information in their pastoral activities—in their preaching, in moral instruction, and in private guidance in the confessional. The primary audience for Catholic moral teaching, then, was not the broad community of faith, made up of married and single persons, women and men. It was to priests and, in particular, to adolescent and young adult men studying for the priesthood, that moral theology was originally addressed. Very likely this audience of young unmarried men intensified the sense of the importance of sexual self-pleasuring.

These various forces in our religious heritage have led to results with which many of us are familiar. Apart from a catechetical prohibition heard now and then, Christians fell into a conspiracy of silence concerning masturbation. If this silence reinforced the sense of shame associated with this action, it did not make the behavior go away. But the silence fostered isolation. Christians bemoaned their weakness by saying, "Surely I am the only one in the world who masturbates! I alone am so wretched and depraved that I persist in this practice." The counsel of the confessor to flee this deadly sin seldom promoted an examination of its motives or circumstances. Isolation and privacy reigned.

A second result of this heritage was a loss of the broader community's experiences. A moral theology developed by priests for priests (and *then* for others) did not learn to listen well to women's experience or to the experience of married persons. When theology neglects so much information, many of us lose confidence in its conclusions.

In an atmosphere of silence, Christians had to come to their own private compromises. Sometimes these were healthy resolutions: a married couple took delight in the mutual pleasuring that did not always lead to intercourse; a widower welcomed the mellow pleasure of this solitary solace; a single woman came, over time, to greater comfort with self-stimulation as an expression of sexuality and self-intimacy. Other compromises were less healthy: a conscientious Christian, bedeviled by this habit, grew to hate himself; a woman in midlife continued to feel, in self-stimulation, shame and loneliness.

These compromises remained private events. When personal resolutions were troubled, their very privacy kept them from being healed. When these resolutions yielded wisdom, this insight could not be shared with the community. Something was badly amiss here. All this invites the Christian community to an honest conversation about sexual self-stimulation.

The Variety of Pleasure

We can rediscover the complexity of masturbation by recognizing the variety of experiences that are brought together under this term.

The mother of two small children takes a leisurely bath at the end of a hectic day. In a mood of quiet reflection, she becomes aware of her own body. Like other "good Catholic girls," she had learned as a child to remain mostly ignorant of this body and its stirrings. Her lovemaking with her husband is generally good, but she still finds much in her experience of arousal and pleasure to be mysterious. Through her twenties and early thirties she has become more comfortable with bodies: her own, her husband's with its different rhythms, her children's with their fragility and loveliness. Sometimes she looks at her four-year-old daughter's body and sees her own, as if for the first time.

In the lazy comfort of the bath, she gives herself permission to touch and to explore her body. She is a bit embarrassed but mostly amused by the pleasure this engenders. She offers a quick prayer of thanks, grateful for the ways she is coming to know and love herself more.

This experience of self-pleasuring has some special nuances: it happens in a mood of quiet introspection, without the compulsiveness that often dominates the stereotypic masturbation of the adolescent male. Its goal seems to be self-discovery, rather than a quick and guilty satisfaction. This action seeks greater self-knowledge as much as a release of sexual tension. But such experiences have had little influence on the discussions of masturbation in traditional Christian theology.

A very different experience occurs in the life of the normal adolescent boy. The fourteen-year-old male is ordinarily thrown off stride by the insistent eruptions of puberty. He is suddenly aroused by persons and pictures and fantasies that seem to surround him. But he remains strikingly alone in this new and confusing experience. He has no sexual partner and will not have one for some years to come. His body is suddenly matured beyond his psyche and his social self. Depending on the moral messages he has received from his environment, his experiences of self-stimulation may be joyous or guilt-ridden. Very often these actions become compulsive: he feels driven or obsessed by this strong erotic arousal.

Most bewildering for this young man is the strange link between sexual stimulation and control. Shame threatens him if he cannot control his erections at a swimming pool or in a locker room. Most often successful at control in these public situations, he is less successful in private. If he has been taught that his sexual activity is a mortal sin, he prays for deliverance from this uncontrollable urge. He may even learn to hate this body that humiliates him with its urgent desires.

A third instance of pleasuring happens in lovemaking. Married for eight years, a couple have come to enjoy just lying close together. Sometimes their embrace leads to intercourse; often it does not. At times their mutual caresses lead to orgasm without intercourse. These experiences are so mutually satisfying that the couple has never even questioned the "moral rectitude" of this behavior. To them the word *masturbation* seems a crude and improper description of this part of their love play. This experience of pleasuring is an important part of lovemaking in many marriages. Couples know that it contributes to the complex fruitfulness of their love. The institutional Church has yet to learn this and to include this experience of sexual pleasure in its reflection on responsible committed love.

A fourth variety of pleasure leads us into a tragic category of sexual release—self-pleasuring as a compensation for loneliness and loss of control. The example here is a forty-year-old inmate in a penal institution. Because of his crime, he is now deprived of his freedom and of control of his own life. In the enforced solitude of this unnatural life, he turns repeatedly to masturbation. His obsessive behavior is less about sex than about control. In a milieu devoid of affection and freedom, self-stimulation acts as a lament, a lonely grieving in which the person can experience some momentary control, some fleeting ability to be aroused, in however wounded a fashion. In his novel *The Falconer*, John Cheever provides a painful portrait of this ritual of pleasure and sorrow. This example bears some similarity to the adolescent's experience in its compulsiveness and isolation. It is strikingly unlike the first example with its gentle self-exploration and the third example with its mutual pleasuring.

A fifth instance of pleasuring brings crisis and healing to centerstage. Theologian Rosemary Haughton, in an essay in *Commitment to Partnership*, exposes a painful and important aspect of sexuality: sexual abuse. Drawing on her experience as the director of a home for women fleeing domestic violence, Haughton describes a common route of healing. These women, some with their children, live together for a time in this haven. Often, as part of their re-entry, two women may move out and share a new residence together. As they care for each other, they continue to heal the scars that years of sexual abuse have left in their bodies. Sometimes this mutual care will include expressions of sexual affection. Tentatively, they learn that sexual contact is not necessarily violent or abusive. Slowly they relearn the loveliness of their bodies, the goodness of sexual pleasure. To call these healing touches "masturbation" reveals a poverty of both vocabulary and theology. These different instances of sexual pleasuring invite us to reexamine our historical judgments about self-stimulation. These stories lead us to questions of motives and meanings.

Motives and Meanings

What meanings do we find in these experiences? What motives stir our own arousals? If we blindly flee our arousals as occasions of sin, we never ask these important questions. But if we are courageous enough to listen to our bodies and our actions, we may learn something important about ourselves.

Traditionally, the chief meaning assigned to self-pleasuring was captured in the term *self-abuse*. In moral discussion the scope of self-abuse was often severely narrowed: sexual self-pleasuring came to be seen as the unique or most important form of self-abuse. There is more candor today in pointing to other potent areas of abuse—such as eating and drinking. Alcohol is now acknowledged to affect one third of the families in America. Whether or not we understand it to be an illness, alcoholism is an exercise in self-abuse with profound and observable social consequences. Eating disorders—from chronic obesity to anorexia and bulimia—are on the rise in American society. In these exercises of self-abuse, people confuse physical and spiritual nourishment. They swallow pain they cannot share, but this private consumption proves unnourishing. Again, the social injury from such abuse is grave.

This discussion reminds us of the family of compulsions that invade and wound our lives. Smoking, begun in pleasure or in an effort to find social approval, becomes an almost unbreakable habit—a compulsion that leads us, literally, to the grave. Smoking may not be a "sin," but it is certainly self-abuse. The compulsive use of food and alcohol also belong to this family. A special compulsion in American life is consumerism—the obsession to buy the newest product or the latest fashion. This exercise in self-abuse has serious social consequences; it diverts our attention and resources from the more urgent needs of others around us.

Self-abuse is an important category of wrongdoing. We judge an action abusive according to its destructiveness—of the individual and of the community. Sexual self-pleasuring, *when compulsive*, may belong in this category. Often, however, it is neither compulsive nor abusive.

PRIVATIZING PLEASURE

Sexual arousals move us toward others. Tentative contact and initial embraces draw us into enduring relationships and life commitments. The goal of these pleasurable stirrings seems to be genuine engagement with other people. Such a goal is not realizable every day, in every arousal. The ideal of our arousals leading us into fruitful contact with others is just that—an ideal.

At times we find ourselves alone, out of touch, solitary. In these periods, we are also stirred and sexually aroused. Acts of self-stimulation do not, by themselves, make us perverted or unclean or unholy. But the danger in these acts is their isolation. Our genital arousals, social in orientation, sometimes find no social expression. This is more an anomaly than an unnatural act or a wrongdoing. Most ordinary, sane folk also talk to themselves with some regularity. Only when people talk *only* to themselves or fail to notice that their conversation has become exclusively solitary do we speak of a disorder.

The possibility of disorder in self-pleasuring lies in the solitary exercise of a social arousal. When this exercise becomes a habit that replaces genuine, sustained contact with others, we have reason to be concerned. Danger lurks when self-stimulation becomes a person's *ordinary style* of sexual expression.

The danger can be real for young men in American culture today. Unsure of himself with women, a young man may slip into a habit of self-stimulation while enjoying fantasies of "the ideal woman." This romantic fantasy is, of course, insistently fueled by American advertising and by media that profitably market this illusion. Fantasies of voluptuous, passive women are not so much "dirty" as they are distorted. The pages of "men's magazines" regularly depict women as extraordinarily beautiful and wonderfully docile. They do not talk back. They do not make demands. At the same time, they display no physical or psychic weaknesses. What a charming world! Its only limitation is its unreality.

A person who lingers too long in such a climate (a natural rest stop for the confused adolescent on the way to adulthood) will have trouble with the women who populate his real world of work and friendship. Their strengths and weaknesses will trouble or offend him. The requests and needs of actual, human females will confuse him. Bewildered by the differences between his inner and outer worlds, he may choose to retreat to a safer, more private domain. Here he can find pleasure with control. He can experience himself sexually with safety. Such a life becomes as self-abusive as that of the alcoholic. The pleasure is private but the damage is social. Increasingly, the ordinary demands of negotiation and conflict imperil the man's necessary, daily interactions with women. His private life—where his sexuality enjoys unrestricted expression—has not prepared him for these challenges. Missed expectations, false demands, and failed commitments: these become the bitter fruit of a behavior that had seemed private and insignificant.

COMPULSION AND CONTROL

We are investigating the motives and meanings of self-pleasuring. This ordinary sexual behavior can become abusive when it distorts our perception and restricts our readiness to face the challenging embraces of our interpersonal lives. It can also become abusive when we engage in it compulsively. We have placed some experiences of self-pleasuring in the family of compulsions in order to glimpse the characteristics these experiences share with overeating, excessive drinking, and smoking. One lesson we learn about compulsive behaviors is that they are often about something else. Overeating, which is about more than food, is an emergency signal about our malnourishment in some other area of our life. Habitual chain-smoking is about more than the enjoyment of tobacco flavor.

The social sciences have yet to fully understand the coded messages concealed in our various compulsions. In these actions that we do again and again, unable to stop ourselves, we both conceal and reveal our distress. What are we trying to announce in compulsive acts of sexual self-stimulation? One common message seems to be that we are out of control. A woman in midlife becomes overburdened by her work; she has no time for rest or leisure or simple, pleasurable friendship. A habit of compulsive self-stimulation appears in or returns to her life. This behavior seems to cry out, "I am starved for affection and rest and pleasure. My life is out of control!" The message does not necessarily demand a drastic reordering of her life. But this activity may signal the need for some significant personal change.

A thirty-year-old man is having a difficult period with his career. He feels less and less effective; none of his recent efforts bring success or bear fruit. A sense of impotence wells up in him, and a habit of compulsive self-stimulation ensues. By these actions he struggles to assert some control or find some potency in his life.

To the person afflicted, of course, the message is seldom so clear. Also, the different messages about love and work are often interconnected. We can tolerate a lack of friends for a time when our work is going well, and vice versa. But when severe difficulty in one area is exacerbated by trouble in the other, we may slip into compulsive habits regarding food or drink or sexual activity. In these peculiarly human and confusing behaviors we both punish ourselves and try to announce an unacknowledged distress.

Significant, Not Sinful

When we touch ourselves to bring about orgasm, we do something significant. Sexuality is too important a part of life to describe this simply as a release of physiological tension. As a growing number of theologians have judged, we rarely sin in doing this, though we may abuse ourselves when the dynamics of compulsion and punishment replace pleasure. Whatever the motive or meaning, we are doing something significant. Even in compulsive actions, we are trying to tell ourselves something. Such actions reveal us to ourselves. They may tell us about our loneliness or woundedness. Shared with a lover or spouse, these actions can express affection and care. Self-pleasuring may, in a very different context, reveal an adolescent fantasy of being totally in control in our sexual life. Recognizing this motive may be the first step of the journey from a self-centered sexuality to a maturity that makes responsible sexual sharing possible. The revelations in our sexual lives are varied and often well disguised. But they *are* revelations, and we need to pay attention to them.

We open ourselves to this important information by not running away from these experiences, by not repressing our memories of this part of our sexual lives. We also open ourselves by changing our vocabulary and our descriptions of these private actions. The term *masturbation,* with its threatening nuances, helps us neither understand nor avoid this behavior. The time has come to retire this word. Self-stimulation and self-pleasuring seem more useful notions. None of these words, however, captures the fruitful sharing of genital pleasure, apart from intercourse, that many committed couples enjoy. A more honest discussion in the community of faith may help generate a better vocabulary for our sexual lives.

Finally, Christian discussion of sexual questions always seems to come back to the tyranny of the ideal. In Jesus Christ we are given an example of a uniquely generous and fruitful life. His is a life of great paradox: brief, but enormously effective; childless, but profoundly fruitful. Jesus' life gives us high ideals without dictating specific life choices.

Christianity, especially in its Roman Catholic tradition, has been deeply suspicious about links between holiness and a fully sexual life. The Church has raised up few married saints, almost none after 1500. Nearly all women saints are described by their sexual status—virgins or widows. Rules and restrictions multiplied in Christianity as our ancestors sought to illumine the path of following Christ. One unfortunate dynamic in this religious history was the tendency to transform ideals into laws. The ideal of a life-long marriage became the law of indissolubility—a Christian marriage *cannot* end. The ideal of having community leaders who are single-minded and lead exemplary lives became the law of celibacy for the clergy. The encouragement of an ideal was often transformed into the enforcement of a law. Freedom and generosity, so abundantly available in the life of Jesus, gave way to strict observance and rectitude. This is the tyranny of the ideal.

The ideal concerning our genital arousals is clear. These pleasurable stirrings ideally lead us toward a partner, a committed companion for life. With this partner sexual pleasure becomes mutual delight, bearing fruit in children and a deepening relationship. In such a relationship, we learn the rhythms and discipline of receiving and giving pleasure. Such is the ideal. Life, however, affords a more complex texture. Not every vocation includes a life partner: death and divorce deprive us of companions; decisions move us toward a single or celibate lifestyle; all of us journey through adolescence—that strange land where we are biologically fit but socially unready for the responsibilities of sexual sharing.

We have been taught that to actively experience genital pleasure in these latter contexts is shameful and wrong. Such pleasuring is so sinful that it removes us from life with God. Here the tyranny of the ideal joins forces with the Church's suspicion of sexuality. This merger binds and bewilders many Christians. Today fewer Christians accept without question formal religious teachings regarding sexuality. The tyranny and suspicion revealed in many official statements are too deeply at odds with the life of Jesus to be believable. Trusting their own experience as it is purified by decades of faithful religious living, more and more Christians are ready to participate in the necessary healing of the Church's understanding of sexual and genital pleasure.

Our responsibility, as Christians, will always be to make our sexual lives generous, instead of selfish; fruitful, rather than manipulative. Our responsibility is also to share the truth of our experiences—whether of divorce or celibacy, marriage or self-pleasuring. In such courageous and honest conversations, we will be revealed to ourselves, and we will better understand the mysterious rhythms that make up our human life.

REFLECTIVE EXERCISE

We have all experienced the inclination toward sexual self-stimulation. It can be useful to reflect on the circumstances of this arousal in our own lives, respectful of the information about our sexual self that we may find there.

Are there particular times or situations in your life (fatigue or loneliness or disappointment) that have moved you toward self-stimulation? What feelings or moods have been part of these situations? Can you see a pattern here?

Has your attitude or behavior regarding self-pleasuring undergone change since adolescence? If so, what factors have influenced the change?

ADDITIONAL RESOURCES

James McCary reports his findings on masturbation in *Human Sexuality*, Third Edition (Van Nostrand, 1978). Domeena Renshaw's evaluation of masturbation from a medical perspective appears in "A Modern View of Ancient Taboos—Masturbation, Oral and Anal Sex," in the journal *Consultant*, September 1981.

Thomas Aquinas' observation on reproduction is found in *Summa Contra Gentiles* IV, 45; see the translation by Vernon J. Burke and Charles J. O'Neill (Notre Dame Press, 1975). For a clear exploration of Aquinas' view of sexuality see Chapter 6 of Lisa Sowle Cahill's *Between the Sexes* (Paulist Press, 1985). Theologian Charles Curran gives a brief and clear analysis of the views that shaped the traditional Catholic view of masturbation in his *Themes in Fundamental Moral Theology* (Notre Dame Press, 1977), pp. 174–81. In *In Pursuit of Love: Catholic Morality and Human Sexuality* (Michael Glazier, 1987), Vincent Genovesi provides a summary and critique of the current discussion among Catholic moralists on the subject of masturbation.

Morton and Barbara Kelsey offer useful observations on self-stimulation in their *Sacrament of Sexuality* (Amity House, 1986); see especially pages 15, 57, 151, 219–24. Rosemary Haughton's essay, "The Meaning of Marriage in Women's New Consciousness," can be found in *Commitment to Partnership*, edited by William Roberts (Paulist Press, 1987). David Mura provides poignant insight into the connections among sexual addiction, compulsive masturbation, and control in *A Male Grief: Notes on Pornography and Addiction* (Milkweed Editions, 1987).

9.
The Discipline of Eros

Eros is absent from the New Testament. Nor does the word appear in the Greek translation of the Hebrew Scriptures. In place of *eros* we meet another name for love: *agape.* This special vocabulary has tempted Christians to imagine that there are two very different worlds of love. One is the world of the erotic body—the realm of genital arousal and sexual passion; the domain of the animal part of us "rational animals." The other is the disembodied world of the soul, where our spirit enjoys the pure affections of agape.

The philosophic dualism prevalent in the Mediterranean world in the third and fourth centuries greatly influenced the Christians of that time. A split between the bodily love of eros and the spiritual love of agape reflected this cultural vision. After all, did not the Christian God demand a love that was, like God's own self, spiritual—that is, nonsexual? Thus, Christians began to exile eros into the narrow confines of genital arousal. Soon the ideal of the celibate ascetic withdrawn from the world replaced the ideal of Jesus, a person immersed in emotional relationships. Such ascetics pursued the spiritual love of agape by turning away from the world of eros. Sexuality and spirituality parted company.

We see efforts in many areas of Christian life today to bring eros out of exile. This journey begins in the recovery of a broader meaning of the erotic. Psychologist Ann Ulanov describes eros as "the psychic urge to relate, to join, to be in-the-midst-of, to reach out to, to value, to get in touch with." Theologian Bernard Lee defines eros as "the life instinct, the large sense of the passionate drive for life and growth." In *Original Blessing* and elsewhere, Matthew Fox attempts to recover a creation-centered spirituality more in tune with the sensuality at the heart of Christian conviction. And the work of theologian James Nelson continues to deepen an appreciation of the intimate connection between sexuality and spirituality in Christian experience.

Embodied Love

As embodied spirits our affection is always stirred within our bodies. These excitations—whether of friendship or of compassion—are not always genital, but they are always erotic. Agape is not the adversary of eros, but the fruit of mature eros.

As we know from our own lives, erotic passion is volatile and ambiguous. In its early immature stages this energy can turn us to selfish and compulsive and destructive purposes. Urges we hardly understand, impulses that lead us to hurt others and abuse ourselves, can sweep us away. In *Identity: Youth and Crisis* Erik Erikson succinctly describes this tendency:

> Before such genital maturity is reached, much of sexual life is the self-seeking, identity-hungry kind; each partner is really trying only to reach himself. Or it remains a kind of genital combat in which each tries to defeat the other.

Traditionally the perversion of our passion has been named lust or concupiscence.

But our ambiguous passion can develop in more generous ways. With good friends and lovers we learn to share pleasure, not just *take* it. Healing touches calm our compulsiveness. We promise this passion to another person and grow stronger by keeping the promise. And as we mature, even strangers can arouse our compassion. This bodily stirring also expresses eros. We experience these movements of affection—traditionally named agape—in our body. Thus they, too, are erotic arousals.

When eros matures into agape, the erotic is not lost. Our ability to love becomes rich and faithful—not because we flee from bodily stirrings but because we befriend them. The desire for contact and more life floods every part of our embodied spirit. The passionate aspiration to be with, to make promises, and to bear fruit energizes both our sexuality and our spirituality. Eros is the gift and promise of creation itself. Because our passion is not an enemy or a demon, we do not need to subjugate it. Because our affections are not essentially selfish, abstinence will not be our ordinary discipline. Instead of mastery or subjugation, we need a discipline that heals the wounds of our erotic life and encourages our passion to be generous.

Naming and Taming

The discipline of eros begins in naming our passions. A variety of inner forces moves us—angers and hopes, fears and sexual passions. But so often these powers stir within us in inchoate, unnamed ways. We become suddenly upset and strike out in violence toward our child; we are plunged into a depression and turn away from our best friend; we are overcome with some strange emptiness that casts us into despair. What is going on here? What are these surging energies that threaten our well-being and imperil our relationships?

Naming is the initial discipline of desire. In many ancient myths the hero demands to know the name of the threatening demon. In a biblical story in Genesis, Jacob, wrestling with an unknown assailant, keeps asking "What is your name?" The message seems to be that by naming these dark demons, we throw off the shackles of their power over us. We see this today in the treatment of alcoholism. The first step toward healing comes in the dreaded acknowledgment: "Hello, my name is Bill and I'm an alcoholic." Until we name the monster, its destructive power goes unchecked in our life. Only by naming our loneliness or depression can we begin to temper its influence on our friendships. Only by bringing to light the hidden forces that compel us to drink can we begin to heal the wounds in our marriage and family. And often, when we are able to name our passion, it loses its threatening shape and becomes our friend.

Naming, of course, is just the beginning. Having identified our hungers and passions, we face the challenge of taming them. Sexual arousal, for example, is not an enemy to be beaten back or avoided. Its passion is a volatile and sometimes dangerous friend. This gift of creation becomes gracious only if we tame its energy. Our wounded history with sex complicates the project of taming our passion. We may have been taught to see our body as suspect and untrustworthy. Or we may have learned to use sex to express our need for control. In lovemaking we must be in charge; both literally and symbolically we have to be "on top." For some of us, unhealed memories of incest or sexual violence continue to haunt our desire to be close to others. If we are to tame our sexual passion, we must heal this heritage of hurt. But the goal here is not domestication. Our taming must take care not to render our sexual energy so docile and subservient that we empty it of its spark and spontaneity.

The great gift of a religious tradition like Christianity should be its savvy and experience. Over centuries of time and grace Christianity has developed a rich store of spiritual disciplines that support the effort to name and tame our passions. Not all these tools remain perennially useful; some, as we have seen, are wounded by negative biases about sexuality. But a heritage remains of tested resources that can support spiritual and sexual integration.

FEASTING AND FASTING

Christian spirituality celebrates the significance of two companion disciplines: feasting and fasting. Jesus spent much time at meals and banquets; the wedding feast was an image he used to describe the reign of God; he celebrated the last days of his life with a special meal. Others on the scene, even his friends, seemed more interested in fasting: John the Baptist followed a rigorous discipline in the desert; Jesus himself admitted that some demons could only be cast out by fasting (Mark 9:29). But Jesus was much more interested in feasting. People challenged him on this, commenting, "John's disciples are always fasting and saying prayers, and the disciples of the Pharisees too, but yours go on eating and drinking" (Luke 5:33). Jesus' reply suggests a rhythm of fasting and feasting in life:

> Surely you cannot make the bridegroom's attendants fast while the bridegroom is still with them? But the time will come, the time for the bridegroom to be taken away from them; that will be the time when they will fast.

In the early centuries of Christianity, fasting became a regular and sometimes extreme practice in monastic life. Feasting fell out of fashion as a religious discipline, as Christians evidently judged that the "time to fast" had arrived. Even the Eucharistic banquet was turned into a highly restrained ritual. Suspicious of our pleasurable appetites—whether for food or for lovemaking—Christians started to stress fasting over feasting. The ideal of virginity and the later discipline of celibacy prescribed a strict fast from sexual activity "for those who would be perfect." As Christians today examine their sexual lives, they see the need for both the disciplines of feasting and of fasting.

When we feast, we celebrate and offer thanks. At a feast we do not just eat; we show off. We bring out new candles, special tablecloths, the best wine. We celebrate both survival and bounty. We use our food to satisfy a nutritional need, but also to nourish other famished desires—especially those for play and gratitude. In our feasts we take more time than at our everyday meals. We do not eat "fast foods." And we do not feast alone, since a major part of our delight comes in sharing.

At its best, feasting is a disciplined performance. We do it well by avoiding excess—eating too much, wasting food, excluding others. Often we fail, turning the impulse to feast into an exercise in selfish and conspicuous consumption. We learn again the limits of pleasure. But the human impulse to feast remains—and may even be a discipline for our sexual lives.

As with food, feasting in our sexuality both satisfies a basic need and celebrates something more. It reminds us that sex is about more than the duty of reproduction. Feasting encourages us to enjoy the play of our sexual passion and to give thanks for its delight. But we must avoid feasting selfishly and feasting alone. Like food, sex can be distorted into abusive consumption. What begins as celebration can turn into compulsive misuse. As a disciplined exercise, feasting refuses both excess and denial. It does not gulp down the fast food of pornography. Nor does it dine, promiscuously, at many tables. And the feast is ruined if we use our sexuality to control or punish other people.

In the life of the erotic, feasting is not an abandonment to the flesh. Instead, as a Christian discipline, it is a response to the gift of creation. If we carry special wounds in our sexual life, feasting can be a healing exercise: with help and encouragement we relearn the goodness of our sensuality; we take time to be nourished again by music or backrubs or even silence. When our erotic life flowers, we naturally follow this discipline. We bring a gift to a friend; we cook a special meal for our family; we spend time in physical exercise and leisure. We can feast on the wide range of our erotic lives only if we believe that pleasure is good and only if we find our passion a friend of our other hopes.

If feasting proves difficult for some of us, fasting challenges all of us. Yet fasting is an ordinary discipline of any maturing life. When we commit ourself to a relationship or career or ideal, we say yes to it. To defend this important yes we will have to say no to many other inviting possibilities. Thus, we fast every day. We pass up wine at supper in order to be more alert for an evening meeting; we turn away from a sexual invitation to honor the yes we have pledged to our partner. The discipline of fasting is not just for monks; it is an ordinary exercise in the taming of our passions.

Fasting developed its bad reputation in Christian history as it became a way to punish the body. But this is an abuse of the human impulse to fast. At its heart, fasting is an exercise not in deprivation but in concentration. We fast—from food or sex or conversation—in order to see more clearly and bond ourselves more surely to our best values. We do not deny our hunger, but we choose not to satisfy it in order to better taste other longings in our heart. People who fast find their senses sharpened and their minds less distracted, less buried under the routines of life. This is partly due to the simple suspension of the basic routine of eating. Physically emptying ourselves encourages other quietings and promotes an increased openness to subtler stirrings in our heart.

Fasting, at its finest, is neither punishment nor denial. We fast not just to avoid evils but to recapture forgotten goods. Not eating food for a day helps us remember all those who do not enjoy a daily plenty. Choosing not to drink alcohol for a time reminds us of our many habits that can both pleasure and imprison us.

Fasting, like feasting, easily goes awry. Fasting can be part of our flight from frightening emotions. It can become an undisciplined compulsion, whether in the medieval ascetic or the anorexic teenager. But even with its dangers, this inclination to fast remains a potential resource.

We fast regularly in our erotic lives. When our spouse is ill, we learn to forgo intercourse for a time. We are sexually attracted to someone, but we fast from this delightful arousal because of other goods we have chosen. Many celibate persons recognize that the discipline of fasting from genital sharing depends on a life that is rich with genuine friendship and is deeply sensual—graced with music or art or other forms of beauty. To fast from sexual contact because eros is evil is not a Christian discipline but an unholy and unhealthy flight from creation.

The no of fasting is fruitful only if we have some deeply valued yeses in our life. The arduous discipline of fasting complements our feasting: we need something *to fast for*. Without some compelling values to pursue and defend, we have no reason to hold back any stirring or impulse. Maturing Christians learn to recognize and honor the seasons of feasting and fasting in their own lives. These erotic disciplines must be integrated into the family of our passions. Fasting from fear we learn to be courageous enough to risk loving. Fasting from the impulses of jealousy and envy we become more generous in our friendships.

Our disciplined efforts of feasting and fasting bear fruit in graceful habits. These habits, which Christians call virtues, are reliable, resident strengths within us. As the habits develop, gradually we find it easier to trust our instincts and to fast from temptation. Saint Augustine was mightily impressed with bad habits—patterns of compulsive and selfish behavior. Our virtuous acts are not habits, he felt, because they are not our doing but the result of God's grace. Thomas Aquinas tried to balance this prejudice, arguing that with grace we can develop good habits—strong and virtuous ways of acting—as well as bad. Our tradition names these virtuous strengths—charity, justice, compassion, hope. These and the other virtues grow in us only as we practice the disciplines of feasting and fasting.

The Play of Intimacy

Eros is a complex and mysterious power. Our passion stirs in the privacy of our bodies but impels us toward public commitments and social care. What metaphor best pictures and illumines this complex behavior? A growing number of theologians and psychologists point us in the direction of the human inclination to play.

The connection between play and intimacy is forged early. Our parents playfully show their affection for us. Our first friends in childhood are our playmates. Falling in love, we learn the wonderful intimacy of love play. The metaphor of play captures the delight and risk and creativity of our efforts at intimacy.

But first we have to confront a profound bias against play in our Christian past. Many of us have learned to see play as childish and irresponsible. In our adult commitments, we must set aside such frivolous behavior. The Latin word for play, *ludere*, shares its root with *ludicrous* and *illusory*, suggesting that play is silly and insubstantial. The serious realm of sexuality leaves little room for play. Religious instruction often speaks of one's sexual "duty" in marriage but rarely mentions play or taking pleasure.

It is true: we can play with intimacy and sexual passion in ways that avoid responsibility and abuse other people. But a deeper, richer sense of human play exists. Theologian John Dominic Crossan argues that the metaphor of play best expresses what being human means. All our actions—our efforts to make sense of our life and our attempts to love—are play. We creatures are players in God's creation. Following the script given us by the play's Author, we enact the next scene in this long-running drama. With delight and inventiveness we play out our vocations. Such roles need not be competitive or manipulative; but they *are* exciting and risky. Each of us plays a part (spouse, priest, worker) that has been done a million times before—but never quite this way. How creative are we allowed to be in these roles?

How much reinterpretation does the script permit? Can we improvise to keep the play lively? Crossan emphasizes that play is much more than repetition. In the Church at the end of the twentieth century, we can feel the strain of invention: we are playing ancient roles in some novel ways. This is especially true in our lives of intimacy.

LEARNING TO PLAY

Psychologist D. W. Winnicott, in a lifetime of studying children, finds profound links between play and maturing in intimacy. His evidence suggests that play is crucial to the discipline of eros. Winnicott focuses his interest on children's use of teddy bears and dolls. With these affectionate playthings (in Winnicott's parlance these are *transitional objects*), the child explores the boundary between self and parent. The child holds on to the doll while gradually letting go of the parent. The teddy bear is both real (something to hold on to) and symbolic (representing the parent that she can no longer constantly hold on to).

In this kind of play the child begins the lifelong dance of intimacy: how we are one with another person, yet separate; how we need both to merge with a loved one and to remain independent. We all "play our way" to our best style of intimacy. Winnicott's study of play in childhood illumines the adult virtues released in the play of intimacy: the ability to risk, to take pleasure, to be flexible, and to trust. The risk and excitement of intimacy arises from its location—in play we explore the boundary between ourself and others. Play is precarious because we are always testing that fine line that both separates us from and connects us to others. How close can I come to you? How much privacy do I need? Each of us can feel both the risk and the pleasure of exploring these questions.

Play is also an exercise in flexibility. Winnicott makes an especially important point here about the discipline of eros. Play,

which is very different from *instinctual* activity, does not impel us
to a quick climax and the gratification of a focused need. Instead
play lingers and dallies; it repeats itself, thriving on an infinite
variability. This is true of the child with the doll and of lovers
exploring each other's bodies. In the vocabulary of C. S. Lewis,
the play of our sexuality leads us beyond biological need to personal appreciation.

Play is a companion of trust. To learn to play, we need a
trustworthy environment. The parent who throws us in the air
will catch us. The big brother who wrestles with us will not hurt
us. In a milieu of disruption or abruptly changing moods, as the
experience of adult children of alcoholics attests, we are unlikely
to learn how to play. But in an atmosphere of trust, children will
feel safe enough to concentrate on play. This concentration—
recall a child's absorption in a toy—is a key part of play and the
fruit of trust.

Winnicott offers a poignant portrait of a child playing with a
toy while a parent sits quietly nearby. Fully absorbed in this play
the child seems *to be alone in the presence of another.* This extraordinary experience is the link between solitude and intimacy. In
the play of adult solitude (and of solitary prayer), we are alone in
the presence of Another. We had learned before about the trust-
worthiness of the environment. We can trust ourselves in such
times of absence because we are not absolutely alone and we are
in a milieu that is kind. We can afford to engage in this special
mode of play—being alone in the presence of another.

Psychiatrist George Vaillant found these strengths of play in
the adults whose lives he studies in *Adaptation to Life.* The
healthiest members of this group were those who, in the midst of
their adult responsibilities, were still able to play. This playful-
ness extended from their participation in sports to their flexibility in loving. Vaillant sums up this connection between play,
trust, and intimacy:

It is hard to separate capacity to trust from capacity to play, for play is dangerous until we can trust both ourselves and our opponents to harness rage. In play, we must trust enough and love enough to risk losing without despair, to bear winning without guilt, and to laugh at error without mockery.

We begin to see play not as frivolous but as a disciplined way of loving.

THE LEAP OF INTIMACY

In his book *Toys and Reasons* psychologist Erik Erikson gives us another forceful argument for play as the best metaphor of adult maturing in intimacy. Erikson follows Plato in picturing play as rooted in the random leap of the child. In such a leap we see the three elements that make this metaphor so rich. Play is, first of all, a leap of delight. It is meant to be pleasurable for its own sake. Second, the leap of play is always testing: how far can I jump; how high can I leap? Third, the leap of play ends in coming down: we fall and sometimes fail. These three elements of play may instruct us in the rigorous discipline of intimacy and eros.

The play of intimacy is meant to be a leap of delight. Falling in love, we make these leaps. The excitement and pleasure we feel encourage us to risk even the leap of a life commitment. Christians today are becoming more enthusiastic about the delight they find in their sexuality. Vowed religious have friends not just for the good purpose of expanding their personalities; they take the leap of genuine friendship for the delight of it, because it is good. This is reason enough. Married Christians are becoming more comfortable with making love not just to beget children, but for the delight of it—for its own sake. A danger in many marriages is not that they will become too playful, but that they will lose this delight. As our relationship becomes immersed in the necessary, daily routines of work and child care, we may lose the ability to play and to delight each other. Many couples use the discipline of a yearly retreat or a weekend away from the family to help them recapture delight. In such a protected space they take the time to revisit and recover the goodness and pleasure of their shared life. They spend some special hours feasting again on their love.

In the playful leaps of our loving, we are also testing the leeway. As we draw closer to another person in affection, we always confront our own limited mobility. We leap against the gravity of our own wounds and hesitancy. We test how close the two of us can come and how much distance we should leave between us. And we leap against the social and religious expectations of our community. The Christian rhetoric of marriage tells us that "two shall become one." As we strive toward such a unity, we come to learn that we must also remain separate. Two becoming one could mean the other being completely absorbed into our own plans and career. But how are we to remain separate, gracefully apart? In the leaps and the testing of our relationship we must play out our own best solution.

Our culture also instructs us in our roles as wife and husband. If our love is lively, we will test the leeway between this cultural ideal and our own best way. Can we find some play in these cultural expectations or must we simply conform to them? If we allow ourselves no play, we force ourselves into a preset mold and role. Our relationship may be dutiful, but it will not be playful.

In this aspect of the playful discipline of eros we face a very robust, challenging part of intimacy. We need to be hardy enough to bump up against boundaries, both our own interior timidity and external rules. As we mature in play, we learn to do this without hostility or petulance. We learn to be at once resilient and respectful. The discipline of eros reminds us that the strain we sometimes feel in our loving is not all due to our immaturity or foolishness. This strain is part of the tension and exhaustion that comes with the robust play of adult intimacy. As part of the discipline of eros, we explore the source of the strain: What expectations, cultural or religious, are we pushing against? What limitations in ourselves are we bumping up against here?

Finally, to leap is to come down. Friendships sometimes end; life commitments can be broken and fail. How do we learn to play in the world of intimacy, knowing that we can fall? Frightened by the possibility of failure, we may choose not to play. If we succeed in avoiding intimacy, we will never fail at it. But this metaphor can remind us that falling is a part of play. We learned this as children when we saw our friends fall down or make an embarrassing mistake and then dust themselves off and keep playing. That must be the way it is done! Crossan reminds us that in play we learn about a certain "disciplined failure." We learn how to fail—and keep playing.

As we grow older we can look back and see, with more comfort, the falls that have been part of our life of intimacy. Blunders, embarrassments, sinfulness—every life is marked with these events in the contact sport of love. In retrospect these falls look more benign. We may even see them as necessary to the journey. They are part of the path we have taken; they are how we have reached this point in our life. We would not have chosen these mistakes and falls but now we can forgive ourself for them.

And we recognize other kinds of falls in the world of eros—necessary falls from the illusions that protected our early loving. We had thought our parents were perfect: our mother's touch could heal any hurt and our dad could beat up anybody on the block. As we grow up we learn the painful truth: some wounds lie too deep for even our mother's healing; some forces outweigh our father's strength. We are invited to let these once-necessary illusions fall away. If we can do this, we can come to love our parents for who they really are; our intimacy with them can take on a mature shape.

Our early intimacy with the Church included a picture of it as a most holy place, a fit dwelling for God. As we mature, we learn the painful truth: the Church is also a fragile place, housing flawed and wounded folk. This is the real Church we are called to love and care for. We can make such a commitment of intimacy only if we let earlier illusions fall away.

How do we dare develop the discipline of such play? Where do we get the courage to play so energetically and boldly? Two convictions seem especially required. First, Christians have the advantage of believing that the play belongs to God. We are players in a larger drama. We do not understand it all nor do we need to. We can be competent players without being responsible for the whole plot. Our part can end before the play is over; not everyone needs to applaud. This conviction should set us free to play with more courage and delight.

Second, Christians know to play in a community. We want to leap among friends who keep us honest; we seek to fall where companions can catch us. In the 1960s people talked of needing "a place to crash." Community is such a place. A community is a network: a netting to break the fall. Playing in community is finally more satisfying than being a soloist or a prima donna. But this, too, is a discipline of eros: recruiting the friends and lovers among whom leaping and testing and falling are safe.

Taming our sexual passion begins in reimagining: how do we picture this lovely but frightening power? The discipline of eros invites our imagination to examine the feasting and fasting in our erotic life. This discipline also encourages us to learn the rules of the robust play of adult Christian intimacy.

REFLECTIVE EXERCISE

Consider the elements of play in your own experience of intimacy. Recall an important relationship, one that enriches your life with affection and meaning and hope. Pause to appreciate the memories this relationship brings with it, before moving on to the questions below. You may wish to share your reflection with your partner.

What important *leaps* have been part of this relationship? Leaps of risk? Leaps of trust? Leaps of delight?

Where do you take delight in your relationship these days? What is the chief obstacle to your experiencing delight?

Where in this relationship do you "test the leeway"? Where do you challenge the limits or question the boundaries: of your own generosity or courage? in the tension between closeness and distance? regarding social roles and expectations?

What does this relationship teach you about falling and failure? What have you learned about forgiveness? What illusions have had to fall away?

ADDITIONAL RESOURCES

Bernard Lee explores the connection between eros and God in his excellent chapter, "The Appetite of God," in *Religious Experience and Process Theology*, edited by Harry Cargas and Bernard Lee (Paulist, 1976). Ann Ulanov discusses eros in *The Feminine in Jungian Psychology and in Christian Theology* (Northwestern, 1971). In *Original Blessing* (Bear and Company, 1983), Matthew Fox gives a comprehensive statement of the theological perspective that supports a creation-centered spirituality. James Nelson's most recent work is *The Intimate Connection: Male Sexuality and Masculine Spirituality* (Westminster, 1988).

Bernard Tyrrell employs the discipline of fasting and feasting in a therapeutic context in his *Christotherapy* (Paulist Press, 1975). For a contemporary spirituality of fasting, see Thomas Ryan's *Fasting Rediscovered* (Paulist Press, 1981).

D. W. Winnicott reports his research in *Playing and Reality* (Basic Books, 1971). For other analyses of play from the psychological perspective, see Erik Erikson, *Toys and Reasons* (Norton,

1977), and George Vaillant, *Adaptation to Life* (Little, Brown: 1977).

John Dominic Crossan, in *Cliffs of Fall* (Seabury, 1980), explores play as the metaphor that describes all we do as humans. In Chapter 1 of *Seasons of Strength* (Image Books/Doubleday, 1986), we use the metaphor of play to describe the maturing of Christian vocation; in "The Practical Play of Theology," in *Formation and Reflection: The Promise of Practical Theory* (Fortress, 1987), edited by Lewis Mudge and James Poling, we use the image of play to illumine the method of pastoral theology.

Part Three

The Arenas of Intimacy

Adults pursue intimacy along many paths: friendship, collaboration in work, marriage, and family life. These avenues of association become, at times, arenas: sites of affection and commitment. And these arenas can become crucibles: places where our ability to love and to be faithful is painfully tested and purified.

In Part Three we explore the arenas of friendship, partnership between women and men, and marriage—examining each to discover the dynamics by which our associations mature and grow strong. We turn to the hopes and challenges of intimacy that are part of the experience of being single, and close with a consideration of consecrated celibacy in the life of the Church today.

10.

Friends and Companions

Wherever you go, I will go,
Wherever you live, I will live.
Your people shall be my people,
And your God, my God.
Wherever you die, I will die
And there I will be buried. (Ruth 1:16–17)

Ruth loved Naomi. In this celebrated passage in Hebrew Scripture, Ruth proclaims her devotion to this woman who was her mother-in-law and much more. Theirs is a fierce friendship, a mutual commitment that moved far beyond the ordinary demands of family concern. The story of their love touches our hearts today, holding out the promise of friendship.

Our everyday lives are filled with acquaintances, the people we meet at work, in the neighborhood, at church. We greet them with civility and even warmth, but we spend little time with them. We know few details of their lives. But sometimes from this crowd of acquaintances something more emerges. By a graced combination of good fortune and personal effort, friends enrich our lives.

Friendship begins in mutual attraction—an emotional spark

ignites between us. We enjoy each other's company and like doing the same things. As we spend more time together, we dare to break through the surface of our relationship. Venturing beyond the casual companionship—of neighbors, co-workers, pals—we move into the more intimate realm of friendship. For a friendship to develop, as psychologist Lillian Rubin observes in *Just Friends*, "there must also be . . . some way in which the friend reaches a part of self not accessible to most others." Such is the heart of friendship. Our friends touch a part of us that is not readily accessible to others, often enough not even to ourselves.

Friendship is a rare blessing today. How do we find the time to build the bonds of trust and affection? Where do we gain the confidence to share our heart with another person? How can we escape the deadly patterns that freeze our conversations in superficial repartee? These questions remind us of the difficulty of friendship in American life. Few structures support a continuing relationship between friends. Friendship does not have the legal protection—or constraints—of marriage. Most friendships lack the familiar ritual celebrations (shared holidays, birthdays, anniversaries) that reinforce ties within the family. Moreover, we do not even have many shared understandings of what being a "good friend" asks of us.

Friendship depends almost exclusively on the ongoing emotional bond between us. This spontaneity is part of friendship's charm. Friends don't *have* to keep in touch; friends *choose* to spend time together. Our relationship grows and deepens not because it *should* but because we both genuinely want it to. But this lack of structure can also imperil our relationship. Our responsibilities at work or in our marriage and family seem clearer and more compelling than the demands of friendship. The claims of other commitments easily crowd out the time we might spend with friends. Absorbing our energy and attention, these concerns leave us drained when we do find time to be together.

Friendship then becomes a refreshing diversion from "real life," with no legitimate demands of its own.

The mobility of our lives complicates friendship even more. Our friendship flourishes when work or living arrangements put us in proximity. But if one of us moves away, the relationship may die. Nothing beyond ourselves exists that we can look to— guidelines, expectations, "rules of the game"—to help us sustain our friendship at a distance.

Yet in spite of the complications, friendships thrive. Those of us with good friends rejoice in their presence in our lives. Those without often sense that something is missing and long to have someone to share life with in this way. In the coming pages we will explore the core and the cost of this privileged relationship and discuss the special complications that can arise in friendships between women and men.

The Core of Friendship

Friends enrich and expand our lives. But what does friendship do for us? Why is it so special? To answer these questions, psychologists Marjorie Fiske and Lawrence Weiss examine the mutually supportive and intimate relationships that most of us would call close friendships. They start by acknowledging that close relationships are not all alike. Friendships between women and men, for example, have different dynamics than those between persons of the same gender. Some friendships are long-standing while others are more short-term. While sexual sharing may be part of a friendship, most often it is not. But more important than these differences among adult friendships is a crucial similarity: as a friendship develops, the partners become *reliable emotional confidants.*

A close friend is, first, a *confidant,* someone with whom we share confidences. We can be open here because we know this person can be counted on, especially in circumstances that involve risk and vulnerability. With a friend, exploring questions that often remained hidden is safe. As friendship deepens, we let ourselves be influenced—even changed—by someone we love.

Friendship links us as *emotional* confidants. Going beyond the enjoyment of each other's company, we enter into one another's inner life. The bond between us is not based just on common activities or similar tastes; we exchange more than ideas. Friendship includes emotional self-disclosure—direct, immediate conversation about what is going on in our heart and mind. Willingness to talk about thoughts and feelings seems essential to a deepening friendship.

And as friendship grows, we become *reliable* emotional confidants. A history of trust exists between us; we have proven ourselves dependable. This heritage helps us approach one another in confidence: here we will not be mocked; here we will not be judged; here we will not be scorned. Dependability does not mean that we will always agree nor does it ensure that we will never hurt one another. Sometimes our words and actions cause pain. Dependability doesn't exclude all conflict or confrontation between us: often only a friend is close enough and courageous enough to tell the truth, especially when the truth is hard for us to hear. But in friendship, we come to count on one other to act *consistently* with openness, understanding, and respect. With a friend, we know that we are *valued* before we are *evaluated.*

Such a relationship lets us relax our ordinary well-guarded stance. We put aside some of our necessary and even useful defenses. With friends, we don't need always to be strong. We can allow a friend to see our wounds. And when friends are not frightened by our weaknesses, we learn to be a bit more comfortable with them ourselves. We may even begin to befriend the frailties from which we have, unsuccessfully, tried to hide.

With friends we don't always have to be consistent. This rare freedom lets us explore the contradictions that are part of our inner life. To a friend we can acknowledge that we are both generous and selfish, sometimes courageous but often enough afraid. The affections of our friends provides a kind of sacred space; here we can explore the parts of life that bewilder us, that challenge us, that seem absurd. Friends help us face the future with less fear.

Friendship is so special because these gifts are mutual. The giving and the receiving go both ways. Friendship may be therapeutic, but it is not therapy. In therapy we talk about what is really important to us, but the self-disclosure is necessarily one-sided. The intimate details of the therapist's life are considered out of bounds. This kind of one-way openness would cripple a friendship. Friends *share* their inner worlds—the special successes and confusions that are not easily available to casual acquaintances. This mutuality may be suspended in a time of personal crisis, when all the energy of our friendship is focused on one of us in need. But soon, even in such trying times, we need to reestablish our pattern of mutuality. A friendship that remains one-sided is sure to falter.

The Cost of Friendship

Friendship welcomes us into a world of mutual support and fidelity. Since friends share a sense about what really matters in life, our friends help hold us accountable for living according to what we believe. The presence and support of friends are often critical in times of significant personal change, when our own hopes or goals put us at odds with "the way things are." By their acceptance and affection, our friends help us face the guilt and blame and social pressure that may accompany our efforts to be different.

But friendship can also present obstacles to personal growth. Some friends are supportive only as long as we agree with them. Our pals and buddies love us for who we are, but their affection demands that we stay the same. In their eyes, change threatens our friendship. The support of friends can exert emotional pressure for a conformity that leads to stagnation.

But if our friends teach us about support, they also instruct us in fidelity. Fidelity means staying with. As a friendship deepens, we seek to spend more time with each other. We want to be there when the other person needs us. Fidelity means that we do not abandon our friends in times of stress or distraction.

Promiscuity threatens fidelity—not always at a sexual level. In friendship, promiscuity means succumbing to the temptation to move on when the novelty of a relationship wears off. As the demands of friendship become clearer, fidelity can feel like constraint. New people await us "out there"; new experiences of spontaneity and discovery beckon to us. And these new relationships are free of the messy compromises that come with commitment. Fidelity roots us in a conviction that can outlast these temptations.

MISPLACED FIDELITY

But even fidelity may be distorted. Sometimes in a friendship, our fidelity can be misplaced. Are we ever willing to let go of a friend? We have all been in a relationship in which a significant problem appears. Perhaps the other person starts drinking more often and more heavily. We begin to fear for his health, as well as the safety of anyone who meets him on the highway at night! We want to bring up the subject of his drinking, but we're afraid to do so. The threat we feel is twofold. First, our image of ourself as a good friend comes under question. "Friends, after all, are supposed to accept one another fully, aren't they? Isn't our love meant to be unconditional? Our friendship shouldn't depend on his acting a certain way, should it? At least not just to please me! Am I just being petty by demanding that *he* change so that *I* will feel better?"

A second threat strikes more deeply—the fear of abandonment. "Suppose I bring up the issue of his drinking and my friend responds by turning away from me? I'm not sure I can bear to lose this relationship. I need my friend's attention and affection. I do not want to risk these by challenging his behavior."

What are we to do? This difficult situation raises disquieting questions: Is there no value for which we will risk a relationship? When does fidelity become something else—an unhealthy collusion or co-dependent behavior? In some circumstances, fidelity holds a severe challenge—it requires that we confront a friend or lover even at the risk of the relationship. A claim of "fidelity to values" can, of course, become a ruse that we use to disentangle ourselves from relationships that demand too much of us. But sometimes genuine fidelity compels us to risk the loss of a precious friend.

A second distortion of fidelity can happen in long-lasting relationships. Let us start, though, by recognizing the importance of old friends, those tested companions with whom we have shared decades of life's journey. Friends like this are irreplaceable. We sense this in the special sadness experienced at the death of longtime friends. With their passing we lose part of our own past. However gregarious we remain as we grow older, we cannot make new "old friends." But sometimes old friends can conspire in a kind of perverted fidelity. Gathering to tell old stories and rehearse ancient complaints (about the economy, about the Church, about "those others") we blanket one another in nostalgia; we defend each other against the winds of change. Nostalgia—our delight and our absorption in the good old days—is an ordinary and honorable form of grieving. Letting go of old ways of seeing and acting takes time. But eventually we need to let go. When we refuse to change, nostalgia can become chronic. Now a hiding place, our shared past protects us from change and its new demands. Old friends remain good friends when they help us draw strength from the past to face the confusions and possibilities of the future.

As friends, our fidelity is not just to an early stage of the common journey. Our fidelity is a faithfulness to the journey itself, with its strange twists and unknown future. Old friends help one another to brave the new.

REMAKING OUR FRIENDS

Among the costs of friendship are the surprises and purifications that await us along the road. One of these surprises is our stumbling upon a secret project of some of our friendships: we have been trying to *remake the other person*, usually in our own image.

The early stages of a friendship are often marked by a startling sense of compatibility. Our interests are similar: we like the same music, the same kind of food. Our needs—for privacy, for excitement, for affection—seem to mesh. With delight, we discover that we are not unique or isolated or odd; we find another person *like me* who *likes me*. In a world that showers us with diversity and conflict, this is a heady consolation.

Gradually, the two of us come to see that we are not so totally alike. We come slowly upon the foibles and habits that make us different. She is not as punctual as we first thought; he seems more restless than we find comfortable. As our relationship continues, we come upon the maddening habits that stretch our tolerance and remind us of the advantages of solitude.

During this discovery of difference, our secret project is likely to begin. We set out, often unconsciously, to remake the other person. We determine that these minor differences between us can be overcome. With some slight adjustments, we can make our friend "perfect" again! If only we can get her to see things our way, we will survive this bumpy period and become lasting friends. We gradually increase the pressure on our friend to change, to be more like us or more like what we need her to be.

Then the moment of purification strikes its blow: we come face to face with this covert operation. Whether our friend assists us in this discovery or we come upon it on our own, we are shocked. We thought we were above that kind of thing! Now we begin to appreciate the difficulty of a mature friendship. Friendship asks us to let those we love be themselves.

But then the problem deepens: How is this covert remaking different from the proper and necessary ways that friends challenge one another? Are we to become passive and utterly uncritical of each other? Is it that "anything goes"? The answers to these questions will not be found within the privacy of our solitary reflection. Only by bringing the secret project out in the open, by talking about it together, will we find a solution that honors our friendship. We should not feel too ashamed to bring up the topic, since our friend has likely been aware of the project for some time! We need to share our concern with our friend. We need to admit, "I want *this* for you but know I shouldn't force you. What most disturbs you in the agenda of this no-longer-secret project of mine? How can we be more honest with each other?" With effort and honest communication, we can forge the compromises that nurture, rather than destroy, our friendship. We can find more mature ways to be faithful to one another.

Women and Men as Friends

Friendships are a source of solace and challenge for all of us—men and women alike. But recent research has uncovered some intriguing differences in the ways that women and men approach friendship. These are differences in style and in expectation.

The differences in style are more apparent. Men friends *do things together*; women friends *talk things over*. Women value their friendships with other women especially for the understanding and emotional support they receive. Women friends tend to spend time together exploring the inner world of personal experience and meaning. This sharing of thoughts and feelings both expresses and strengthens their emotional bond.

The bond that develops between men friends often has more to do with solidarity than with self-disclosure. Among men, friendship is based more on common experience—at the workplace, in the army, in school—than on intimate conversation. As friends, men stand shoulder to shoulder more than face to face. Confronting a common task, they come in touch with each other. Gradually and indirectly, this association can grow into a deep friendship.

Many men hesitate to discuss their personal life with another man, especially if the conversation might touch on areas of personal weakness or vulnerability. Men often find that expressing strong positive emotions—affection, gratitude, joy—among their men friends is difficult. They rely, instead, on a growing sense of loyalty and camaraderie.

This familiar difference in friendship *style* reflects an underlying difference between women and men in their *expectations* of friendship. In a close relationship between two men or between two women, the gender difference is not a factor. But as a friendship develops between a woman and a man, this difference in expectations can cause confusion.

Most confusing, as Lillian Rubin's study revealed, are expectations about emotional sharing and sexual attraction. Many women report that a male friend is not as forthcoming as they would like him to be in terms of emotional sharing. Many men indicate that they sometimes feel pressured by a woman friend to reveal more of themselves than is comfortable for them. Men and women agree that, in most cross-gender heterosexual friendships, the issue of sex has to be resolved before the friendship can deepen.

THE EROTIC POSSIBILITIES

Rubin and other psychologists suggest that these expectations are rooted in our interpretations of the erotic possibilities of friendship. As we have seen in earlier chapters, the erotic includes the full range of attraction and responsiveness that draws people toward one another. This delightful dynamic spans the incredible range of arousals that we experience as embodied persons. Thus eros encompasses the sensual pleasure of a hot bath as well as the emotional companionship of a good friend; both the delight of a good meal and the joy of genital sharing express eros. But as women and men, we often learn to interpret the erotic possibilities of friendship in quite different ways. In relationships between men and women, these differences often come to the fore.

For many men the erotic possibilities of friendship tend to be understood in explicitly sexual ways. The excitement of a friendship with a woman is closely associated with genital arousal; the "chemistry" that they experience is interpreted as explicitly sexual. Men learn, both from their physiological arousal and from culture, to first ask of this friendship a sexual response. Only as the friendship progresses will they feel safe enough to explore the possibility of emotional intimacy—that deeper sharing of self through significant self-disclosure.

Many women interpret relationships differently. As a friendship begins, most women respond first at the emotional level. They look forward to connecting with this other person in experiences of empathy, care, and companionship. While a woman may be physically attracted to a man who is a potential friend, the emotional attractions she feels toward him is what tells her that friendship is possible here. As the friendship deepens, she may want to include sexual intimacy as part of the relationship. But for most women, emotional closeness comes before and opens the way for genital love. Many men experience these two aspects of eros in the reverse order: for them sexual attraction comes before and opens the way to a deeper emotional connection.

This difference in erotic expectations can complicate the effort of women and men to develop deep friendships with each other. Feeling drawn to a woman, a man may sexualize the relationship in a way that surprises the woman. As she views their relationship, sex is not what brings them together. His obvious sexual interest seems inappropriate and confusing to her. In turn, her disinterest confuses him. He reasons that her reluctance to move the relationship toward genital expression must be because the relationship means less to her than it does to him.

The erotic possibilities of friendship—the opportunities for closeness, affection, mutual support, delight, concern—are vast and complex. As we become more aware of each other's expectations (and our own), we have a better chance of untangling our hopes in friendship. In a particular relationship we may find the bond of friendship between us expanding to include sex. More often, friendship between women and men thrives in the decision to exclude sexual sharing. In *Among Friends,* social analyst Letty Pogrebin confirms this finding in Rubin's research. Sexual tensions often complicate close relationships between women and men. When these feelings arise, they must be acknowledged in some way, either by joking about them or by discussing them directly. In the man-woman friendships that she studied, Pogrebin found that sex became less an issue as the relationship grew. The partners often explained that they suspected sex between them would change things in ways that would ruin their friendship. For these partners, their friendship was too important to take that chance.

American culture often complicates friendships between women and men. Its bias, evident in the media and other forms of popular culture, suggests that affection between a man and a woman always and inevitably leads to genital expression. Because of this bias, we suspect our own friendships. We begin to second-guess ourselves: "If we really like each other, we ought to be sleeping together, or at least struggling with the question. Maybe we are not being honest with one another." Both history and personal experience testify to the reality of significant emotional relationships in which genital sexuality has no part. Attraction and affection are strong, as are mutual concern and care. But the communion of these friendships does not include genital love. Another sign of our culture's preoccupation with sex is that we must reassure one another that such a friendship is possible.

Our mobile lives in a competitive society endanger the gift of friendship. When we are blessed with a friend, we are invited both into another's life and more deeply into our own. In the arena of friendship the virtue of intimacy is refined, as we experience the benefits and demands of this gifted love.

REFLECTIVE EXERCISE

Reflect for a moment on your own experience of friendship. Who are your closest friends and companions these days? Drawing up a list that mentions them by name may help you to savor their presence.

Keeping these people—your own close friends—in mind, consider the issues we discussed in this chapter. Focus on each person in turn, spending time with the rich quality of this particular relationship.

How would you name the core of this friendship—the bond that links you together? Be concrete: What attraction drew you together at the start? What commitment holds you together now?

Recall something of your history together, its ups and downs. How have you faced the costs of friendship?

Finally, is there an image—a symbol, a quote from Scripture, the title of a song—that captures this friendship at its heart?

ADDITIONAL RESOURCES

Novelist Cynthia Ozick offers a wonderful reflection on Ruth's friendship with Naomi as her contribution in *Congregation* (Harcourt Brace Jovanovich, 1987), a collection of essays by Jewish authors on the books of the Hebrew Scripture, edited by David

Rosenberg. Marjory Zoet Bankson reflects on this biblical story in *Seasons of Friendship: Naomi and Ruth as a Pattern* (Luramedia, 1987). Eugene Kennedy's *On Being a Friend* (Ballantine, 1982) is a valuable resource for prayer and discussion. Paula Ripple writes movingly on the experience of friendship in *Called to Be Friends* (Ave Maria Press, 1980).

Lillian Rubin's compelling analysis of the role of friendship in the lives of American women and men is found in *Just Friends* (Harper & Row, 1985). In *Among Friends* (McGraw-Hill, 1986), Letty Cottin Pogrebin explores the shape of friendship today.

Marjorie Fiske and Lawrence Weiss report their findings on the role of emotional intimacy in psychological well-being in "Intimacy and Crises in Adulthood," in *Counseling Adults* (Brooks/Cole, 1977), a collection of essays edited by Nancy Schlossberg and Alan Entine. Their focus expands in a consideration of friendship throughout the life cycle in *Four Stages in Life* (Jossey-Bass, 1975).

In *Love in America* (Cambridge University Press, 1987), Francesca Cancian discusses the effect of gender roles on commitment. Stuart Miller focuses on the male experience in *Men and Friendship* (Houghton Mifflin, 1983); Janice Raymond examines women's experience in *A Passion for Friends: Toward a Philosophy of Female Affection* (Beacon Press, 1986). In *Between Women: Love, Envy, and Competition in Women's Friendships* (Viking, 1987), Luise Eichenbaum and Susie Orbach draw from personal experience and research findings to explore friendships between women. See also their earlier *Understanding Women: A Feminist Psychoanalytic Approach* (Basic Books, 1983).

Important insights into the costs of close relationships come from the theoretical and therapeutic literature in the fields of alcoholism and other addictive diseases. See, for example, Anne Wilson Schaef, *Co-Dependence: Misunderstood, Mistreated* (Harper

& Row, 1986); Sharon Wegscheider, *Another Chance: Hope and Health for the Alcoholic Family* (Science and Behavior Books, 1981); Charles Whitfield, *Alcoholism, Other Drug Problems, Other Attachments, and Spirituality* (The Resource Group, 1985).

11.

Women and Men as Partners

The "battle of the sexes" seemed simpler when we thought we knew the rules. Our understanding of the differences between women and men gave us guidelines. The world, as we knew it, was stratified vertically. Social life was hierarchically arranged, with certain roles essentially superior to others. In this worldview, men were "natural leaders"; women were more suited to supportive roles. A woman's place was in the home, a man's in the marketplace. These expectations allowed only very guarded forms of partnerships.

In such a world, the lives of women and men intersected only rarely, seldom as peers or equals. In marriage, for example, husband and wife were to become one, but the husband was still the head of the household. The marriage vows reminded a wife of her necessary obedience to his leadership. In their relationship, she was the emotional core while he was the reservoir of logic. Thus, the man should be more directive and the woman more willing to accommodate. The husband was not, of course, to "lord it over" his helpmate, but he still exercised lordship or dominion in the relationship. Experience showed that frequently enough this dominion slipped into domination—to the defeat of intimacy.

New opportunities exist today for women and men as partners. In personal life—as friends and spouses—and in the public
realm—as colleagues and competitors—men and women are together in new ways. The new terrain of partnership reveals not a
vertical world but a more horizontal realm. In friendship, marriage, and the world of work, partners recognize that their differing talents do not automatically rank as superior or inferior. The
image that guides partnership is not a hierarchy of strong and
weak but a network of multiple strengths. Seen through the lens
of partnership, our differences do not just set us apart; they
reinforce our need for one another.

The Shape of Partnership

Partnership is an experience of shared power—the genuine interplay of strengths and limitations in the movement toward common goals. As partners, we learn to count on each other's
strengths. This does not mean that we each bring the same thing
to our relationship or even that we each contribute equally.
While equality of opportunity is an essential goal in social life
and equality under the law provides a necessary safeguard against
the prejudices engrained in human society, equality is a tricky
objective in close relationships. Equality stresses sameness; partnership delights in diversity, knowing that our differences can
expand and enrich our relationship. Concern for equality carries
the hint that we should be keeping score. But measuring our
respective contributions is more likely to defeat partnership than
to enhance it.

Partnership, while not demanding strict equality, does require
real mutuality. The giving and receiving go both ways. In partnership each of us brings something of worth to the relationship;
each receives something of value as well. As partners, we recognize and respect this mutual exchange of gifts.

But cultural ideals make this kind of interdependence suspect.
In the images of the rugged American, self-reliance replaces col-

laboration; autonomy is valued over the ability to cooperate. Thus, appreciating interdependence as a mature response becomes difficult.

To many of us, *interdependence* suggests that we are not sufficient for ourself, that we *need* other people. Such dependence seems shameful. To look to other people for emotional support or practical assistance contradicts the prevailing norms of adult maturity. Our culture's commitment to the frontier virtues of "making it on my own" and "being beholden to no one" can be seen most sharply in the tendency to consider dependence a feminine trait. To need support and assistance is to be "womanly"—hardly a preferred attribute for the red-blooded American man. Yet the ability to depend on other people is crucial in both love and work. And it is a requirement of partnership.

To depend on other people is to rely on resources beyond our own. This dependency can be a problem if it arises from a sense that our own resources are inherently deficient—that on our own, we cannot make our way in life. An adult who is dependent in this way is seriously at risk—to exploitation by others and to the threats against self-esteem.

But dependence does not always arise from weakness; it can be a sign of strength. In the long-term relationships of marriage and friendship, for example, we must be able to trust ourself and our needs to others. In healthy partnerships we learn that other people can offer us help in ways that do not diminish us. We can count on his concern; we can rely on her care.

Our ability to depend on other people in this way says a good deal about them—how they have treated us in the past, how trustworthy they have proved to be. But the ability to trust says even more, perhaps, about ourselves. To depend on someone else requires a capacity to be open, confident that we are strong enough to display our need: being vulnerable in this way does not demean us in our own eyes. To depend on another also means that we are strong enough to risk rejection. We can survive if the other person cannot or will not respond. If we have to, we can carry on with just our own resources—even though this is not what we want to do. With this strength of independence, we are less likely to have our neediness contaminate a relationship. We are not so desperate.

The Dynamics of Collaboration

Collaboration teaches us to rely on other people. If we can trust only our own strength, we will probably not risk working so closely with others. We do not want their efforts to actually affect us. If we can count on only our own talent or our own judgment, we are likely to retain direct control of as many elements of our job as possible. As a member of a work group, we will insist on distinct areas of responsibility and autonomous spheres of action. In this we avoid having to depend on other people to "come through."

Collaboration demands that we depend on one another. This kind of dependability is built on a sense of personal power. To be dependable, we must be able to trust our own ability. We must trust that our resources will be there when we need them, when other people need them. This confidence is rooted in an appreciation of our strength—the conviction that our own resources are adequate to the tasks we face.

But more is required. Mature "depend-ability" means that we can rely on other people. We have learned to count on more than just ourself. We have come to realize on occasion—in love, in work, in faith—we can share a power that goes beyond our own. At times we cannot "go it alone." These incidents invite us into a wider experience of power. We learn to participate in processes that escape our exclusive control. These experiences prepare us for genuine interdependence.

To experience the interplay of power is to know that we need other people. For many of us this need is not easy to acknowledge because it forces us to face our limits. We have to recognize that in some areas of life our own strengths are not sufficient. Gradually we must come to accept our limits, even our weaknesses, without undue shame. Accepting ourself, we learn to depend on others in ways that enlarge rather than diminish us.

Here is the core of interdependence: we can count on the resources of other people as well as our own. We do not possess alone all that brings meaning and joy and accomplishment to life. We need strengths beyond our own. To ask for, to accept, these resources does not demean us. Rather our acknowledgment of interdependence opens us to the experience of partnership.

Tensions in Partnership: Attachment and Autonomy

Many factors help defeat partnership between men and women. Lillian Rubin, an astute chronicler of adult relationships, reminds us that cultural attitudes toward autonomy and attachment complicate our efforts to be together. Attachment is about being close to others, feeling connected with people. Attachment refers to all our hopes for *belonging*, our strategies for linking up with others, our efforts to be included in their affections and their plans. Women and men share the need for attachment; both benefit from the sense of security that comes when we join our lives with other people. Both women and men need autonomy, too. Autonomy is about relying on our own resources, knowing that we can take care of ourself. For both men and women, the conviction that we can stand on our own is a foundation of self-confidence and an important source of self-worth.

But our culture gives women and men different messages about attachment and autonomy. The man who does not seem to need other people (especially as portrayed in the cultural stereotypes of the cowboy, the private detective, the wealthy and successful "self-made man") is powerfully attractive. Such a man, we learn, will be admired, courted, and accepted. Under the influence of these cultural images, this man connects his masculinity with an independent stance that says, "When I appear strong and independent, others will find me desirable." This independence shields him from the demands of partnership. His strength and distance protect him against the risks of attachment, the threat that he may lose himself in coming too close—especially to a woman.

In the cultural expectations of femininity, a woman hears a quite different message. To appear autonomous, to act independently, is to jeopardize her opportunities for closeness. She learns that dependency is attractive, that "needing to be taken care of" makes her desirable. In many situations, "being taken care of" is the easiest way or even the *only* way she can establish connections with a man—especially if he is suspicious of emotional closeness or wary of a woman who appears too strong. Many women, then, learn that being dependent on men is rewarding.

These constraints conspire against partnership in the work setting. Under the sway of cultural images of masculinity, a man may feel that he must preserve an image of autonomy and self-sufficiency on the job. He may be able to develop an effective working relationship with a woman whose position is clearly dependent—a secretary, even a junior colleague. The obvious power differences here will protect him from the risks of professional parity or the even more threatening demands of emotional mutuality. In such a world, a man will experience a woman colleague who moves toward greater partnership—in which both mutual need and mutual strengths are explicitly acknowledged—as a challenge.

A woman, too, may feel some strain in the move toward partnership in work. She is likely to be well acquainted with both the limits and the benefits of being in the subordinate role. The scope of her contribution may be narrow, but so is her responsibility if things go wrong. Unable to pursue her own vision or test the full range of her abilities, she is nonetheless shielded from the embarrassment of public failure. As learner, as apprentice, as protégée, she participates in the interplay of power from a protected position. The move toward genuine partnership increases her vulnerability. She cannot so easily absent herself from conflict or challenge. In the face of a difficult decision she can no longer defer to those others who are "really in charge." Her own talent and courage are on the line. When these prove sufficient, the praise and sense of accomplishment are clearly hers. However, if her abilities fall short, she is clearly accountable. As a work partner, she participates more directly in the contact sport of effective collaboration—and she has both its victories and its injuries on her record.

Partnership can be threatening in the more personal relationships of friendship or marriage, as well. For example, so long as a man's wife is dependent on him financially, he feels safe in the emotional web of attachment and belonging that holds them together. If her economic dependence is less clear (should she decide to go back to work or pursue advancement in her career), the emotional bonds between them are upset. The balance of power has been disturbed. A shift in her obvious financial dependence jeopardizes their mutual attachment.

Both women and men feel the stress of this shift toward partnership. When his wife goes back to work, a man may complain that she doesn't need him anymore. At the same time his wife senses that she needs him even more now—for emotional support to build up her confidence, for practical assistance around the house, for collaboration in parenting. Or a woman, clearly competent to take care of herself and her job, will lament, "I don't want to do this without him." She wants to stay connected with her partner; she wants their attachment to endure in this new context of interdependence.

For many men, the challenge of effective partnership is to allow themselves to acknowledge greater dependence—to be willing to admit that they need others. For most women, the challenge is to develop greater strengths of mature independence—the ability to trust their own power. For both women and men, partnership will demand more flexible styles of autonomy and attachment.

The Conversation About Needs

Men and women, in their personal lives and at work as well, increasingly have partnership as a goal. We have explored friendship between women and men in Chapter 10. In Chapter 12 we will examine marriage. Here we will look more closely at a dynamic between men and women that affects collaboration in the world of work.

Partnership, while not always a goal for women and men who are working together, is more and more often a hope, an expectation, a demand in the work site. The world of work today is increasingly interdependent. Team work, effective planning, shared decision making—these require that we work closely with other people. Sometimes the interdependence is structural, built into the situation. To accomplish our goals we depend on others: we need his active support or her formal approval. His project is affected by our priorities; her budget influences our access to funds. Frequently we have to coordinate our work schedules or negotiate how we will share limited resources—the secretarial pool, the staff car, the parish list of willing volunteers.

To work together well, we must be able to talk about what we need from one another at these practical levels. The management disciplines are working hard to develop tools that help. In some factories, for example, workers and supervisors meet regularly in quality circles to discuss issues of joint concern. Staff members in service agencies develop and discuss their job descriptions so that they can understand the ways in which their tasks overlap. In the hope of more comprehensive long-range planning, corporations form project teams that bring together managers from several different departments. Strategies like these help women and men who are working together become more comfortable with the conversation about what we need from one another to do the job well.

But partnership often requires that the discussion go deeper, to include what we need from one another personally. As we work together, we need to ask, "What do I need from you to feel that I belong to this group? What do you need so you will know that your contribution is appreciated?" The deeper vulnerabilities we face demand this more difficult conversation. We are concerned here with more than a question of job description. This dialogue affects much more than our professional competence. Our conversation involves greater immediacy for it is about "you and me" more than about the job "out there."

Effective collaboration does not require that women and men who work together must become close friends or lovers. (In fact, as most of us know, the dynamics of romance complicate a working relationship and add considerably to its strain, both for the lovers and for the rest of us on the team.) But collaboration does raise the question of how close we want to be as co-workers and what we can confidently expect from one another.

No automatic "right answer" comforts us here. Our expectations of closeness and collaboration have to be worked out "in particular"—taking into consideration the persons involved, the scope of our commitments, and the larger values we hold. A small group of people who share a strong value commitment (working with the poor or directing a local campaign for political reform) may develop strong ties of emotional support. A group that is more highly structured and more diverse in values—say, a university faculty or a business office—may display much cooler patterns of collaboration and concern. Neither one of these is necessarily the preferred pattern for partnership. But, either by choice and negotiation or by default, *some* pattern will develop as we work together.

Who are we for one another here? What can we confidently

expect of each other? For people to work together as genuine partners requires that they be able to talk—directly and without manipulation—about their expectations of interdependence. This conversation, which can be difficult for all of us, is a special source of tension between women and men who are colleagues.

Considerable evidence today suggests that women and men tend to respond differently in the discussion of emotions. This is not true, of course, for every man and every woman. But the work of Nancy Chodorow, Carol Gilligan, and other students of gender differences notes a strong cultural trend. Many women have learned to be aware of their emotions; most have developed a working vocabulary that helps them to identify what they are feeling. This awareness makes many women, if not always comfortable with their feelings, at least sensitive to the emotional dimensions of what is going on around them. This sensitivity has implications for partnership. Most women want to know where they stand emotionally as they work out the other practical details of effective collaboration in the workplace.

The case is different for many men. Most American men report an upbringing and education that urged them to deny or downplay their emotions, especially those judged to be "womanly"—fear, dependence, tenderness, affection, appreciation. As a result, some men come to adulthood with little awareness of their emotional lives and a limited vocabulary for identifying how they feel. These men are often at a disadvantage in discussions about emotions. Beyond that, they have been socialized to see such a discussion as irrelevant or as a sign of weakness. Neither attitude is likely to put a man at ease in a conversation about what we have a right to expect of one another as we work together.

For many women, exploring issues of emotional interdependence early in a relationship is important. In team work and other collaborative settings, then, a woman often feels the need to initiate a discussion of "who we are for one another here," since she sees the clarification of this question as the *foundation* of genuine partnership.

For many men, such a conversation is not the foundation but the *fruit* of partnership. Any discussion of "what we need from one another personally" seems out of place in the early stages of collaboration. For these men to feel comfortable with such potentially threatening topics, a tested atmosphere of trust and acceptance must already be in place. Practically, then, this means that many men find the conversation about personal needs to be appropriate only *after* a period of effective collaboration. Some men would say that such a discussion is *never* appropriate.

This difference in expectations can be a source of considerable strain between women and men who work together. A woman may expect to have this discussion with her male colleague early on, since she wants to know where she stands with other people. Although this discussion is threatening for her (as it is for the man), she judges that the conversation is nonetheless necessary. After an honest discussion of what we need from one another and what we have a right to expect of one another, she is more willing to invest herself in the demands of genuine partnership. Without this opportunity to clarify expectations, she may remain uneasy about her place and uncertain of her own contribution. This uncertainty can eventually dissipate her energy and erode her commitment to the common endeavor.

On the other hand, her male colleague will likely consider this kind of direct conversation premature at this point. He expects it —accepts it—feels up to it—only later. For him, a working relationship does not *start* here; co-workers have to *earn* the right to this kind of self-disclosure. If a woman colleague introduces the discussion too soon, he is likely to respond with resistance and confusion. He may misinterpret the request, seeing it as a need for reassurance on her part (weak woman that she is) or as an inappropriate demand that they become emotionally involved. He may even consider her request as a sexual advance. The woman is likely to interpret his resistance as defensiveness (as a man he is, of course, "frightened of his feelings") or indifference ("after all, most men just don't care").

None of these responses is likely to support our efforts at partnership. Instead, we must be aware that, as women and men, we may be interpreting the situation between us differently. We have to be willing to explore these differences. But finally, we have to be ready for the risky discussion of what we need from one another.

REFLECTIVE EXERCISE

Take a look at your own experience of partnership between women and men. Recall the different settings in which you have been part of men and women working closely together. It may be helpful to list these experiences, especially if you have several. Spend some time with your memories of these situations—the people involved, the circumstances that brought you together, your own participation. Then consider these questions:

In your own experience, what are the benefits of partnership between men and women—benefits to you, to others, to the work?

What are the problems you have experienced in these settings, the tensions or concerns that make partnership difficult?

From your experience, what works? What factors—whether attitudes or behavior, strategies or structures—support genuine partnership between women and men?

ADDITIONAL RESOURCES

Nina Colwill examines the benefits and burdens of collaboration in the corporate world in *The New Partnership: Women and Men in Organizations* (Mayfield, 1982). Rosabeth Moss Kanter reports her findings on the dynamics of power in organizations in

Women and Men of the Corporation (Basic Books, 1976). Heinz and Rowena Asbacher bring together several of Alfred Adler's articles on interaction between men and women in *Co-operation Between the Sexes* (Norton, 1978).

Jennifer Coates reports the findings of her research on patterns of communication between women and men in *Men, Women and Language* (Longman, 1986). In *No Contest: The Case Against Competition* (Houghton Mifflin, 1986) Alfie Kohn draws implications for social collaboration, based on his research on the effectiveness of competitive and collaborative learning styles. With her colleague Bill Page, Carol Pierce describes the processes of personal transformation involved as women and men move beyond relationships marked by dominance and submission; see *A Male/Female Continuum: Paths to Colleagueship* (New Dynamics, 1986).

Theologian Letty Russell challenges religious institutions to hold themselves accountable to the gospel call to collaboration in *The Future of Partnership* (Westminster Press, 1979) and *Growth in Partnership* (Westminster Press, 1981). Beverly Wildund Harrison explores questions of partnership and more in *Making the Connections—Essays in Feminist Social Ethics* (Beacon, 1985), edited by Carol S. Robb.

Jim Heller, John Reid, and Mary Savoie have prepared a planning guide to assist ministry teams and staffs to implement greater collaboration among themselves; see *The Gospel Call to Collaborative Ministry*, available from the National Association for Lay Ministry (1125 W. Baseline Road, Mesa, Ariz. 85202). We discuss the theological foundation and practical challenge of collaborative ministry in "Women and Men: Partnership in Ministry," available in videotape with accompanying workbook from the National Federation of Priests' Councils (1307 S. Wabash Avenue, Chicago, Ill. 60605).

12.

The Maturing of Romance in Marriage

In our society the primary human symbol for a
committed relationship, with permanent intentions
and promise for mutual fulfillment, is marriage.
(Robert Shelton, *Loving Relationships.*)

Many of us find intimacy in marriage. Even more of us expect to
find it there. As a cultural ideal, marriage holds so much promise. Most Americans, whether married or not, see marriage as
the preferred setting for intimacy. No other adult relationship
seems so serious or so sustained. Even those who are aware—
sometimes from personal experience—of the perils that marriages face still carry images of married love that are remarkably
positive.

As a result, most of us have high expectations of marriage. We
want romance—the emotional and sexual attraction between us
that will keep our lovemaking passionate. We want to be friends
—enjoying each other's company, discovering in one another
the comfort and challenge, the solace and stimulation that we

need. We want devotion, too—the loyalty that we can count on, the trust that we are safe in one another's care.

Marriage did not always carry such high demands. As recently as a generation or so ago, wives and husbands did not generally expect to be one another's chief emotional companion or best friend. Couples today feel the additional pressures that come with the "companionate marriage." Yet few among us would be satisfied with a style of marriage that did not have friendship and mutual devotion as major goals.

Marriage and Romance

To Americans, romance stands as the source and seal of the decision to be married. But marriage and romance have not always been bedfellows. For many centuries Christians and others knew that while marriage might lead to love, it did not necessarily start out there.

The accepted norm for marriage today is personal selection based on romantic love. The understanding is that *we choose* whom we shall marry, and the person we choose is someone with whom we have fallen in love. Across different periods and in other cultures, a range of factors have been accepted as appropriate reasons for marriage: the decision of parents, the advice of matchmakers, concern for dynastic purity, or the effective transfer of property. Today most Americans would feel uneasy about a marriage motivated by these concerns. The sophisticated or the skeptical among us may be aware that these factors remain influential, but most of us feel that a marriage is well begun only when the spouses choose for themselves and when the choice is based, at least in large part, on a shared experience of romantic love.

THE INGREDIENTS OF ROMANCE

What is going on in romantic love? Three elements are central. The first is powerful *attraction*. Romance draws us together, physically and emotionally. When we are apart, we long for the other's presence; when we are near, we feel exhilarated. The allure can be overwhelming; we feel "swept away." The forces at play are "bigger than both of us"; they are outside—even beyond—our conscious choice. We speak of the "magnetism" we feel, the "chemistry" between us. These images capture the sense that we are caught up in something beyond our control. In this excitement and attraction, the sexual component is strong. Lovers may choose to reserve genital expression until after the formal commitment of marriage, but sexual energy is high.

Second, romance celebrates a sense of "fit." In romantic love a strong (even if not always accurate) awareness of *congruence and compatibility* emerges. We are convinced that we are perfectly suited for one another: "we fit together well." We like the same things; we have the same hopes for our love; we agree on what is important in life; we never argue. Romance, then, links us in values and vision as well as in affection and attraction.

Third, romance holds out the *promise of the future*. If our shared present holds such delight, surely a common future holds even more. This sense of promise fuels the decision to take on the broader commitments of married life. Romance leads us into marriage with powerful hopes of what our future will hold. Together, we want to shape a life that guarantees the love we know now and realizes our shared vision of an even richer future.

THE VALUE OF ROMANCE

We have fallen in love: this is how most marriages in our culture start. And all things considered, romantic love is not such a bad place for a marriage to begin. Romance is a legitimate and important early stage of love. Sexual longing is linked with genuine concern for the other person; the seeds of mutual devotion are planted here. The powerful attraction we feel for one another fuels the movement toward commitment, encouraging us to be open to the risks and possibilities that marriage will bring. A sense of compatibility reinforces the hope that this love will last. Our dream of a shared future nurtures a "we" that is larger than our separate ambitions.

Romance, then, is often love's ally. It is not simply, as the cynic would say, a deception. Romance is more than just a delightful distraction, to be set aside once we become involved in the "serious business" of marriage. Still, romance remains ambiguous. Two proverbs capture the ambiguity. Most of us know —from our own experience and from what we see in the lives of others—that these adages are true. "Love is blind," one proverb insists. Caught up in the excitement of romance, people can overlook even what seems obvious to others. Lovers respond selectively, sometimes blocking out what they do not want to see. Most of us have learned the sober lessons that come from being blinded by love. We have become properly suspicious of love's enthusiasms, if not always in our own lives at least in our judgments about other people's affairs.

But this is not the only conviction we have about romance. Most of us know equally well that "only the lover has eyes to see clearly." This proverb, too, has been true in our own experience. When we are in love, we see things—in the person we love, even in ourselves—that are lost on others. The lover knows the truth about the beloved. In the eyes of the one who loves us we see reflected the parts of ourself that we have been unable or unwilling to accept—our goodness, our loveliness, our dream.

Love is blind and love sees clearly—we know both to be true. The experience of romance that brings us to marriage is likely to include both these dynamics. Our own love is part insight and part illusion. As we begin our marriage, it is not clear how much insight and how much illusion are involved. Over the early years of our married life some of the illusions gradually surface. We start to see things differently; our romantic expectations are tested against the reality of who each of us is and the patterns of life that we develop together. Discrepancies arise between what we expected and how things are really turning out. These discrepancies begin to erode the euphoria of romance. The honeymoon is over.

The emergence of these initial discrepancies marks a critical point in the maturing of our marriage. Marriage matures as love becomes an active choice. We come to appreciate that marriage is an action verb—something we *do together*—not just something that we are "taken up in." This realization moves us beyond the exhilarating but largely passive experience of "falling in love" toward love as a cultivated and chosen commitment.

The commitments of marriage are the promises we make—to ourselves, to one another, to the world—to do whatever is necessary for our love to grow. Our commitments, of course, do not control the future. That sober lesson we learn as we move through life. Gradually, the events of our days challenge us to give up one by one our adolescent images of omnipotence. Maturity modifies both our sense of power and our sense of control. We discover that we are both stronger and weaker than we had realized. Our promises may be fragile, but they still have force. This vulnerable strength of commitment can transform romance into a love that sustains marriage for a lifetime.

This transformation, while it need not signal the loss of romance, does point to its purification. Committed love grows as we are able to acknowledge and appreciate our spouse "as is," beyond the idealized images that may have been part of our early attraction. The challenge is not to keep on loving the person we thought we were marrying, but to love the person we did marry! We come to know our spouse more completely and more clearly, as perhaps more gifted than we had dreamed but also as more limited than we had hoped.

The religious rhetoric surrounding marriage can help or hinder a couple from facing this purification. If this rhetoric portrays Christian marriage as necessarily free of conflict, we are not encouraged to confront the difficulties that unavoidably arise between us. Imagery that pictures marriage only as an institution —a "state" of matrimony that we inhabit—does not equip us for the surprising changes in this shared journey. The greatest gift that Christian faith may have to give to a married couple is the expectation of forgiveness. The move beyond infatuation often includes false starts; the purification of romantic love forces us to face our failures. Forgiveness becomes a powerful resource for this journey. If we can summon the courage and skill to forgive and to accept forgiveness, our married romance will have a future.

Season of Struggle

Romance, as we have said, is not a bad place to begin a marriage. But a marriage cannot thrive only on romance. Early romance has gotten us to this point on the journey, but by itself it can take us no farther. In fact, romance can become a stumbling block. Afraid that the loss of romance signals the end of our marriage, we may deny the new information that emerges from our life together. Trying to hold on to the good feelings that accompany our early infatuation, we look away from any evidence that contradicts these romantic ideals. We are afraid to acknowledge differences between us; competition must be masked, conflict suppressed. The struggle to live up to our own romantic images (our spouse as perfect; ourself as unselfish lover; our marriage as conflict-free) leads us to ignore the truth of our relationship. We try to force ourself and our partner to fit the increasingly illusory "ideals" of our romantic expectations.

We then face a time of considerable confusion and strain. Most of us come to marriage nurtured on fairy tales of "happily ever after." The songs and movies that celebrate the sexual bliss of romantic love have forcefully shaped our expectations. We may even have learned in our religious upbringing that good marriages successfully avoid all conflict. Under the tyranny of these ideals we turn away from our own experience and look outside ourselves for signs of what our relationship "should be." Panic arises as these romantic images betray us. To sustain these illusions involves considerable strain, but we have nowhere to turn for more realistic models of what marriage is or can be.

For our marriage to mature, our love must expand to include bonds between us that are stronger than romance. Our early enchantment hinted at this expanded love. The purification of romance allows these broader links of love to emerge and be strengthened. But as we are forced to face some of the illusions that are part of our relationship, purification often generates tension.

In some marriages, this is a time of conflict and disillusionment. Our sense is that we have been lied to; even worse, we have lied to ourself. We give a lot of time to assessing blame for the disappointments we experience when things have not turned out as we had hoped.

We may then devote much effort to getting our spouse to be different, to "live up to" the promises, hopes, illusions of romance. We may use overt and subtle power tactics (threats, accusations, silence) to buttress these demands. We may withhold affection, using sex as a power ploy between us. Or we may become bitter and spiteful, trying to get back at our partner for the disappointments and hurts (real and imagined) we are experiencing.

For both men and women, the reassessment of our marriage is a time of challenge, questioning, and change. But often, husband and wife are on a different timetable. One of us may move into disillusionment while the other is trying hard to hold on to the illusions. A friend of ours, whose divorce stunned all of us, gave this example: "The first year I said, 'There's something wrong,' and she said, 'No, there isn't.' The second year I said, 'There's something wrong,' and she said, 'I don't think so.' The third year she said, 'Something is wrong,' and I said, 'Yes, but it's too late.'"

For many marriages, though, reassessment brings not disillu-sionment (with the emotional trauma this term suggests) but de-illusionment. Romantic love, after all, is a kind of enchantment. Enthralled by one another, we delight in every detail and man-nerism. *This* person, we are convinced, can rescue us at last—from our parents, from a dull life, even from ourself.

Romance often involves falling in love with love. Part of what we see in the other person is our ideal of "man" or "woman," especially of the woman or man we want to marry. This vision, partly a statement of our values and partly an expression of our needs, energizes us toward the commitments of marriage. But if enchantment starts us out on the journey of love, the route to maturity often goes by way of disenchantment. As we live to-gether, our larger-than-life ideals come under closer scrutiny. We realize that our partner doesn't correspond perfectly to this ro-mantic vision. The prince (or princess) does not always turn into a frog, but experience begins to challenge idealized expectations.

De-illusionment brings the mellow realization that giving up some of these illusions of early romance is safe. We now recog-nize many of our initial assumptions about marriage as burdens we have shouldered unnecessarily. We are glad to let them go. Other assumptions we had—about who each of us is, about what we could expect from one another, about what our marriage would be like—seem silly now. We have simply outgrown them. Some of our romantic illusions, we know, were genuinely useful to us. They helped get us this far together, but we do not need them anymore. A stronger basis for our continuing love now exists—our growing ability to commit ourselves to one another as we actually are.

TRANSFERENCE AND PROJECTION

The assumptions we bring to marriage sometimes have compli-cated origins. Some of us choose a marriage partner as part of a larger effort to deal with troublesome issues we faced in our original families. We use our mate to act out an old and still unresolved conflict with a parent. The unspoken, often unconsious, hope is that "this time we will get it right." For example, we may still bear in our heart the wounds of being too controlled by our mother. Her embraces always meant restraint: she often held us back or held us down. This confusion of intimacy and control still rankles. In the close contact of marriage, we experience the echoes of this constraint. We feel the threat of suffocation whenever our spouse draws close, whether in affection or in anger.

This pain, inherited from our family of origin and still harbored in our heart, makes us push away from a spouse's efforts of intimacy and closeness. The trouble, of course, is that this problem is not really "out there" between ourself and our mate; the problem exists "inside," in the painful memories that still surround our earliest experiences of intimacy. Trying to rework the troublesome issue, we deal with our marriage partner "as if" our spouse were our parent. But, in fact, our partner is not our parent. Our spouse is a unique person, responding to us here and now. If we insist on continuing to use our spouse as a stand-in for our parent, then we must react to our mate selectively. We must focus on the qualities in our partner that remind us of our parent; we have to deny those characteristics that are genuinely different. Psychologists call this process *transference.*

Transference distorts relationships. The unfinished business of our emotional past intrudes into the present, screening out whatever does not fit the old pattern. In transference, as psychologist Michael Cowan explains, "then and there" overshadows "here and now." When we push away from intimacy with our spouse, we are really trying to push away our parent. Again in Cowan's words, an "absent other" intrudes into our relationship and threatens its survival. This distortion can occur not only in marriage, but in any significant relationship.

Another psychological process may be at work between us,

imperiling our efforts to move beyond the illusions of romance. This is the dynamic of *projection*. In projection, we see in another person a feeling that really exists in ourself. Projection is rooted in a serious discomfort with the inner world of our own emotions. We find unacceptable some part of ourself—our anger or our neediness or our desire for independence. To feel good about ourself, we must not have this feeling. When the feeling arises, we cannot acknowledge it as our own. So, we project the feeling onto someone else.

An example may help. A woman cannot admit a growing anger toward her husband, because "being angry" is unacceptable to her. To admit that she feels anger, especially toward a loved one, would diminish her sense of self-worth: she's not that kind of person! At a deeper level, her childhood experience may have taught her that to be angry with a loved one is dangerous. The loved one (in this early case, an all-powerful parent) can withdraw love and protection, leaving the angry person vulnerable and alone. This memory remains, though seldom at a conscious level. And this memory carries a message—anger is a threat to her well-being.

So, when her anger arises toward her husband, this woman feels the threat even more urgently than the anger. To contain the threat, she must repudiate the anger. She withdraws emotionally from her husband, hoping her angry feelings will go away. This strategy is likely to increase the tension and distance between them. But now she can identify the source of the strain outside herself: "My husband is so withdrawn and hostile these days, and it frightens me."

Projection defends this woman from unacceptable emotion by distorting her experience. The distortion happens in two steps. First, she "splits off" any conscious awareness of her anger, since she judges that this emotion is bad. Second, she projects her anger onto her spouse. Now she can identify the problem: it is his! Dealing with anger in him is less threatening than having to face it as part of her own experience.

The problem here, of course, is that it is *her* anger that is causing her trouble. Dealing with it vicariously, through her spouse, is unlikely to be of any help since the real conflict is *inside her* not *between them.* But by refusing to recognize her own difficulty in dealing with the anger she feels, she is likely to create a problem between the two of them, as well.

In intimate relationships such as marriage and close friendship, transference and projection seldom happen on one side only. For the distortions to continue, we must both buy into the arrangement. In *Intimate Partners,* Maggie Scarf offers moving examples of the "trade-off of projections" that develop as spouses use one another to rework inner conflicts held over from their original families. The spouses "collude" with one another to reproduce in their own marriage the problems each brings from the family of origin. What most often results from this unconscious collusion is a continuing pattern of conflict. The tension between them remains unresolved, since the husband, for example, will never become the father his wife wanted but didn't have, and she can never finally make up for the mother who did not love him enough. And since the spouse is *not* the real cause of the inner tension that either of them feels, the conflict is basically unresolvable. They hold each other captive in a vicious cycle of familiar but unsatisfying interactions. Marriage therapists call this pattern "the game without end." It is also a game without winners.

To end this destructive pattern we must change the rules of the game. This process starts with the realization that neither of us is an "innocent victim" here. Each of us must acknowledge our part in the collusion. We will have to deal with the hurts we carry from the past, recognizing they are *in us.* We must start to take responsibility for our own feelings and needs, rather than forcing them out of awareness or focusing them on the other person. As we come to recognize our captivity to the wounds of "then and there," we will be better able to appreciate the hope of "here and now." This relationship can be different because this relationship is different. We are not held hostage to our emotional histories. Change is possible; we can learn to hold one another in new, more life-giving ways.

Now our marriage becomes a place of healing. Love's power is released as we start to separate *this* relationship from the projections of the past. Marriage can be a relationship of injury and pain, as many of us know. But marriage can also be a place of great healing. Marriage is where most of us learn our most profound lessons of forgiving and being forgiven. We even learn how to forgive ourselves. Scarf summarizes this potent possibility:

> When it becomes possible for partners to take up the unfinished work of childhood and to reown parts of self that once had to be disavowed and discarded, then marriage becomes a therapeutic relationship in the best, most gratifying sense of that word.

Beyond the Struggle

The maturing of romance often includes a time of reassessment. In some marriages this takes the shape of "the calm after the storm." Tired of the constant tension and conflict between us, we strike a truce. We are not yet really at peace, but we have determined to stop fighting. Our insistent efforts to change each other have failed; we need time to catch our breath, to let some of the wounds heal. Through stalemate our relationship moves into a kind of stability. Weary of the struggle, we resolve, "I'm not going to continue to give more than I get in this relationship. I haven't been able to get you to change—to be different, to meet my needs, to come up to my expectations. But what I can do is set limits on what you ask of me. This is the bargain: I won't continue to make demands on you, but in return I will give only this . . . and no more." Marriage therapist Susan Campbell calls this "the contract of limited expectations."

But most of us find such a standoff unsatisfying. Surely marriage must mean more than this! Wary and exhausted, we back away from demands that our partner be different. This is less a time of passivity than of "active pacifism." We start to assume more responsibility for ourself and, especially, for the expectations we have been carrying of our spouse and of our marriage. As we explore what *in ourself* needs to be different, our gaze turns inward. For many women, especially, the reassessment of marriage is part of a midlife dynamic of individuation. We step back from the emotional commitments and close relationships that, as women, we have found so central to our awareness of who we are. We need time and emotional distance, so that we can savor the internal resources of integrity—our own needs and values and hopes.

This period of personal assessment marks a critical point in marriage. We must decide if our relationship is worth the work involved. We ask ourselves, "Am I willing to invest the necessary energy to come to a new relationship with my spouse, one less crippled by unreal expectations, one more shaped by who we really are? Am I willing to be open to the kind of personal examination and change that might be demanded?"

Many marriages move from a romantic experience of excitement and youthful generosity through this more cautious sense of commitment. Often this transition coincides with the exhausting years of childrearing. Burdened by career responsibilities and family demands, we learn about false expectations and genuine limits. Marriage research indicates that many couples emerge from the family years into a new experience of intimacy. Forgiveness seasons our affection. As spouses we are now more comfortable with the balance of strength and weakness we find in one another—and in ourselves.

This movement often includes an appreciation of the paradoxes of our relationship, the parts of one another that we both love and hate. We say, only half in jest, "You are so wonderfully dependable, and sometimes it drives me crazy!" Or "Your sense of humor delights me, but must you always turn everything into a joke?" And "I love being able to count on your love but sometimes I wish I didn't need you so much."

The paradox deepens as we recognize how interrelated these experiences are; we cannot have one side—the "good" side of the paradox—without embracing the other side. We begin to appreciate that this is the way reality comes: strength and weakness together, disappointment and delight as parts of a more complex affection that binds us to one another. Our marriage is rooted in this paradoxical strength, the love of these two flawed persons, lovely and limited as we are. This realization takes us beyond truce and stalemate into a covenant of grace.

The Authority of Our Marriage

Over many years we sort out the expectations that have haunted our marriage. As we reexamine the demands of our family and culture and religion, we begin to enter into the authority of our marriage. We are not jettisoning these cultural and religious values, but we are personalizing them.

In our early years of marriage, our parents were important authorities. Whether we chose to imitate or oppose our parents' relationship, their marriage still powerfully influenced the shape of our own. In those early years we were still susceptible to cultural imperatives: how a good wife "should" act; what a responsible husband is "supposed" to do; what a "happy family" looks like. Gradually we come to *our way* of being together. We decide to have this many children; we allot family tasks and household chores this way; we make these value choices about the use of our time and money. Slowly we craft the particular shape of our marriage. We become the authors of this commitment. We enter into the authority of our love. This can be a scary notion if we understand authority solely as an external force that belongs to leaders and to the law. But in truth, our conscientious decisions over several decades of our marriage make us authorities too. We do not simply repeat the ideal of marriage. We give our marriage its special shape. This is the authorship of our marriage.

As we mature into the special authority of our marriage, the "we" of our commitment comes into clearer focus. Gradually we accept the truths of our shared journey: we are in this together; our spouse is not the enemy; we both want this marriage to continue, to grow; both of us are responsible for the troubles we have experienced, both of us will have to be involved in the survival and success of this marriage.

This purification of romance is expected—even inevitable—in marriage. But the loss of love is not. The expectation that the quality of our commitment to one another will change does not mean that we must fall out of love. Instead romantic love expands to include the strengths of mutual devotion. This maturing love of choice is strong enough to sustain us in the moments of strain and confusion that are part of our ongoing life together.

The experience of mutual devotion is the fruit of a maturing covenant. But the word *devotion* can be vague. What does it mean? Devotion is that feeling that is aroused as we look across the table at a spouse with whom we have shared our life for a decade. We have stood by this person in illness and in anger, in childbirth and in the tedium of dressing toddlers. The feeling that stirs in us is different from youthful passion; it is a sense of *being with*. We belong with this person more profoundly than we had realized before.

In devotion, the "active" and "passive" sides of love seem to merge in an experience of both caring and being cared for. We are together deeply, and we each feel this is a strength. In our awe at this unexpected gift we confess, "You know me so well, and still you love me. You care for me in ways that go beyond what I could ask for. You call me out to what is best in myself. I

know you hold my life as important as your own. And all these
gifts I give to you as well."

Sexual Maturing in Marriage

The commitment of marriage, while it matures into a love that is
larger than romance, remains a love in which affection and sexuality are central. We approach sexual maturity in our marriage as
we develop our capacity to share physical affection and erotic
pleasure. Sexual maturity, too, is more a process than a state, for
learning to be good lovers takes time.

To give ourselves to this process of sexual maturing we must
each move beyond the experience of love play and intercourse as
chiefly competitive—an experience of proving ourself as a "real"
woman or man or of "winning out" over our partner. These
interpretations of sex keep the focus on ourself and make mutuality difficult. And without mutuality, sex is often a barrier to
intimacy.

In contrast to many marriages of a generation ago, couples
today generally approach marriage with greater awareness of
their own bodies and with more information about the details of
sexual performance. Although a boon to marriage, this intellectual sophistication is more the starting point of a satisfying sex
life than its guarantee. Married sex is a process through which
we both learn to contribute to what is, for us, a mutually satisfying sexual experience. We learn the physical and emotional nuances that make lovemaking special for us. We develop the patterns of expression that fit us—patterns of frequency, of time
and place, of initiation and response. We discover the ways in
which passion and affection, humor and intensity, play a part in
our own love life.

The exhilaration of sexual discovery is usually strong early in
marriage, at least if we are able to move beyond an initial embarrassment. For most of us, our spouse gives us the gift of knowing
that our sexuality is beautiful. Loving us in our body, our part-

ner invites us beyond the shame we still carry. Together we can explore our passion and expose our vulnerability and self-doubt. Having risked the self-revelation of sex—and survived—we can approach with greater confidence the other, even more threatening, process of self-disclosure upon which the quality of our life together will depend.

After this early period of exploration, our sexual life can begin to level off. We have found a pattern that works for us. But, especially in the press of the other responsibilities of our lives, this pattern may become routine.

Only gradually do we realize that, although our love is strong, our lovemaking somehow falls short. An aura of romance surrounded our early sexual sharing. Frequently this romantic aura made our experiences of sex more satisfying than our lovemaking skills would otherwise justify! Now sex has lost its savor. We know that the substance of our love is more important than our sexual style, but the questions of sexual style and satisfaction become important.

American culture's current interest in sexual techniques reinforces this concern over our sex life. We are more aware of the richness of human sexuality and of the diversity of sexual expression. This new awareness can work destructively, setting up yet another standard of success against which to evaluate our own intimacy. But our expanded awareness need not have this negative effect. Instead it can remind us that the patterns of mutually satisfying sexual experience differ from couple to couple and that only *we* can best discover which pattern is best for us. In sex, as in most other aspects of marriage, to be mature does not mean to fit some general criterion of performance but to have a developing (and perhaps changing) sense of what is appropriate *for us*, what works *for us*.

Sex research shows the contribution that diversity and surprise make to long-term sexual satisfaction. This realization can be liberating, inviting us to expand the ways in which we celebrate the sexuality of our marriage. A sense of exploration can help us move beyond a point of sexual boredom or routine and stimulate our own creativity in lovemaking. The expanding literature of sexual functioning can assist this process of sexual maturity in marriage, not by giving us a norm of what is "best" but by providing information that can enrich our own experimentation and choice.

Information about the normal problem areas in sexual function can also be of special help in marriage. Often, as many therapists know, sexual dysfunction is a "presenting problem" that points to deeper troubles around intimacy in a marriage. But real changes in sexual function, many of them the result of normal processes of aging, can disrupt a previously satisfying pattern of physical lovemaking. A husband who begins to find that maintaining an erection is difficult or a wife who starts to experience pain in intercourse may be confused, even frightened, by this disquieting development. Too embarrassed to bring up the symptom for discussion, a spouse may simply avoid lovemaking. This one-sided and often unexplained decision cannot fail to affect the intimacy of the marriage! A couple's commitment to marriage for a lifetime finds a strong ally in a physician or psychological counselor who can provide information and assistance at this time. Those of us concerned about marriage—our own or other people's—should stay current with this now readily available information about sexual functioning throughout the lifespan.

The Covenant of Marriage

The image of covenant illumines Christian convictions about matrimony. From the beginning Christians and Jews were quick to compare the marriage relationship with the covenant between God and humans. This covenant, a commitment of unconditional love, combined enormous affection with great responsibility. A covenant was a lifelong gift exchange between lovers.

Soon, however, Christians felt the cultural pressure to see marriage in a different light. This important social commitment, on which property transfer and future heirs depended, needed legal and clearly defined rules. Therefore, marriage was best pictured as a contract. Church law, following this cultural interest in contracts, began to neglect the imagery and vocabulary of covenant. Instead, the precise, unromantic vocabulary of a contract was generated: Christian marriage became a matter of rights and duties; such a commitment was legally binding if the two parties were baptized—whether they had any genuine faith, or not; this contract was consummated in the first act of intercourse—whatever the dispositions of the spouses.

Then, in the revolutionary changes initiated by the Second Vatican Council, the imagery of covenant returned. Catholics began, again, to picture their love commitments as the exchange of gifts, rather than legal rights and moral duties. In such a vision, a vital faith life becomes more important than a ritual baptism in childhood; a mature self-giving in love becomes more important than the physiological consummation of a contract. Christian marriages are covenants of human love and, as sacraments, they are signs of the enduring commitment that binds us to our Creator.

REFLECTIVE EXERCISE

Recall a marriage that you know well—your own or your parents' or that of close friends. Be patient as you let your memory move over the course of this relationship: the early attraction, the decision to wed, the movements of life and love since that time. Then consider the maturing of romance in this marriage.

Look first at the early face of romance. Romance, we have suggested in this chapter, involves three ingredients: strong attraction, a sense of compatibility, a shared hope for the future.

How were the elements of romance alive early in this marriage? Be as concrete as you can; give examples.

Can you identify the dynamics of purification in this love? Perhaps a season of struggle? A time for letting go of illusions, even for disillusionment? What demands were made on the couples' love during this time of purification? How was their relationships strengthened? Were there ways the relationship was wounded?

Is romance part of this relationship now? In what ways? Again, be as concrete as you can, giving examples of the seasoned face of romance as it enlivens this marriage today.

ADDITIONAL RESOURCES

Maggie Scarf offers an instructive, if sober, look at the complex dynamics of marriage in *Intimate Partners: Patterns in Love and Marriage* (Random House, 1987). In *The Couple's Journey* (Impact Publishers, 1980) and *Beyond the Power Struggle* (Impact Publishers, 1984), therapist Susan M. Campbell provides a range of practical exercises to help couples explore tensions that can block the development of their love. Robert Butler and Myrna Lewis give a useful summary of current information on sex in middle and late life in *Love and Sex After Forty* (Harper & Row, 1986).

Michael Cowan provides a penetrating analysis of transference in "Sons and Lovers in a Patriarchical Predicament," *Journal of Pastoral Counseling*, Vol. XXII, no. 1 (1987): 46–64. See also the valuable discussion of mutuality in Bernard Lee and Michael Cowan, *Dangerous Memories: House Churches and Our American Story* (Sheed & Ward, 1986). Thomas J. Tyrrell's reflections on the connections between infatuation and intimacy, in *Urgent Longings* (Affirmation Books, 1980), are helpful to an understanding of romantic love. In *The Future of Marriage* (Yale University Press, 1982), Jesse Bernard introduces her now-classic distinction between "his and hers" marriages and explores the causes and effects of this discrepancy. John Money examines research findings on issues of sex and gender difference in love relationships and beyond in *Love and Love Sickness* (Johns Hopkins Press, 1980).

Joan Meyer Anzia and Mary G. Durkin explore the role of sex in a developing marriage in *Marital Intimacy: A Catholic Perspective* (Loyola University Press, 1982). We reflect on the shape and spirituality of marriage today in *Marrying Well: Stages on the Journey of Christian Marriage* (Image Books/Doubleday, 1982).

13.
More Than Single

Christians model their lives on a person who was single. Jesus was not married; he took no public vow of celibacy. He was simply single. And he was more than single. Strong personal relationships and generous concern for other people distinguished his life. So fierce was his fidelity that he laid down his life for his friends.

These days being a single follower of Jesus has its hazards. A friend who teaches in a Catholic school shares this experience:

> I start out each day feeling pretty good about myself and my life. But sometimes by the time I get home at night, I'm really depressed. Throughout the day people are asking me questions that seem to suggest something is wrong! Have I met anyone yet? How come I'm not dating seriously? Why am I working at that dead-end job? Am I planning to join a religious congregation? If not, why am I "still single"?

The voice of single people—those who have not married, those who are widowed or divorced—is often muted in the community of faith. With so much parish activity focused on the family and the education of children, those who are not married can feel excluded. The concerns of single people are seldom directly addressed in the religious context; even more rarely is their religious experience consulted. When the Church does speak explicitly to lay people who are not married, the issue is often sexual and the tone moralistic—even punitive. Its message seems to suggest that, especially for women, "outside marriage there is no salvation."

Our goal in this chapter is to give voice to the experience of single Christians. Priority is given to statements by single people —friends, colleagues, participants we have met through our workshops. We do this, first, to recognize the limits of our own knowledge. Only recently, and with some prompting, have we begun to give serious consideration to many of the themes in this chapter. More importantly, we want to acknowledge our indebtedness. We are grateful to many people who have—with both candor and grace—helped us come to a deeper appreciation of the shape of their lives.

All around us today we hear about singles. More and more adults are living alone. Americans today tend to marry later than they did a generation ago (the Census Bureau reports that the percentage of Americans in their early thirties who have not married has more than doubled since 1970). An increasing number of people do not marry at all (current estimates are that the number of adults who remain unmarried throughout their lives will soon reach 10 percent of the U.S. population). Others become "single again" through divorce or the death of the spouse.

These changing statistics are seldom reported as neutral facts. Some see the increase in a positive light. Trendy magazines tout the advantages of the single lifestyle. Housing, vacations, social clubs are offered "for singles only." Economists point out that the spending habits of single working people contribute to robust retail sales. Others interpret the data more negatively, emphasizing that the largest groups of the "new poor" in our country are older people living alone and single women with small children in their care. And those with more affluent lifestyles, as well, sometimes find cause for concern in the increase in singles. A few years back panic ran through the heart of many young career women (and their parents!) as figures appeared suggesting that—statistically speaking—a woman still single in her late thirties was more likely to be involved in a terrorist incident than to marry. (Surely only the cynical asked what the difference would be!?)

For all its prevalence, the notion of *single* is in trouble. The term groups together people who in fact are very different. A recently divorced woman living with her preschool children, a seventy-five-year-old widower in an affluent seniors' condominium, a twenty-three-year-old graduate student still living with his parents, a woman in her fifties with a successful career who has been on her own for some thirty years: the lifestyles of these people have little in common. And none matches the media version of the swinging single. The diversity is so great among those who are lumped together under the category *single* that dropping the term is probably a better—and certainly a more accurate—approach to this discussion. But the term is unlikely to be replaced soon. We will try, however, to be sensitive to the limitations of the word as we use it ourselves.

Into the Box

Being single is . . . a technicality. Yes, I am the one responsible for getting things done. Nobody else will pay the bills, do the groceries, fold the laundry, change the oil, buy new tires. But those are *external* ways in which I'm single. In terms of who I *am*, being single has very little to do with it. *Single* is not part of my identity; I don't wake up and say to myself, "I am single." But I do wake up and say, "I am Christian." (Actually, my exact words are "good morning, God," but you get the point!) I don't walk to work knowing that I am single. But I do walk to work knowing that I am a woman. Christian? *Yes!* Woman? *Yes!* Single? Oh, now that you mention it, yes.

This comment by a friend of ours in her thirties is echoed frequently by others with whom we have talked. One of the problems with the term *single* is that it is a social classification more than a self-description. "Being single" is a mental category; something we construct in our minds. Because categories help us make sense of the complexity of the world, they are useful. But categories also distort. When we classify, we simplify; we group together things that are in many ways different. This makes categories dangerous, especially when we use them to describe people.

Categories are dangerous because they are always partial. When we put a person in a particular category, we ignore all the other factors that make up the person. Using a category may blind us to what is most important about the person. This is perhaps easiest to see with categories that carry a strongly negative connotation, such as "cancer patient" or "unemployed" or "alcoholic." But other classifications can also blind us. Identifying people as "Southerners" or "suburbanites" or "senior citizens" may be accurate and still not say anything very significant. In addition, the process of classification is often external to the person being categorized. People usually do not assign themselves to a category; others do this *to* them. A colleague's explanation may make this distinction clear:

I'm always surprised when I realize people think of me as single. It's true that I am not married and that I live alone. But I rarely think about that in any explicit way. "Being single" is as little a part of my sense of myself as "having blue eyes"; as a statement of fact, it's accurate enough, but it has little to do with who I am.

Thus, being single is more an external classification than an aspect of personal identity. Many people who fit the definition do not describe themselves that way. When people do use it to describe themselves, the sense is often negative. Consider the anomaly of the singles club: Most people join a singles club in the hope it will help them become "unsingle"!

The category of *single* stumbles at the start, since it defines people by what they *are not*: singles are unmarried. In *Loving Relationships*, Robert Shelton reminds us that this way of thinking has things the wrong way around:

> After all, we are all born single; even if we marry, we spend from sixteen to thirty or more years single before we enter into marriage, and may well spend many more years in one or more states of being single after that. We could, in fact, think of marriage as being "un-single," rather than submitting without thinking to the common practice of labelling those who are single as "unmarried."

While the phrase *being single* does not carry much content, it does carry negative connotations. The meaning of *single* expands to include some of society's subtle prejudices: those on their own are uncommitted, irresponsible, ungenerous. An attorney in her fifties relates her frustration: "It's getting harder for me to respond civilly to people who say they envy my 'uncommitted' life. I am committed—to the gospel, to my vocation, to my work!"

However, despite its distortions, the category of *single* is not likely to disappear. As more and more Americans live in one-person households, the term has become important in demographic analysis. The category is also important in economic analysis, as manufacturers and advertisers identify the goods and services needed by people living alone. But *single* is not just a description; it has become a cultural image. The term *being single* is loaded with certain expectations, a set of social "shoulds." These social imperatives tell a single person how to act (the sexy single with a self-indulgent lifestyle) and what to want (the single person as conspicuous consumer; the ultimate yuppie with no dependents—financial or emotional).

For a more accurate sense of what being single means, we will draw on the experiences that have been shared with us. We look first at several concerns that single people often raise. Then we turn to a broader discussion of vocation and lifestyle.

Issues in Living Alone

Single people voice particular concerns. Our friends and colleagues have emphasized several interrelated themes: self-reliance, loneliness, work, sexuality. Self-reliance can be a special gift of being single. A divorced man finds, to his amazement, that he can survive as a single parent. In the midst of the demands made on him, he discovers unexpected strengths of patience and nurturance. A woman who has grown up with a sense that "girls need to be protected" comes to recognize that her own resources are considerable; she can manage very well on her own. But such self-reliance is not always an uncomplicated achievement, as a friend in her late thirties notes:

> As a single person I constantly live with the tension between self-reliance and dependency. One of the real joys of my life has been learning that I can survive and flourish "on my own." But at the same time, I have a deep need to be connected to others, to be loved and cared for as well as to give of myself. Too much self-reliance leads me into isolation and a "lone ranger" mentality. Too much dependence leads me to feel lonely and unfulfilled. It's a tension I hold delicately these days.

Like married folk, singles struggle to balance independence and a sense of belonging. Those who live alone usually have less of the built-in companionship that many married people take for

granted. As a result, single people often give more explicit attention to their relationships. For some this feels like a burden:

> In the past few years I've become aware of how much work is
> involved in staying in touch with my friends. I think most single
> people would agree. Real friendship takes a lot of time and energy.
> Even a casual evening with people I like seems to involve a lot of
> planning. Sometimes I resent the fact that I have to take so much
> initiative.

Most single people we know are quick to mention that having
strong ties with their families and friends is very important to
them. Many acknowledge that initiating and maintaining close
relationships takes real effort. But more often they focus on the
rich benefits that these friendships bring to people living alone.
The rewards make the effort worthwhile. And important relationships are not always studied and planned. A colleague in his
thirties appreciates the spontaneity he feels with friends:

> I'm single, but I'm not a loner. It means a lot to me when my
> married friends let me know that I'm welcome at their homes; for
> example, I can feel free to stop by for supper unannounced.

The care devoted to eating is an important element of an adult
lifestyle and can be an intriguing indicator of one's sense of self-
worth. Observers of the single lifestyle would have us look to the
kitchen. Is the refrigerator stocked with a range of healthy food?
Does the person take care and time to prepare a meal for "just
me"? An empty refrigerator and a habit of never preparing a
meal for oneself suggest an unhappiness with one's own life. Our
colleague explains this phenomenon:

> I've come to see that when I start eating poorly or always eating
> out I'm really protesting my singleness. When I'm comfortable

with myself I nourish myself, with good food and other ways too. I rely on friends and, sometimes, on fast food. But I can also care for myself; this is part of my self-reliance and self-acceptance as a single person.

LONELINESS

"I like my life, but loneliness is a real problem for me." In saying this, a friend in his early thirties voices a concern shared by many people who live alone. Without a spouse and most often without children, single people face the fact of their solitariness more frequently. A colleague, successful at midlife in his career as a therapist, observes, "However exciting my workday is, I still come home alone." A writer finds that, despite many friends, her work finds her often alone and sometimes lonely. But most people who live alone recognize that loneliness is not a concern only for them. A woman in her twenties remarks:

Loneliness is an issue for me, but I'm not sure that makes me different from other women my age. Married women can be lonely; vowed religious can be lonely. From the divorced people I've met at work I've learned that marriage is no lifetime guarantee against being lonely.

A divorced mother of four teenagers agrees: "I was much lonelier during the twenty years of my marriage than I am now!"

Loneliness is as much about how we are with ourselves as about how we are with others. People who live alone often develop personal strategies to help them deal more effectively with this everyday demon. A friend in her thirties confides:

There are things I've learned to do when I feel lonely. I refuse to turn on the television just to have the sound of voices in the apartment. Feeling sorry for myself just makes things worse. Instead I do something to treat myself as I would a good friend: buy flowers, spend time to prepare a nice meal, settle in to read a book I've been looking forward to. Most of all I remind myself that this sorry mood will pass!

Beyond that, many people who live alone have come to recognize loneliness as more than a "problem." It can be seen as a positive signal, alerting us to examine ourselves and our relationships. A friend in his early forties acknowledges:

> I've come to realize that for me loneliness is an opportunity to learn about my intimacy needs, to help me clarify and get more realistic about my expectations of marriage.

We will look again at the experience of loneliness in Chapter 15.

WORK

Work is of concern to most adults—married or single, women or men. The kind of work we do determines a lot about our adult identity, from the practical issues of income to the subtler questions of social worth and self-esteem. Evidence suggests that these work-related questions are of special relevance to single women.

In *Life Prints*, social scientists Grace Baruch and Rosalind Barnett and journalist Caryl Rivers report the findings of a wide-ranging study of women approaching midlife. Included in the study was a large group of women, ranging in age from thirty-five to fifty-five, who had never married. The authors' discussion of their attitudes toward work makes great reading, confounding much of what is accepted as conventional wisdom about the fate of unmarried women. Based on an analysis of factors that contributed positively to the lives of these women, the researchers conclude that the sources of well-being in the single life are not mysterious and unreachable but are in large part within the control of the woman herself. Since a life of "drift" can cost her dearly, the unmarried woman should take care to get involved in a job that she finds challenging, where she can advance, and where she can earn a good salary.

Employment in the workplace is one of the characteristic ways in which an adult identity is established. However, this means of testing and developing an adult identity is often lacking for young women. In past decades many women married just after completing their high school or college education. Thus they had no young adult involvement in the world of work or career. Many of those women who did work in their late teens or twenties saw this as a period of "waiting to be married" more than as a period of personal investment in a project that had a meaning of its own. Thus work did not establish identity; rather it was a stopgap, something to do until the "right" man came along.

Today both pragmatic and psychological reasons urge women to delay marriage until they have tested themselves in the world of work. A look at the contemporary scene yields the pragmatic reasons for this. Today the majority of adult women in the United States is employed. In over half of American families both wife and husband work outside the home. In most of these families, especially in the face of economic uncertainty, two paychecks are needed to maintain the standard of living. Every year thousands of women who are divorced or widowed find themselves suddenly responsible for their own economic well-being and, often, for that of their children as well. Women head 90 percent of the nearly 5 million single-parent families in our country. Pragmatically then, a woman today needs to obtain not only the education but the subsequent work experience that will enable her to support herself and, quite possibly, others as well.

But an even deeper reason moves many women to seek employment. A job is a vehicle of self-expression and self-transcendence. In the course of our work we find out and affirm who we are. We also learn how to engage ourself in social issues, to involve ourself in questions of public concern. An experience of financial independence and work autonomy can be crucial to the psychological development of women, many of whom are still socialized to evaluate themselves primarily in terms of their relationships—who they are with and who wants to be with them. Work involvement through the twenties helps young adults develop greater self-awareness and confidence. These psychological assets are valuable, whether one's future includes marriage or not. Perhaps especially for women, this critical experience of self-exploration and growing self-confidence must be safeguarded and promoted.

SEXUALITY

Another genuine concern for singles is sexuality. Several questions arise: Can a Christian be single and sexual, or is singleness equivalent to celibacy? (In French, one word for single is *célibataire.*) Is sexuality's sole meaning to be found in reproduction? If not, how does a single Christian share this pleasure in a responsible and fruitful way? But Christian circles seldom encourage these questions.

In a world that defines responsible adulthood preeminently in terms of marriage and family, a single person never quite belongs. Such an individual is likely to be seen as waiting to marry or as failing to marry. In either case, the single woman is a special worry. An unattached woman floats between the socially acceptable roles of daughter and wife. She is not accounted for. As one social commentator has observed, the single woman is "socially indigestible."

Traditionally women have been encouraged to understand themselves in terms of relationships: I am daughter, wife, mother. Thus the interpersonal relationship of marriage came to figure very prominently in the identity of women. Marriage and especially motherhood were what women *were for.* To have children, to nurture life, to care for others—these were the concerns of a woman. Her highest privileges and weightiest responsibilities were rooted here. Not to be married, not to have children, was to be "unfulfilled as a woman." In the double standard of society and Christianity, a man could be excused from marriage and parenting because of some important social calling (as doctor, scientist, or priest). But for a woman not to be a mother was not to be fully woman.

If this negative evaluation of single women seems dated, consider the subtle ways it still survives. The social status of a single man is often positive; as an available escort, he is even in demand. The social status of a single woman is interpreted in different ways, often as a threat or an embarrassment. A friend notes:

> It amazes me that there is still such concern to "balance" me at a party. It's not true among my close friends, but in many social situations I am aware that a single man has to be added to the party or I can't be included. It seems there can be an "extra" man or two without any problem, but an "extra" woman breaks the etiquette.

In other settings, the unmarried woman is "sexually available." A woman in her late thirties shares her experience:

> This past year I've dated four men, two are Catholic. One goes to church every Sunday, the other almost every Sunday. Both wanted me to have sex with them on our first date. These guys wouldn't be willing to change a tire for me, but they expect me to be willing to sleep with them.

The traditional cultural and religious remedy for a woman's singleness is to get her married. But what if she chooses to remain

single? With little support from culture or religion, single women
—and men—are often left alone as they struggle to find trustworthy guidelines to shape a mature sexual lifestyle.

THE GAY AND LESBIAN EXPERIENCE

Another challenge faces the lesbian and gay Christian. This is
the experience of *enforced singleness*. A friend in his late twenties
reports:

> I speak from the experience of the gay and lesbian community. We
> are the only group who are compelled to stay single. The legal
> system insists that we can't marry. The church insists that we
> remain celibate. There is no "option to marry" for us; so there is
> no real "choice" to remain single.

Society and Christianity define homosexual adults as necessarily
single. Because their sexual orientation is seen as a threat, they
are encouraged to remain separate, isolated, uncommunicative.
Their sexual inclinations, if not sinful, should at least be kept
secret. However, a strong indication of adult maturity is a growing comfort with one's identity and lifestyle. If, as is often the
case for the lesbian or gay person, singleness is made to feel like a
quarantine, psychological and religious maturing will be im-
paired. By enforcing singleness, society and the Church suggest
that commitment and fidelity are unachievable for gay or lesbian
adults. To contest this punitive singleness, some lesbians and
gays are tempted to act out an erratic or compulsive sexual style.
But this just defeats hopes for genuine intimacy. Society's prejudice becomes a self-fulfilling prophecy: the homosexual person is
left not only single but alone.

When homosexual Christians do attempt to forge a lasting
union, both Church and society refuse acknowledgment. A gay
couple who have lived in a committed, faithful union for seven
years must present themselves in the larger community as two

single men who just happen to share a house. Two women whose life together is a major source of their creativity find that being known as a lesbian couple in the parish they attend is too risky.

Pressures from within and from without may push a homosexual Christian toward a heterosexual marriage. Against such pressures, the lesbian or gay Christian tries to discern a sense of vocation and identity and asks, "What kind of intimacy and lifestyle fit who I am and how God has gifted me?" For the lesbian and gay—as for the heterosexual—Christian, the challenge of intimacy begins in the invitation to come to know and then to love and trust who we are. Our ability to be faithful to who we are—and this includes our sexual identity—grounds our ability to be faithful to other people and to values.

Vocation: The Choice to Be Single

Getting married is no longer an automatic sign in American life that a person is fully adult. Remaining single or at least delaying marriage until the late twenties or thirties has become a more acceptable option. As young adults more deliberately choose when and whom to marry, they also find greater freedom to choose a single life. A colleague in her mid-thirties reports:

> I've not determined that I will not get married, but I can't operate with the sense that I'm "waiting." I can't put off other decisions about myself and my life because I'm waiting to get married.

As young adults shape their lives through commitment to work and friendship, some find that marriage will probably not be part of their future. Does a person *choose* to remain single or is this something that just happens? The answer to this question is different for each person but the comment of a colleague in his mid-forties seems representative of many:

I did not really start out with a choice to be single or not to marry.
I made decisions about my life and my work as choices came up,
and these have given shape and direction to my life. One of the
results of these decisions is that I am not married.

For many people, then, being single is not a direct or explicit
choice. Nor does one's life as single happen only by default—
because "Prince Charming" or "the girl of my dreams" did not
show up. In reality, a subtler evolution guides the maturing of
many single adults.

Single adults often express a special affirmation of this lifestyle
in their forties. They come to the point where they can say,
"This is who I am. I recognize and accept that I am unlikely to
marry. This feels good and right for me." With such an affirmation, single adults can let go of the family and cultural pressures
that may still haunt them. They can turn away from a lingering
sense of self as "still not married."

In both theology and spirituality, the Catholic understanding
of vocation has been undergoing a dramatic transformation. In
the piety of two generations ago, "to have a vocation" meant to
be a vowed religious or a priest. The rest of us, married or single,
had to muddle along without any special religious identity or
sense of calling. Today a more adequate theology of Baptism
insists that every adult Christian has a vocation—a personal invitation to live one's life transformed by grace. Grounded in the
gifts and inclinations we discover in ourself, our vocation calls us
to give ourself in a particular way.

A vocation, then, is both an invitation from God and a response to this call. Our vocation, which welcomes us into our
identity as a Christian, is an invitation to live a life shaped by
two powerful influences: the values of Christian faith and the
qualities—strengths and limits—we find in ourself. Our religious
identity becomes real in particular choices. We must discern how
we will love our neighbor, care for the world, witness to justice

and mercy. Through these acts of our vocation, we are revealed to ourself.

Gradually, Christians are coming to a more fruitful distinction of *vocation* and *lifestyle*. A vocation refers to that profound and continuing call that each of us, with effort, can discern. God invites us to give our life's energy to *this* way of loving and working and contributing to the world. A vocation, like a dream or life ambition, is our deepest and best hope for our life. Our dream may be very clear (we want to become a public official devoted to social reform, or a scientist working for peace) or remain somewhat vague (we would like to help make the world a better place). But it moves us to become our best self. As Christians we recognize that this dream, our vocation, comes as gift; it is part of God's hope for our life. This holy ambition runs deeper than any particular job; it survives the detours and failures that are part of any journey of faith.

On the other hand, our lifestyle points to the patterns we develop as we attempt to live out our vocation. Our lifestyle includes the value commitments that guide our decisions, the choices we make about friends and work and leisure, the way we organize our time. Whatever our vocation, we must each determine the lifestyle that best supports this calling. For many single Christians, expanding the idea of vocation and distinguishing it from lifestyle is helpful. This insight encourages singles to explore and trust their emerging vocation, whatever it is. They are also invited to examine how being single will be part of their unique vocation. Their vocation is not "to be single." Their vocation—like that of celibate or married Christians—is the larger plot and purpose of their life, through which God gradually reveals them to themselves. Being single—whether for a time or for one's life, by choice or by circumstances—is part of that larger movement of grace, but seldom the defining characteristic of one's identity or vocation.

VOCATION AND FIDELITY

Beneath our social roles and beyond all social expectations, we must affirm and follow a unique and God-inspired vocation. Revealed to us through our relationships and our action in the world, this vocation is personal but not private. A vocation is a call from God, but not a single call given only once at the beginning of adult life. We hear our call repeatedly in the various challenges and crises of our life. Such a vocation becomes a lifelong conversation with God. Most of us recognize that at the age of twenty-one we could not have understood all that our lives would bring. We are grateful that God takes a lifetime to show us who we may become.

Fidelity to a vocation is not an act of clinging to what God once said. Instead, fidelity means staying in the conversation, remaining alert to new suggestions and demands. Fidelity to others and, ultimately, to ourself is rooted in faithfulness to this lifelong conversation. Fidelity is—like identity—a question of congruence, of fit between who we are and how we live. Fidelity is also related to confidence—having faith in ourself. Coming gradually to a clearer sense of self and vocation—what we can and should do with our life—we learn to trust ourself. Trusting ourself and believing in the direction of our life, we gain confidence to meet the surprises and changes that life may have in store.

Self-confidence, as an important part of the strength of fidelity, is also related to conscience. Conscience—the ability to discern and decide what is right for us to do—is grounded in a sense of who we are and what we are for. A well-developed conscience allows us to trust ourself and our decisions; we know our actions and commitments are right because they fit, they are faithful to who we are as *this Christian adult*.

Conscience allows us to make choices about our lifestyle, not out of a compulsive *should*, nor mainly to please others, but because this action is faithful to who we are as *this* Christian, with this set of commitments and gifts. Both religious wisdom and psychological conviction demand this movement beyond conformity to external norms and rules as a sign of personal maturity. In fact, Erik Erikson defines conscience as that independence that makes a person dependable. We have so thoroughly incorporated the best values of our faith and culture that we can make independent choices. Because we embody these values, others can rely on us. As Christians we believe that God invites each of us into our particular vocation. And these invitations lead not to individualistic self-expression, but to a common pursuit of gospel ideals.

In a culture like ours—which insists on marriage as *the* adult lifestyle—some Christians find that fidelity to their own vocation, to who they are being revealed to be, does not include marriage. Thus, a young man or woman in the late thirties begins to suspect that marriage will not be a part of his or her life. This can be disappointing or confusing. A woman may ask, "Should I marry, even if this means going against my judgment?" A man may scrutinize his motives minutely and wonder, "Am I just being selfish? Am I afraid to make a commitment?" The challenge here is to discern and then to trust this developing shape of our vocation. We need to discover and accept who we are becoming and the direction that seems most genuine for our life. Fidelity challenges us to be faithful to the unfolding story of our own life with God.

As Christians, our fidelity is not a static but a moving reality. A vocation is a lifelong conversation rather than a single cosmic command. During the course of our life we may expect to hear new invitations and face unexpected demands. This means that fidelity is not a virtue that allows us simply to hold on doggedly to a remembered commitment. Instead, fidelity is a virtue that provides resilience and courage in responding to where life leads us. Unforeseen changes in ourselves and others—whether new discoveries or failures—impel us to revise, deepen, or alter our commitments. Then we are drawn into the mystery of a life still being revealed to us, a life we do not fully control. A friend in his forties sums up his sense of discovery by saying:

> There is a mystery in my life. For a long time I've wanted to be married and I still have a sense that I'll marry some day. But I realize now there is a mystery in life. It may be that I won't marry. I don't know what the unfolding may be. I think I will welcome however my life goes. But the problem comes in the anxiety I pick up in our society. I feel good about myself, but I feel strangely "incomplete" in terms of the subtle norms I know are operative— at work, among my family members, even among some of my friends.

Single Christians face a special challenge in separating the cultural messages about the superiority of marriage from the deeper intimations, given in grace, that guide their own movement of integrity. When they can do this, their vocation and lifestyle come together in a life that is both satisfying and fruitful. Beyond this, their lives become a gift to the Church, teaching the rest of us about the diversity of God's design for generous love.

REFLECTIVE EXERCISE

List the single people who are part of your own life these days— family members, friends, and co-workers, perhaps yourself as well. Drawing on your experience of these lives, consider the following questions:

As you see it, what are some of the benefits of being single? What do you find attractive or satisfying or admirable?

From your perspective, what are some of the burdens of being single? What strikes you as troublesome or difficult or undesirable?

Where do the single people you know best find support for their lifestyle and vocation?

Is the Church part of the lives of single people you know? If so, what shape does this participation take?

ADDITIONAL RESOURCES

Throughout his helpful discussion in *Loving Relationships* (Brethren Press, 1987), Robert Shelton takes up explicitly the experience of those who are not married. Dorothy Payne focuses on women's lives and spirituality in *Singleness* (Westminster Press, 1983). In *Creative Singlehood and Pastoral Care* (Fortress Press, 1982), John Landgraf sensitively considers the variety of single lifestyles and recommends creative pastoral responses.

Grace Baruch, Rosalind Barnett, and Caryl Rivers report the findings of their research into the lives of women approaching midlife in *Life Prints* (New American Library, 1983). Cargan Leonard and Matthew Melko examine the situation of singles today in *Singles: Myths and Realities* (Sage Publications, 1982).

Karen Lebacqz suggests a fresh starting point for the discussion of sexual morality in "Appropriate Vulnerability: A Sexual Ethic for Singles," *The Christian Century*, May 6, 1987, pp. 435–38. In *Living Alone* (Crossroad Books, 1983), Martin Israel looks at some of the possibilities and concerns of the single lifestyle. Paula Ripple explores the experience of those who are separated and divorced in *The Pain and the Possibility* (Ave Maria Press, 1982). In Part One of our *Seasons of Strength* (Image Books/Doubleday, 1986), we examine the challenges and crises through which a Christian vocation unfolds.

14.

The Gift of Celibacy

Christian faith proclaims its deepest truth in paradoxes. Like the grain of wheat, we must die in order to find life. We meet Christ in the unlikely guise of the sick and the imprisoned and the stranger. Celibacy is another of our faith's paradoxes. As Christians we know that we can love one another well apart from sexual sharing; we recognize that, even without offspring, we can live fruitful and generous lives. But in a culture obsessed with sexuality, this paradox provokes surprise and disbelief.

Celibacy is a durable mystery. From early on, some who follow Jesus have chosen a path that excludes marriage and family. Over centuries of Christian history and across a wide range of cultural contexts, many people have experienced committed celibacy as a grace. This lifestyle has nurtured Christians in their personal journeys of faith. In addition, celibacy has borne fruit in generous service to the world as celibate women and men served in the formal ministry of the Church.

A consideration of the lifestyle of vowed celibacy is essential in any discussion of Catholics and sexuality. As we turn to that consideration, let us offer an initial clarification. Although we—the authors—are married, the reality of committed celibacy is significant to us, personally and professionally. Our ministry puts us in touch with the convictions and concerns of many religious and priests; our friends who are vowed celibates share with us the wisdom of their own experience. So it is as interested and sympathetic companions that we observe the ongoing conversation about the meaning of celibacy for the Church today.

In reevaluating the meaning of sexuality, the Christian community comes to reexamine the lifestyle of celibacy. In the process, some earlier understandings of celibacy have come under question. These images and expectations no longer provide celibate Christians with a compelling explanation for their own lives. And they no longer provide the basis of a genuine appreciation of celibacy in the larger community of faith. Catholics today struggle to come to a renewed vision of celibacy as an authentic Christian way of life.

The vitality of the gift of celibacy has been repeatedly proven in its ability to take on new meaning, to be persuasive, in many different historical and cultural settings. The challenge now is not to do away with celibacy but to find what meaning this gift holds for the future. Like other parts of Christian faith, celibacy will survive by being purified. Our goal in this chapter is to examine where we are, as a community of faith, in the conversation about the purpose and practice of celibacy today.

The Why of Celibacy

The why of celibacy raises questions of meaning and motive. What is the religious significance of the lifestyle of celibacy? Why do some Christians commit themselves to this way of following Jesus Christ? In the Church of the 1940s and 1950s, the religious meaning of celibacy was clear. The Church recommended this special way of life to those who would follow the path of perfection. Celibacy, or consecrated chastity, was understood to be one of the evangelical *counsels*. It was evangelical because it was rooted in the gospel. It was a counsel or advice that Jesus issued to his followers. To the rich young man who inquired about holiness, Jesus replied, "If you would be perfect . . . leave all and follow me." In Catholic spirituality, the vowed life of poverty, chastity, and obedience came to be seen as the principal way in which this gospel call to perfection could be followed. Most Christians would seek God by the ordinary way of life and work in the world; consecrated celibacy was an option for those who would seek the "better way."

But why was the choice of celibacy a "better way"? In the piety that had come to prevail in Catholic life, virginity was seen as preferable to marriage. Both Mary and Jesus were virgins. Moreover, the choice of celibacy helped one avoid the snares of sexual engagement and the entanglements of human love. Many Christians had been taught that sex was inevitably involved in sin and that human love was a distraction from a wholehearted devotion to God. True, these suspicions were seldom stated so baldly. And our best theology constantly battled against these aberrations. But many of us who grew up Catholic before Vatican II were influenced by these powerful, even if unorthodox, sentiments.

The problem with linking the religious significance of celibacy to these convictions is, of course, that they are heretical. That is not what Christians believe. Some religious traditions *have* judged sex to be evil—Manicheanism tempted the early Christians in this way. Christians, however, have consistently, even if not always successfully, insisted that sex—like all that God has created—is good. Christians also dispute that the love of God is in competition with human love. In truth, some early proponents of an enforced celibacy for the clergy argued that the demands of marriage and family would distract the minister from his constant occupation with God. These advocates of celibacy were profoundly suspicious of the compatibility of the sacred and the sexual. But the best and most enduring conviction of Christians is that the love of God and the love of neighbor are essentially linked. In the love that others show us, we come to know the love of God. And only by loving other people is our love of God purified and matured.

The renewal of Catholic life generated by Vatican II brought with it a rethinking of the meaning of celibacy. The Council's reaffirmation of the spirituality of marriage challenged earlier understandings of celibacy as the "better way" or "higher calling." Church historians showed that the lifestyle of vowed celibacy has emerged gradually, its meaning and purpose understood differently at different times in Christian life. Earlier explanations of celibacy no longer seemed adequate. Even when they were not in error, they could no longer persuade.

Over the past twenty years the vocabulary of the evangelical counsels has undergone profound purification. Vowed religious do not live in poverty as much as they do in simplicity. Their shared responsibility in community life is better understood as mutual accountability than as obedience to a quasi-parental authority. And the chastity to which they aspire is not meant to deliver them from the dangerous demands of friendship, affection, and charity that other Christians face.

The spirituality of a "higher calling" drove a wedge in the community of faith, creating different classes of Christians. Recently this understanding has fallen into disuse. More and more celibates find that such a spirituality neither reflects their religious experience nor energizes their continuing commitment. An interpretation of celibacy as the "higher way" does not serve the rest of us either, since it no longer reveals to the larger community of faith the religious significance that celibacy can hold.

This leaves the Catholic community at a loss. Our understanding of celibacy is moving away from the image of the evangelical counsel, but as yet no well developed or widely accepted interpretation of celibacy replaces this image. Such a new consensus is sure to emerge, but only as we listen to the living tradition of consecrated celibacy as it takes shape in our own time. In the meantime, we are all at a disadvantage. Here, as in so many other areas of sexuality, we sense that we know more than we are able to say. Our religious vocabulary has not kept pace with our religious experience. Fortunately, the images used today in the discussion of celibacy hint at an emerging theology.

We will examine three of these images that are used most often in theology and by celibate Catholics. In each image, we will point out the positive understanding of celibacy as well as some of its limitations. The images we will consider are celibacy as a charism, as a choice, and as a call.

Celibacy as a Charism

The image of celibacy as a charism is often part of current discussion. Sometimes the term is simply a rhetorical flourish but often it holds more substance in its use. The intent here, as in the understanding of celibacy as an evangelical counsel, is to root the lifestyle of consecrated celibacy in the gospel. This is a fruitful direction for the discussion, since every Christian lifestyle finds its source and significance in the witness of Jesus Christ. The understanding of celibacy as a charism will surely be strengthened if it can be shown to bear the marks of the other gospel charisms.

Recent biblical scholarship clarifies the meaning of charism. Saint Paul reported the charisms that enlivened the church in Corinth: preaching, healing, prophecy, administration. These vital activities in the early Christian communities had three essential characteristics. These were, first, *personal abilities.* Charisms are specific strengths, identifiable talents, activities that a particular member of the community does well.

Second, these abilities are experienced as *gifts.* A follower of Jesus who finds herself capable in these ways is drawn to acknowledge that more than just herself is involved. She readily admits, "This is something I do well, but I am not the sole or even the principal author of this talent. I experience myself as gifted and I am grateful." These gifts, Paul reminds us, come from the Spirit (I Corinthians 12:11). They are not the result of administrative decision or official largesse. Instead they are discovered throughout the community, owing to the generosity of God's Spirit.

Third, genuine charisms have a *distinctive purpose.* These talents are not for private satisfaction or personal aggrandizement but for the building up of the body of Christ. A charism is a gift that is meant to be given away. Acknowledged in gratitude, it is exercised in generosity. Charisms reside *in* particular persons but they exist *for* the community of faith.

If the image of charism is to serve as the basis for a more adequate appreciation of the religious significance of celibacy, then celibacy must be shown to meet these scriptural criteria. While celibacy is not listed among the charisms that Paul cites explicitly, that in itself is not the critical issue. Catholics are not biblical fundamentalists; our appreciation of God's action in human history is not limited to proof texts. But if the powerful scriptural category of charism is to be used to explore the meaning of celibacy in our own time, the lifestyle of consecrated celibacy will have to display the three characteristics of a charism. We will have to show how this way of living is rooted in personal ability, how it is experienced as a gift, and how it serves the larger needs and hopes of the community of faith. Many of us are confident that celibacy—at least in a purified form—can show these characteristics. But the Christian community needs to expand this discussion and make it available in a persuasive way.

Celibacy as a Choice

Another image figures significantly in current theology and spirituality: celibacy as a choice. Here the discussion is especially sensitive to the negative attitudes toward sex that so easily creep into a piety of celibacy. Historically this piety had often urged

Catholics to choose celibacy for negative reasons: to avoid the temptations of sex and the demands of a family. But as Catholic theologians insist today, only if sex is evil, only if marriage is a "lesser way," is it praiseworthy to choose celibacy for these negative motives. The choice of celibacy must be a decision not *against*, but *for* something. The person must choose not just to avoid, but to engage. As with every Christian choice, the motivating force of this decision must be love for something. Christians make the decision to be celibate for the sake of the kingdom of God.

In some discussions celibacy is chosen for the sake of the eschatological kingdom, the reign of God at the end of history. Celibates live among us as witnesses to the end time "where there will be neither marriage nor giving in marriage." This perspective, which acknowledges the goodness of sex and significance of married love, reminds us that these are only limited and partial realities. At its best, human love reveals God's love for us. But the immediacy of sex and the complexity of our relationships often blind us to the larger transcendent presence of God who is love. The lifestyle of committed celibacy is chosen for the sake of the kingdom. The committed celibate serves humankind as a sign of contradiction, forcing us to confront the deeper issues of human existence and meaning that are so easily masked in our culture's obsession with sex.

This argument is not persuasive with everyone, but it has a powerful influence on many whose ministry brings them into contact with persons whose lives have been devastated by our culture's sexual compulsions. To know strong, mature, caring celibates is a liberating experience for those who have been sexually abused, for young people caught in prostitution, for people grown sated with sex and yet cynical of any other source of personal worth. The eschatological or symbolic value of celibacy in our sex-crazed culture is an area that deserves much more thought. But a theology of celibacy that focuses on its witness value also remains accountable to the important questions: who is looking, and what do they see?

The credibility of the Catholic Church in the area of sexuality is not unquestioned. Recent statements and actions make many persons of goodwill suspicious of what religious officials have to say on these issues. We must acknowledge that not many people today are looking to Catholic celibates for guidance and revelation concerning their sexuality. And some who do look at celibates do not find their lives to be signs of love or generosity or joy. This theological interpretation of celibacy will become more credible as it confronts the practical question of what persons of goodwill see when they come in contact with the lives of religious celibates. Some suspect that many celibates are not faithful to their vows or that most are faithful only under duress and would marry if given that option. These perceptions undermine the persuasiveness of religious celibacy.

Another understanding of celibacy for the sake of the kingdom carries weight today. Participating in the mission of Jesus Christ, some Christians are drawn into demanding work in potentially dangerous circumstances. They choose to share their life with the poor, care for the critically ill, work for social justice in the midst of a politically repressive regime. Devoting one's life to these efforts is often all-consuming; it can be perilous as well. Here the choice for celibacy may be part of a larger sense of vocation. A person reflects on the implications of his calling:

> Weighing the circumstances that surround my own life's work, I realize that wholehearted devotion to this mission will make it impossible—or at least difficult—for me to honor the practical and emotional commitments of marriage and family life. So, aware of the demands and dangers associated with my vocation, I've decided not to marry.

Celibacy is chosen not "for itself" but "for the sake of the kingdom."

This can be a powerful and persuasive argument for committed celibacy. Some tasks in our time make these demands; some roles require such courage; some responsibilities ask for this kind of generous response. We have only to recall the patient heroism of the four women pastoral workers murdered in San Salvador or the witness of others who risk imprisonment and disgrace by speaking out for justice in the face of repression.

But we must acknowledge that most of us involved in the mission of Jesus are not engaged in this kind of difficult and dangerous work. Most persons who are celibate today are in fact involved in work that does not, on the face of it, exclude the commitments of marriage and family life. The experience of other Christian denominations shows us that effective religious leadership does not always require a celibate clergy. Protestant missionaries, usually married and often with families, have a long history of generous service in remote and dangerous settings. Within the Catholic community, more and more married persons are found in roles of pastoral ministry and religious leadership once available only to celibates. Catholics who are celibate, single, and married work side by side in ministry these days—doing similar work with similar results of success and failure. In this closer collaboration, many celibates recognize that in the lives of their lay colleagues the commitments of marriage and family life often do more to support effective ministry than to distract from it.

Another understanding of celibacy as a choice must be mentioned here. At issue is the linking of celibacy with priesthood. Scriptural studies have made clear that celibacy was not an essential element of Christian leadership in the New Testament: Simon Peter and others of Jesus' closest followers were clearly married; in the Pastoral Epistles bishops are described as married men (I Timothy 3:2, 3:12; Titus 3:6). The study of Catholic history, however, shows the gradual development of the celibate priesthood: in the fourth century married priests were exhorted to abstain from sexual intercourse; gradually, fewer and fewer bishops and priests married; then in the twelfth century celibacy was made mandatory for priesthood in the Latin Rite. Because of this biblical and historical evidence, most theologians have concluded that celibacy is not a necessary part of the ministry of priesthood. Rather, celibacy is a religious discipline required by the Catholic Church.

Compulsory celibacy is part of Catholic priesthood today. To be ordained, a candidate for priesthood must accept the requirement of celibacy. Seminarians know this from the outset; over the course of training they are made aware of the practical and spiritual requirements of the celibate way of life. Therefore, it is said, celibacy is a free choice made by those who are ordained.

Among many diocesan priests and seminarians, however, this discussion of celibacy as a choice rings hollow. Their experience is not that celibacy is a choice open to them in the Spirit. Rather it is a formal requirement demanded of them if they are to move forward toward ordination. For many, the choice they have made is for the ministry of community and liturgical leadership to which they know themselves to be called. In order to be allowed to exercise that ministry, they have accepted the stipulation that goes with it—that they will not marry. Many diocesan priests do not, in fact, experience celibacy as a personal charism or a vocational choice. They experience it neither as a gift of the Spirit nor a personal strength. They would choose to marry if that were possible. Since marriage is not an option at this time, these priests strive courageously to live in a way that is faithful to their public declaration of celibacy, even though their own spiritual gifts and personal temperament do not offer them much support for this lifestyle.

Celibacy as a Call

We have been exploring the images that are part of the discussion of celibacy today. For many people, the most important image is celibacy as a call. The strength of this understanding of celibacy is its close connection with spirituality: celibacy is experienced as an integral part of one's personal journey of faith. This can be the experience of the young adult who feels drawn into a deepening relationship with the person of Jesus. Through prayer and discernment, often assisted by a spiritual director or other religious guide, she comes to recognize that her own spiritual journey includes remaining celibate. For her, celibacy is part of God's call. Here the decision for celibacy is rooted in an openness to God's mysterious action in one's own life.

For another person, the decision for celibacy is part of a call to live in religious community. He feels drawn to share life with this religious congregation. Their vision and values, their mission and spirit, the work they do, the way they live together appeal very strongly to him. After a period of reflection and evaluation, he comes to the conviction that this way of life can be for him a way to God. His commitment to celibacy is made as part of a larger commitment to share life with this particular religious group. Here again, celibacy is seen as part of one's personal journey of faith. The decision to remain celibate is made because it is seen as part of God's call *for this person* rather than because celibacy is objectively a higher or holier way to live.

The mature witness of celibate persons in midlife and beyond offers us another rich experience of celibacy as a personal call. This experience is an especially significant source of renewed appreciation of the meaning of celibacy today. These people have lived the celibate life for many years. Their experience bridges the gap between the earlier understanding of celibacy as the "higher calling" and the current confusion over the validity of the life choice of celibacy. Their personal experience includes the early motives that brought them to the decision for celibacy as well as the convictions that support their continuing decision to live this lifestyle today. These maturing members of the community of faith bring both candor and confidence to the discussion.

In moments of reflection, the midlife religious muses:

> The reasons that brought me to religious life are not the reasons that see me through today. My understanding of myself, my sexuality, what celibacy means, what it demands—all these have changed significantly. I am aware of the mixed motives that were part of my earliest decision for celibacy: generosity and fear, guilt and idealism, openness to God and susceptibility to social pressure. However, this hodgepodge of motives does not mean I made the wrong choice. I am aware that all important life choices combine a range of motives. But I also recognize that I have been able to face some of the shadows, to purify some of the compulsions that made my earlier decisions less than free. The convictions that hold me in this lifestyle today are in many ways different from the beliefs I held twenty years ago. But I remain celibate, or better, I continue to choose celibacy because it fits. As a celibate, I have grown and deepened and learned to love. The celibate life, with its joy and sorrow, has given me much of what is best in myself. This is the way I have been led; this has been the path of my own journey to and with God.

Mature celibates like this testify most convincingly to the adequacy of the celibate commitment today. The American Church is blessed with thousands of such mature religious and priests in whose lives the contemporary significance of celibacy is lived out. This is a rich source of information to bring forth more explicitly into the larger ecclesial discussion of celibacy. Such lives serve not as justifications of a questionable theology of the "higher way," but as witness to the power and purpose of celibacy as one of the trustworthy ways in which the Christian journey may be followed in faith.

Two Challenges

Christians continue to acknowledge that celibacy is an authentic way to live our religious faith. In the community of faith today we recognize how fruitful this paradoxical lifestyle can be. However, two special challenges for the survival of celibacy arise from our shared history.

The first challenge we face is to unyoke the gift of celibacy from biases against sexuality. Celibacy first flowered in a milieu of hostility toward sexuality and the body. Virginity was judged to be the one genuinely pure way to live the faith. Marriage was a poor, second best—a concession to nature and a sure distraction from Christian virtue.

Because sexual activity was portrayed as unavoidably stained by selfishness and compulsion, many Christians were attracted to the choice for a celibate life. As the bias against sex is healed, the negative motive for celibacy is removed. Increasingly Christians choose a celibate life, not to avoid the threat of sexuality, but because this style of life fits their temperament, career, and spirituality. Such a lifestyle allows them to love well and generously. This purifying of our motives will make celibacy a healthier and more graceful path for following Jesus.

The second challenge we face is to disengage the lifestyle of celibacy from the ministry of priesthood. Catholics have been allowed to forget that the linking of celibacy and the priestly ministry was a pastoral strategy introduced hundreds of years after Jesus' time. When the discipline of celibacy was first applied to priesthood, many priests and bishops were married. The two sacraments, Matrimony and Holy Orders, had not previously been seen as incompatible. In the fourth century, for the first time, an incompatibility was asserted as Pope Siricius, Saint Augustine, Saint Jerome, and others urged the married clergy to abstain from intercourse with their wives. Not until almost eight hundred years later, in the Second Lateran Council of 1139, did the discipline of celibacy for priests become part of official Church law.

Historical research shows that the conviction that priests ought not to marry was strongly influenced by negative attitudes toward sexuality. These attitudes no longer prevail. Only slowly and painfully are we returning today to a more authentic confidence in the compatibility of sexuality and spirituality.

The time has come for Catholics to disengage the choice for celibacy from the community service of the priestly ministry. Both celibacy and the priesthood will survive this separation. The ministry of the priesthood will profit by the influx of generous and gifted married persons and celibacy will be appreciated as the special gift it is meant to be. This paradoxical grace will be a more convincing witness in those Christians who freely and courageously choose to follow the Lord in this way.

REFLECTIVE EXERCISE

Consider your own experience of committed celibacy. First, take a moment to recall a celibate person who has influenced you—a teacher or a pastor, perhaps a member of your own family or a close friend. What do you find most attractive or admirable about this person? In what ways has this person been influential for you? What is the chief conviction about celibacy that you draw from this person's life?

Next, broaden the focus of your reflection by responding to these questions. What contribution does the Christian vision of celibacy make to you personally? As you see it, what contribution does celibacy make to the community of faith? To humankind?

Finally, are there any concerns you have about the vision and lifestyle of celibacy in the Catholic community today?

ADDITIONAL RESOURCES

Sandra Schneiders provides an excellent analysis of the different motives for celibacy in *New Wineskins* (Paulist Press, 1986); see especially Chapters 7 and 8. In *Celibate Loving* (Paulist Press, 1984), Mary Anne Huddleston brings together a valuable collection of essays on the experience of living celibacy today.

The ongoing discussion about consecrated celibacy can be traced across several of the significant contributions from the 1970s. Donald Goergan's classic treatise on sexuality and celibacy, *The Sexual Celibate* (Seabury Press, 1974), remains an important part of the ongoing discussion. Philip Keane deals specifically with moral issues of sexuality and celibacy in his *Sexual Morality* (Paulist Press, 1978). *Sexuality and Brotherhood* (Christian Brothers National Office, 1977), edited by Martin Hellsdorfer, includes contributions from several perspectives in theology and spirituality. The challenges of celibate living are discussed in an issue of *Studies in Jesuit Spirituality* devoted to "Affectivity and Sexuality" (March–May 1978). Henri Nouwen reflects on "Celibacy and the Holy" in *Clowning in Rome* (Image Books/Doubleday, 1979).

Biblical scholar Carolyn Osiek explores the New Testament meaning of charism in "Relation of Charism to Rights and Duties in the New Testament Church," in *Official Ministry in a New Age*, edited by James Provost (Canon Law Society of America, 1981), pp. 41–59. Jo Ann McNamara examines the early history of consecrated celibacy in *A New Song: Celibate Women in the First Three Christian Centuries* (Hawthorne Press, 1983).

Three studies that trace the appearance of celibacy as a requirement for priesthood are: Edward Schillebeeckx, *Ministry* (Crossroad, 1981), pp. 85–99; Roger Balducelli, "The Apostolic

Origins of Clerical Continence: A Critical Appraisal of a New Book" in *Theological Studies* 43 (December 1982): 693–705; and Daniel Callam's "Clerical Continence in the Fourth Century: Three Papal Decretals" in *Theological Studies* 41 (1980): 3–50.

Part Four
The Hope

Intimacy invites us into unforeseen experiences. Conflict and loneliness are two of these painful surprises. If conflict is one of the ways we hold one another as intimates, how can we get better at this difficult embrace? If loneliness is so normal a part of our intimate lives, how can we let this painful emotion instruct us in loving well? In the initial chapters of Part Four we explore ways to befriend these sometimes troubling companions.

Part Four concludes with a look at two central virtues of intimacy: compassion and gratitude. We trace the expansion of eros as solidarity becomes compassion. We end by examining the links between gratitude and generosity. In giving thanks and becoming generous, both eros and caritas find their fulfillment.

15.
Facing Conflict

Our first fight was the worst. Jack and I had been working together for over a year. Things seemed to be going so well between us; we were both amazed at how well matched our working styles seemed to be. Then, one day a minor misunderstanding blew up into a big argument. Things came to a head in the middle of an important planning meeting: he made a series of sarcastic remarks, and I yelled at him and stomped out of the room. I was furious, embarrassed, confused. I had just assumed that mature adults would always be able to work things out before tempers became involved. My feeling of defeat was worse than the argument. Things are a lot better between us now. But a long time passed before we could even talk about what happened.

The Scandal

Our lives are flooded with images of harmony: Good friends do not quarrel. Lovers live happily ever after. Mature adults do not become angry. These romantic fantasies, forcefully marketed in parts of our culture, promote the ideal of affection without conflict. Still we have daily experience of our own stumbling efforts to love well, efforts often accompanied by tension and distress.

We have good reason to hate conflict—nations in conflict disrupt lives and people die; violent quarrels break up marriages; arguments end friendships. These dangers have taught many of us to avoid conflict—at any price. We speak softly, stifle anger, look away from the distress. But our effort to ignore conflict usually does not work. The mounting tensions endanger our relationships and erode our love.

We need to know that conflict, as threatening as it feels, is normal in close relationships. When people come together at a level that touches their significant values and needs, conflicts are expectable, even inevitable. In fact, conflict is not "all bad." Its effects in a relationship are not simply or necessarily destructive. As many marriage counselors know, conflict may be either a sign of health in a relationship or a symptom of distress. Conflict between us indicates that we are at least engaged with one another, that something is going on here that is important to both of us. We can harness the energy of our conflict so that it does not work against us. A friendship in which there is nothing important enough to fight about is more likely to die than one in which arguments sometimes occur. Somehow we know that indifference is a greater enemy of intimacy than is conflict.

Conflict is a critical part of life, an honorable dynamic of change and growth. This is true at the personal level and beyond: adolescence brings us into conflict with the constricting safety of childhood; our adult commitments put us in conflict with the limitless possibilities of adolescence; new hopes in our marriage challenge the equilibrium we have established between us. Whenever a new value appears in society, whether it is equal rights for blacks or just wages for women, its demands are likely to conflict with the status quo. But for us to appreciate conflict as more than a scandal to be avoided, we will have to find strategies for facing it.

The Virtue

Conflict is ordinary and inevitable. In any relationship that brings people close—friendship, team work, marriage—conflict is sure to arise. It becomes destructive only when we fail to face it virtuously. But to become virtuous in handling conflict we need both vision and skills. We must learn to see conflict more optimistically and to manage its sometimes frightening force.

A positive vision of conflict depends on three insights. First, we need to realize that conflict is an honorable adult embrace; it is one of the ways that we hold each other. Adult intimacy includes many embraces. We hold our friends in affection; we hold one another accountable in collaboration at work; we embrace in making love. And at times we hold one another in conflict. This unsettling embrace can be part of our intimacy. Willingness to confront the growing tension between us can be a face of fidelity, a way of keeping our promises instead of fleeing them. Befriending conflict begins with the recognition that this embrace is one of the demands of close relationships.

Second, we heal our vision of conflict by seeing more clearly the underlying dynamic involved. Conflict is a response to discrepancy. We realize that things are not as we expected or as we wanted them to be. When a relationship is in conflict, we see the other person as somehow involved in, or responsible for, this discrepancy. We find ourselves saying, "You are not as I expected; it is your fault that things are not as I want them to be." At times like this we must resist simply blaming our partner or refusing to admit any differences between us. Instead, we must recognize the areas in which we differ—expectations, values, needs—and develop ways of dealing with these differences so that our relationship is enriched rather than destroyed.

For us as Christians, the third source of a more positive vision of conflict is the image of conflict in Scripture. Religious piety often favors an idyllic view of harmony and calm, but our religious history is quite different. Jesus' way of life stirred up much conflict for him and for his followers. His favorite stories were parables that caused consternation and confusion among his listeners. Parables delight in conflict: we think we know who our neighbor is until we hear about the Good Samaritan; we are content building our own fortunes until a voice says, "Tonight your soul will be required of you." Jesus' parables overturn our plans; they hold us in the uncomfortable embrace of conflict. But Jesus did more than speak parables. He lived a parable that argues that some values are more important than life itself, that life can be found even through death.

Biblical scholars remind us of the centrality of parables to Jesus' message in the gospels. In every age, authentic Christian faith is a countercultural challenge: it proclaims values and raises hopes that undermine cultural demands—whether for profit or individualism or even national superiority. Conflict is at the center of Christianity.

Both the Hebrew and Christian Scriptures brim with stories of conflict. But religious piety and institutional control conspire to "forget" these tales in favor of images of harmony and obedience. To recover a vision of the graceful side of conflict we need to revisit these sacred stories, and be attentive to their revelation to us now. Perhaps the best story of conflict and intimacy is that of Jacob wrestling in the dark with God.

> And Jacob was left alone; and something wrestled with him until the breaking of the day. When it saw that it did not prevail against Jacob, it touched the hollow of his thigh; and Jacob's thigh was put out of joint as he wrestled with it. Then it said, "Let me go, for the day is breaking." But Jacob said, "I will not let you go, unless you bless me." And it said to him, "What is your name?" And he said, "Jacob." Then it said, "Your name shall no more be called Jacob, but Israel, for you have struggled with God and with humans, and have prevailed."

Then Jacob asked it, "Tell me, I pray, your name." But it said, "Why is it that you ask my name?" And there it blessed him. So Jacob called the name of the place Peniel, saying, "For I have seen God face to face, and yet my life is preserved." The sun rose upon him as he passed Peniel, limping because of his thigh. (Genesis 32: 24–31)

This evocative tale, which is about Jacob's relationship with God, portrays intimacy through the metaphor of wrestling. One night two partners fall into the ambiguous embrace of conflict. This very ancient account captures all the anxiety of such an encounter. Jacob is alone in the dark. Something grabs hold of him from behind. Struggling with this unidentified combatant, Jacob demands to know what it wants of him. Jacob cannot escape this embrace nor can he control this nocturnal assailant. In the dark these two struggle, with injury and complaint, toward a new day and a changed relationship.

The heart of this story seems to be the ambiguity of this wrestling embrace. Jacob is threatened but not destroyed; in the struggle he is seriously injured, but he also strengthens his resilience and comes to a new sense of himself. For modern readers, this story resonates with the ambiguous embraces of our own lives.

A friendship begins to deepen, and we are apprehensive about this change. We wonder, "Will this friendship demand too much of me? What if this friend wants to hold me in a way that I find too close for comfort?" Or a colleague wants to work with us on a new project. We question ourself: "What if her presence crowds my fragile plan? Will her energetic collaboration transform my idea into something closer to her own?"

Or in our forties we feel a stirring deep inside ourself. Some neglected part of ourself (an ambition, an aspect of our sexuality, a long-untended value) wants attention, demands to be more thoroughly embraced. But we do not know where acceptance will lead. We have been doing just fine (we thought) by ignoring this part of our life. We are not sure that we can remain in control if we risk change.

Our adult lives demand so many different embraces of us. Many are ambiguous and beyond our control. Like Jacob's combative embrace, they invite us to a new and frightening partnership. We find ourselves asking, "What are the rules here? Will I survive such an encounter?"

In the unpleasant and sweaty embrace of Jacob and his assailant, each is changed. Jacob finds his identity challenged; he loses his name and becomes Israel (meaning "one who has struggled with God"). Also he is seriously wounded, limping for the rest of his life. But even his powerful adversary (whom he will later learn is a strange, nocturnal form of God) is forced to give up something: upon Jacob's demand God surrenders a blessing. This exhausting night changes both combatants. They have embraced in a new way. But again we demand, "What are the rules? How are we to hold on, or let go, in these trying embraces of partnership?"

As we muse on this odd struggle, we recall the temptations that come to all of us in these embraces of conflict. First, we may be tempted to flee. Facing the conflict seems too frightening. We fear to confront our differences for then our relationship might explode, we might seriously injure each other. So we flee. We might physically leave the partnership but, more likely, we avoid conflict with subtler strategies such as using humor to deflect the tension, absenting ourself from a stressful meeting, changing jobs. We distance ourself to avoid the embrace of conflict.

Sometimes, of course, flight is a wise response. An unfair fight, at the wrong time, is not a good idea. And in many instances— in marriage, at work, in the Church—flight becomes the virtuous, the only, response because of an imbalance of power. Yet if flight is our *regular* response to conflict, the story of Jacob might invite us to reexamine our interaction.

Others of us are drawn in a second direction. Frightened by an arising conflict, we feel compelled to dominate the situation. We devise strategies to control the potential conflict in a relationship. We tightly monitor the agenda of the meeting; we avoid any conversation that is not protected by clear boundaries.

The conflicts that unavoidably arise between partners in love and work are a part of the dance of mutuality. In adult intimacy we find ourselves moving in rhythm, close to others. Sometimes this dance includes the strenuous embrace of conflict. With the metaphor of dance we get a clearer glimpse of the differences between the temptations of flight and of control. The "fleer" within us says, "I don't dance. Dancing is for girls, for sissies." And so we avoid these complex social occasions. We skirt the embarrassment that awaits the dancer—being out of step, perspiring in public, kicking others in the shins. But we do not get to dance. The remedy is expensive; to avoid conflict, we sacrifice intimacy.

The controller within us says, "Let's dance, but I get to lead." Here we dance, but only when we can control the tempo and the direction of the relationship. We enter into conflict but only with an edge, an advantage (of authority or muscle or cash) that allows us to control this dangerous dance. To outsiders we may appear to be moving in harmony. For our partners, caught in this manipulative movement, the dance will not refresh.

A third temptation that comes to us in the embrace of conflict arises from a special cultural conditioning—we avoid conflict by giving in immediately in any dispute. Many women have learned that wrestling is unladylike and that conflict is unchristian. The ambiguous embrace of conflict—with a spouse, a work colleague, or a church official—triggers in these persons the impulse of immediate surrender. We give in and comply; we roll over and play dead. By calling this behavior docility, meekness, even obedience, Christians have sometimes tried to sanctify it.

Returning to the metaphor of dancing, we see the special liability of this response. Dancing with a corpse is difficult. The contest fizzles when one of us refuses to engage in the struggle. And the conflict, uncontested, goes unresolved. Moreover, many women, made unnaturally meek and docile, learn underground methods of manipulation to even the score with their more dominant partners.

A fourth and very different response to conflict appears in the story of Jacob. Murkier than the other reactions, Jacob's response was to hold on for dear life. Unable to flee or to control the encounter, he seizes hold of the other and will not let go. In sophisticated vocabulary, he is sustaining the ambiguity of this peculiar, nocturnal embrace. In ordinary words, he is trying to outlast the night. Bewildered but determined, he holds on to his partner until it dawns on him who this contestant is and what it wants of him. In this dark tale the metaphor of "dawning" begins. Jacob's tenacity (his faith?) tells him that from this night of struggle will come illumination and grace, but only if he holds on.

Alas, even Jacob's reaction fails to give us a sure rule for conflict. Holding on is not a magic, guaranteed solution. It takes two to dance, even in the embrace of conflict. Sometimes a person may cling to a partner who is no longer psychologically present. Or a person will clutch at a friendship or marriage already dead. Or a person may hold on to a crisis year after year until what was meant to be a purifying passage becomes a chronic disorder. In every embrace, with or without conflict, we learn new rhythms of holding on and letting go. But we learn to trust these rhythms only as we dare to share and compare our histories of intimacy and conflict.

This story of Jacob and the parable of Jesus' life can give us a renewed vision of conflict. But to live this vision we will need to develop patterns of graceful response.

Rescuing Virtue from Rhetoric

Conflict can be positive, but it is seldom easy. Whether conflict strengthens or erodes our relationship depends in large part on how we respond. To deal well with its ambiguous power we must first appreciate that conflict can be more than simply negative. We must believe that the benefits of working through our distress outweigh the discomfort we feel. We need the maturity to face strong emotion and the flexibility to look at ourselves in new ways that may force us to change. We must learn to act in ways that are effective, even in the heart of our disagreement.

In an ongoing relationship—friendship, family life, close collaboration in work—partners develop a characteristic way of dealing with conflict. This style is conjoint: all the parties are involved. It becomes their way of handling the discrepancies that inevitably arise. Two basic conflict styles are avoidance and engagement. While either may be useful under certain circumstances, each carries its own hazards.

Avoiding Conflict

Some relationships avoid conflict by ignoring any distress. Partners here seem unable to face anything that might arouse negative feelings between them. At work, colleagues carefully avoid certain topics or turn away from them quickly as soon as emotions are aroused. Friends refuse to accept any information that might point to a problem between them. A wife prefers not to know about her husband's extramarital affair. This conspiracy of silence blocks both reconciliation and growth.

Avoidance often comes from a fear of strong emotion. We find ourselves saying, "I am afraid of what will happen—to me or to you—if I let myself get angry." Sometimes avoidance stems from a sense that our relationship is fragile. We admit, "Things between us are strained enough as it is. We'd better not risk getting into something that might just push us farther apart." Avoiding conflict keeps a relationship stable at the cost of keeping it super-ficial.

As a tool of discretion, though, avoidance can help us handle conflict well. In many mature relationships, partners face conflict but they do so carefully. Aware of conflict's ambiguous force, they take steps to ensure that they are equal to a confrontation. When circumstances limit their ability to face conflict effectively, they try to avoid it: Aware that we are particularly tired one afternoon, we ask a colleague to postpone our conversation on a touchy topic until tomorrow. Or with in-laws visiting us for the weekend, we put our disagreement aside until a more opportune time provides privacy to confront it. Discretion makes us sensi-tive to factors of time and place and personal vulnerability. This style of avoidance is neither flight nor denial. The proof of its virtuousness arrives when we actually face the conflict. Discre-tion does not mean we never confront our difficulties; it does mean that we are careful to face them when we are at our best.

ENGAGING IN CONFLICT

Engaging in conflict, too, can take different forms. A confrontive style is likely to be destructive when we take on the issues in a way that escalates the tension between us. Sometimes this hap-pens as a minor problem is allowed to expand. Your bringing the staff car back late to the office causes me to miss an important appointment. As we start to discuss this, I shift the focus from this event to the many *other* times that you have inconvenienced me. These incidents, in turn, remind me of your (reputed) gen-eral selfishness. My angry response excites you to come up with your own list of how demanding I am or how many times I have inconvenienced you. The conflict has escalated and will be much more difficult to resolve.

Another risky response in conflict is to shift the focus from an objective problem to the relationship itself. Here the specific is-sue in conflict becomes a sign of something much larger. Close relationships seem especially susceptible to this emotional escalation. Issues of practical decision ("What shall we do?") become tests of our relationship ("If you really loved me . . ."). The discrepancies we feel ("Things are not right between us") become occasions for personal attack ("And it's your fault").

In another engagement style, conflict becomes cyclic. Some partners take up the conflict, even lustily, but seem unable to go anywhere with it. They quickly become polarized, and move to nonnegotiable positions in which neither one is able to offer a way out. Their way of dealing with one another strikes an observer as especially damaging and bitter. The strife between them rises and falls but is never really resolved. As with the couple in Edward Albee's *Who's Afraid of Virginia Woolf?*, conflict becomes the common but wounded form of communication and contact between them.

A more useful style of engagement leads toward the resolution of the conflict. This stance requires that we acknowledge the problem between us rather than simply denying our distress. If we are willing to explore the discrepancy, we may be able to learn something new about ourselves and one another. Caught in conflict, we recognize that things are not as we thought. But panic can turn us away from this disconcerting information, as we try to mask the truth or fix blame. Or we can seize this opportunity for growth. We can view conflict as a chance to come to a better sense of what is really going on between us. Being willing to engage in conflict, we still need both great flexibility and specific skills to guide us on this perilous path.

FLEXIBILITY

Our willingness to take on the troublesome issues between us does not automatically ensure a successful resolution. Without some flexibility in how we respond to the problem, engagement may leave us more frustrated and angry. For example, our initial discussion may reach an impasse. The scenario may go like this:

I want us to ask my parents to help us make a down payment on a new house. You refuse to do so. I see things one way; you see them another. We share little common ground. So, we must reformulate the problem. I need to understand and appreciate what is at stake from your point of view. For me, to ask for money from my parents expresses my sense of belonging to them and being secure in their care. Besides, I know that they would love to do this for us. But for you, to take money from them seems like an admission of inadequacy in making our own way; it is humiliating. Besides, you feel that seeking my parents' help just continues my pattern of looking to them first whenever we face a difficulty instead of working things out on our own. Thus, I discover new ways of interpreting our standoff: for you, the issue is not so much one of money as of independence and self-esteem. By reformulating the problem, we can move beyond our earlier impasse. I can be sensitive to the potentially "hot" issues that may be involved here for you . . .

The above scenario shows us how flexibility helps us reformulate the problem and arrive at a workable solution. We may need, however, to explore a range of options before we reach a resolution that satisfies both of us. Under stress, many of us find that thinking creatively or coming up with alternatives are difficult to do. We feel stuck, with few possibilities open to us and none of these acceptable. The more ideas we are able to generate in the midst of conflict, the more likely we are to evolve a decision that respects both of us and also solves the problem. Now the scenario continues:

We will not start with my parents as we look for down payment money but will explore other possibilities first. Perhaps we can get part of the money from several different sources and thus not be so dependent on my parents. Maybe we should approach them for a loan rather than a gift, or we can ask your parents for help as well as mine . . .

Thus, to come up with new possibilities under the stress of

conflict requires personal flexibility. We resist becoming totally involved in defending ourself and our original plan. We explore other alternatives, whether they come from our partner or ourself. We remain flexible enough to compromise, to work toward a decision that is satisfying for both of us. We accept a resolution that may ask something of each of us. Our sense that this conflict is resolved does not depend simply on either of us having the last word.

We know that conflict is expectable, even inevitable. So, what is important is how we deal with one another and what we learn about our relationship through conflict. The solution we come to, even "who wins," is less significant than what happens between us. A year from now we may have forgotten what we decided today but we are likely to carry with us a sense of whether we can work out the problems that arise between us. What is said and left unsaid, with what level of care and skill, how power is shared, and whether healing or hurt prevail are the elements that make up our conflict style. And these are what our hearts remember.

SKILLS FOR RESOLVING CONFLICT

A virtuous approach to conflict begins in vision as we see our painful disagreements as more than simply negative. Strengthened by this vision, we will need some practical, interpersonal skills to assist us in resolving the disputes that are an important part of our relationships.

The discussion of skills is still suspect in some areas of the Christian community. Strategies of effective communication can become techniques for manipulating others. We do not trust the huckster's smooth talk and the salesman's ingratiating smile. For Christians the skills of dealing with conflict must be bound to a religious vision and value. We learn the skills of interpersonal communication to help us live the Christian values of intimacy and committed love.

Two skills that are essential for handling conflict are appropriate self-disclosure and effective confrontation. Self-disclosure begins in self-awareness. We must know what we have experienced and what we are feeling. Very often, of course, we do not—this churning emotion inside us has no name; we do not know if we are fearful or guilty or depressed. The ability to name our feelings and emotions is part of the discipline of eros discussed in Chapter 9. This skill in naming the different movements of our heart makes available to both ourself and our partner the dense and ambiguous information of our own life. But we will give careful attention to learning about these half-submerged hopes and feelings only if we value them. We must believe that these inner movements have worth and weight and that they are not just signs of our inferiority. Only when we can name these stirrings are we able to share them with loved ones.

An important skill of self-disclosure is our ability to speak concretely. We must be able to say "I," to acknowledge our own ideas and emotions. Skillful communication with loved ones is often thwarted by a retreat to phrases such as "most people want" instead of "I need," or "people have a hard time with" instead of "I don't understand." In the midst of a conflict between us, the question is not what "most people want." The concern is what *we* need from this person right now. Only if we have the courage and insight to name this need concretely are we likely to heal the conflict.

Beyond this willingness to own our experience, we can also learn to provide more specific details about our actions and emotions. To share with a friend we need a broad and nuanced vocabulary of feelings. We must be able to say more than "I feel good" and "I feel bad." When we say, "I feel bad," our friend must guess whether this is a feeling of anger or disappointment or loneliness. Our friend must guess who or what is the source of our distress. Such guessing does not improve the chances for our dealing well with a conflict.

Skills of confrontation help us share information, positive or negative, in a way that encourages the other person to explore his or her behavior rather than defend it. When we speak descriptively rather than judgmentally, we give others more room to examine their action. To tell a co-worker that we missed our meeting when she did not return the car at the agreed time is a *description*; this is something we need to talk about. To call our colleague inconsiderate and selfish is a *judgment*; she will then most likely defend herself and remind us about some of our own selfish behavior. Now, discussing today's conflict becomes more difficult. For us to say, "I am intimidated by you" is an admission of a concrete distress. For us to announce, "You are intimidating" is a judgment. Whether our co-worker is generally or always intimidating is a difficult question to settle and not quite to the point. The issue for us here and now is the feeling that happens *within us* when we are together. If we can accurately name and discuss this particular specific experience, we have a much better chance of healing our conflict.

Through practice with a skillful teacher or experienced friend, we can get better at these particular abilities. We can learn to name concretely the anger or sorrow that arises in a conflict. Rather than blaming or punishing our companion or colleague, we can look into the discrepancy together. Then we can face and heal the conflicts that are part of adult intimacy.

The Gifts of Conflict

We have been trying to appreciate conflict as a normal part of intimacy. To love well we need to face conflict. As we get better at entering this frightening embrace, we come to recognize that it offers us three gifts.

One gift of conflict is the hard-earned insight that *the good emerges*. When we commit ourself in love we think we know what we are doing. But as we live these commitments, life expands and unfolds. Our partner discovers new hopes hidden within herself.

And these sometimes conflict with an earlier, safer sense of who she is. Neither of us had seen these hopes when we made our commitment. Now, new possibilities conflict with old arrangements. Our love will grow only if we confront, together and skillfully, these changes. The good is not given fully in our first commitments of affection; the good emerges.

The good emerges in our larger commitments as well. As we become active in parish life, we start to notice that the Church is largely controlled by men. Women are seldom allowed in leadership positions. This realization threatens our comfort with the Church. We try to ignore the issue, but it will not go away. The belief that Christianity itself is growing and conflict is a part of growth can help us face this unsettling situation. Adult faith prepares us to acknowledge the good wherever it emerges and encourages us to face the institutional conflict that an emerging good may provoke.

A second gift of conflict is its ability to reveal us to ourselves. In a disagreement with a friend we are made to see our limitations—our possessiveness or our unwillingness to forgive. We may resent this revelation, but it is a great gift. Made more aware of our weakness, we can be motivated to change. We can become a more forgiving friend and a less possessive lover. But conflict also gives us some happier revelations. Through a prolonged struggle with a friend we come to appreciate our surprising courage. We can endure this distress; we are tougher than we had thought! Grateful for this unsuspected strength, we are more willing to face future conflicts.

A third gift of conflict teaches us about the shape of fidelity. In our early innocence we believe that true love lifts us beyond arguments and disagreements. In our maturing we learn that the embrace of conflict is an ordinary and expectable part of loving. And this painful embrace can even be a form of our fidelity. In the midst of a painful struggle, we do not run away. We strain not to injure each other. Like Jacob, we hold on. Our fidelity to those whom we love cannot mean our insistence that they remain the same. It cannot mean forcing others to do things our way. In adult intimacy fidelity means staying in the conversation. It means not letting go and walking away. We find no sweetness or romance in these periods of conflict, but we hold to a dogged conviction that this struggle can bring us together to a better place.

This third gift is an important part of our life in a changing Church. Experiencing the heated debate these days about sexuality or the role of women or the function of authority, we may be tempted to walk away. But something good is emerging in this painful conflict. So we hold on to the Church and refuse to let her go. The bewildering embrace of conflict becomes a way of being faithful.

REFLECTIVE EXERCISE

All of us have "horror stories" of conflicts that were simply destructive. We invite you here to revisit an experience of conflict that had a more positive result. Begin by recollecting yourself in a restful place, during a quiet time in your day.

First, let the richness of your past few years come back to you. Then gently listen for an experience of struggle or conflict. It may have been with a friend, with a co-worker, with a part of yourself, or with God. Initially, just let the memory of this wrestling return, with the emotions that come with it. Feel again the confusion and pain. Then consider these questions:

What was most threatening to you in this struggle? Were there ways in which you were wounded?

What did you learn about yourself in the struggle? How was the conflict a revelation?

In retrospect, was there a special gain from this conflict? Was it, in some way, graceful?

ADDITIONAL RESOURCES

John Dominic Crossan explores the revolutionary nature of
Jesus' parables in *Cliffs of Fall* (Seabury Press, 1980). Also see his
In Parables: The Challenge of the Historical Jesus (Harper & Row,
1973). For an excellent analysis of the story of Jacob's wrestling
with God, see biblical scholar Gerhard Von Rad's *Genesis: A
Commentary* (Westminster Press, 1961).

Psychologist Gerard Egan continues his significant contribution to the understanding and practice of effective communication; see his *The Skilled Helper* (Brooks/Cole, 1985) and *You and
Me: Skills of Communicating and Relating to Others* (Brooks/Cole,
1977). Fran Ferder draws connections among scripture, psychology, and effective communication in *Words Made Flesh* (Ave Maria Press, 1986). In *Communication Skills for Ministry* (Kendall/
Hunt, 1983), John W. Lawyer and Neil H. Katz provide a practical overview and training tool; see especially their treatment of
conflict in Chapter 6.

Jean Baker Miller examines the complex role of conflict in
women's experience in *Toward a New Psychology of Women* (Beacon Press, 1987). Mark Juergensmeyer discusses strategies for
resolving everyday conflicts in *Fighting Fair* (Harper & Row,
1986). Pastoral psychologists John Faul and David Augsburger
examine the connections between assertion and affirmation in
Beyond Assertiveness (Word Books, 1980). We explore the role of
conflict in Chapter 18 of *Marrying Well* (Image Books/Double-
day, 1983) and Chapter 9 of *Community of Faith* (Harper & Row,
1982).

16.

Learning from Loneliness

Loneliness is our response to the anguish of being alone. Separated from those we love, we experience sorrow, longing, helplessness. We may be angry or resentful; we are likely to sense frustration, even bitterness. Most of all we feel abandoned. Our distress becomes especially acute in the face of loss—the death of a spouse, the betrayal of a trusted colleague, the gradual erosion of a friendship that was once strong. In these experiences our dismay deepens. A relationship of great significance to us is now gone. Confronted by this searing absence, we respond in the pain and panic of loneliness.

Loneliness passes judgment on our interpersonal world by signaling that our links with other people are not sustaining us. Sometimes this emotion reminds us of the difficulty we have in making contact—reaching out to another person, even when we want to, is hard. Sometimes we feel estranged from those who are nearby—we do not fit in here, we just do not belong. Often loneliness points out a painful conflict between us and a friend—some important disagreement separates us from one another.

Loneliness makes us question our connections with other people. Perhaps our ties are too few; perhaps they are too superficial. Maybe we are asking too much from people; maybe we are settling for too little. Oddly, the painful emotion of loneliness can be a special ally of intimacy. The distress loneliness brings can serve a good purpose by challenging the illusions we harbor about the place of other people in our lives.

Loneliness, then, is a bad feeling about something good—relationships. The bad feeling works like an alarm, putting us on notice that something is wrong. But too often this powerful emotion causes us to focus solely on ourself. Then our life comes to a halt. As an ally, however, loneliness acts as a warning signal rather than a stop sign. The pain that grabs our attention points beyond itself to an important area of our life that demands scrutiny. By facing this uncomfortable emotion, we can examine the causes of our distress.

Times to Be Lonely

While the feelings of loneliness are common to us all, the circumstances that give rise to these feelings differ in important ways. Most of us recognize loneliness as a common companion. During a quiet evening at home we feel a twinge of sadness or a stirring of regret for being alone. But this mood does not overpower us. We are familiar with this emotion: we simply acknowledge it and turn our attention elsewhere. Knowing the mood will pass, we can be patient with it and with ourself. In this instance, loneliness does not disrupt our life in any serious way. Sociologist Robert Weiss estimates that as much as one quarter of the population feels "extremely lonely" at some time during any given month. For most of us, this experience passes.

However, as loneliness stirs within us, we are frequently tempted to take the emotion too seriously. We make too much of this temporary mood by allowing it to pull us in upon ourself and our pain. Then loneliness escalates into self-pity. By feeling sorry for ourself we neglect the information that our loneliness might bring. For in the mellow mood of loneliness we can savor the separateness of our lives and acknowledge the incomplete-

ness of our relationships. Such a response recognizes the truth of
this emotion but is patient with the transient negative feelings
that accompany it.

But we also experience other types of loneliness. Changing
circumstances, for instance, may trigger *situational* loneliness. A
job transfer takes us away from our hometown. As our initial
excitement subsides, the realization suddenly dawns—we have
left old friends behind! Panic arises and emptiness assaults us:
will we be able to make any friends in this new location? Some
instances of loneliness are easier to deal with because a cause can
be identified: a dear friend dies, leaving an enormous gap in our
life. But in our grief we at least know why we feel lonely. A
significant change has seriously altered our network of sustaining
relationships. We have experienced a clear rupture in our interpersonal world.

Other experiences of loneliness are more *developmental:* the
necessary losses in life trigger this kind of loneliness. When a
young adult leaves home, both child and parent are likely to be
lonely. But this loss is more than situational. Each party of the
separation leaves behind something significant, a part of their
life that will not be regained. Both the young adult's and the
parent's loneliness is tinged with nostalgia for the good old days.
For both, maturity demands a leavetaking of which loneliness is
a normal companion.

The young adult experiences the loneliness of being a stranger
in a strange land. Suddenly she must rely on herself in new and
unfamiliar ways. On some days this experience of independence
exhilarates her. But often she feels alienated from her past and
even from parts of herself because of this new and necessary self-
reliance.

Developmental loneliness can also be part of a reassessment
that comes at midlife. A husband in his early forties feels a growing dismay. He shares a house with his wife and three teenagers,
but he feels strangely alone. Questions plague him about his job:

"Is this really what I want to do for the rest of my life?" He wonders about his relationship with his wife: "What will our life be like when our children are gone?" These questions frighten him and may isolate him from his family. A painful mood of loneliness often accompanies these important midlife reevaluations. He needs to face these questions, not flee them. By finding his own rhythm of letting go and recommitment, he can recover the energy and affection he has lost.

But some loneliness becomes *chronic*. We fall into a mood of alienation and sorrow that seems to have no apparent cause. No special situation, no developmental challenge is involved. We have just slipped into a pervasive mood of estrangement.

This devastating mood often moves us toward self-blame and self-contempt. When we are lonely for a long time, we typically start to blame ourselves rather than the circumstances for the situation. We conclude, "I am alone because I am unattractive and unlovable. I *deserve* to be lonely!" This self-castigation further depletes our energy to do anything to change the situation. We can see no way out, since our wretched self—not the situation—is at fault. A sense of our unworthiness limits any attempt to establish satisfying contacts. In a mood of chronic loneliness we may develop unrealistic expectations about friendships and intimacy. As we long for the ideal partner who would rescue us from this crippling mood, we overlook the familiar companions who could support us.

Lonely Men; Lonely Women

Both men and women experience a need for closeness, a desire to be able to depend on others, a sense of personal vulnerability. But many men have learned that these feelings are unacceptable for the "real man." This conflict between personal needs and cultural demands often leads to an ambivalence about relationships. Afraid to appear vulnerable, a man may hesitate to admit, to himself or others, that he needs other people. This reluctance generates a cautious interpersonal style: he acts somewhat diffident, a bit distant, emotionally cool.

A painful experience of loneliness can shatter these illusions of self-sufficiency. For the man who has been pursuing the cultural ideal of the autonomous and self-sufficient male, the pain reminds him of how he wants and needs other people in his life. Loneliness energizes him to change the way he deals with other people, especially those close to him. This emotion can make a man more respectful of closeness, more grateful for the companions along the journey. Loneliness benefits a man when it encourages him to acknowledge his need for other people and readies him to respond to the requirements of real mutuality.

For many women in American culture, loneliness often invites a different purification. Both men and women learn much about themselves from the responses of people who are close to them; women and men alike depend on relationships for solace and support. However, the evidence of contemporary gender research indicates that many women rely in a special way on their relationships to nourish an adult sense of who they are and what they are worth. This reliance on relationships does not mean that competence and career are meaningless to women. Rather, it signifies that the world of work is not as exclusive a source of personal identity for women as it is for many men.

Typically, then, women develop self-esteem and a sense of security primarily in the give-and-take of the interpersonal world. Most women are keenly aware of how much they need other people. Some women, in fact, carry an overwhelming sense of their psychological dependence on other people and may lament that without a close relationship—particularly a relationship with a man—they feel empty and worthless. What these women are saying is not that they prefer close relationships or that they thrive when their relational world is rich. Instead, they are telling us that apart from a close relationship they do not know who they are. Or, more poignantly, they feel as if they do not exist.

Taken to its extreme, this dependence on relationships leaves a woman convinced that outside a close relationship she will not survive. She fears that her own resources are not sufficient to sustain her. This is more a question of psychic survival than it is of economic survival, even though the crisis is compounded when a woman is unsure that she can earn enough to support herself. Since her sense of self has become so dependent on relationships, the real question is whether there is a "self" that can survive outside these bonds.

Thus, her relationships hold her captive. In a friendship, for example, she cannot risk making demands because she cannot face the possibility that the relationship will end. Even an unhappy association—physically violent or emotionally arid—is better than no relationship at all.

For a woman like this, the distress of loneliness may be an opportunity to examine her relationships more critically, to reassess the imbalance between what she gives and what she receives, to challenge her conviction that she cannot survive on her own. Loneliness then becomes an ally, because not until a relationship disappoints her is she able to question her assumptions. She assumes that she must look outside herself for self-esteem and self-definition because she has no meaning or value on her own. When a relationship disappoints her by not giving her a sense of personal meaning and worth, initially she feels lonely. But if she can face her panic and resist self-destructive behavior, the woman starts to question the basic assumption that she cannot find these essential strengths within herself.

"I can survive on my own!" For many women, this affirmation is a gift of loneliness. With this new strength comes a sense of freedom, as a woman recognizes choices: "I may choose the give-and-take of close relationships, with the personal accommodation and sacrifice that are often required. But I do this because a life of intimacy is worth the trouble; it is rewarding and life-giving even as it is demanding. But I have a choice, since I know that if I have to, I can survive on my own. This makes me freer in my associations. I can be less demanding and more flexible, since my very survival is not at stake as I try to make this relationship work—for both of us."

Loneliness, as a special ally of intimacy, invites us to purify our expectations of other people. This purification equips us for genuine interdependence. For some (men), loneliness helps us become more open to the risks and demands of genuine interdependence. Admitting our vulnerability, we can let others know how important they are to us and how much we need them.

For some (women), loneliness helps us become more confident in our ability to stand apart from the demands of relationships. Acknowledging our strength, we realize that we can care for and sustain ourselves. Recognizing the legitimacy of our needs, we approach those close to us in ways that do not make us subservient and unduly submissive.

Exploring My Interpersonal World

Loneliness sometimes seems so unjustified. "How can I have this empty feeling," we ask ourselves, "when my life seems to be going so well? I have friends, my family appreciates me. So why do I feel so alone?"

We can be well loved and still feel lonely. We can feel lonely in a crowd. These paradoxes remind us of the richness and complexity of our social world. In his comprehensive look at the dynamics of loneliness, psychologist Robert Weiss explores how different kinds of relationships contribute to our lives. For example, we all need people we can count on, no matter what. Whether or not they are blood relatives, these folks are like family to us.

Other relationships bring other benefits: the acceptance we receive from a trusted confidant, the sense of solidarity we feel with people who share our values, the delight we experience as we enjoy an evening with good friends. We are nurtured by the unwavering devotion of our intimates. However, we also need more objective colleagues who can recognize our competence and appreciate our skills. The support of a mentor, the love of our spouse, the affection of our children, the respect of co-workers—each of these gifts comes from a *particular* kind of relationship. These benefits, however, are not interchangeable. A friend's devotion enriches our life, for example, but does not cancel out the isolation we may feel at work.

Loneliness signals a relationship in pain. Relationships come *in particular*, each with different benefits and burdens. When we are lonely, then, our distress points to some inadequacy in a particular part of our relational world. Our anguish over a failed marriage is different, to be sure, from our disappointment that none of our friends share our passion for political reform. But both these experiences can provoke the unease of loneliness— the sense that we are adrift, without the bonds that effectively link our life with others.

To deal effectively with loneliness, we must identify where the pain is pointing. The remedy is easier to find when we know where the hurt is. The reflection exercise at the end of this chapter will help toward an assessment of our interpersonal world.

Invitations to Solitude

The Christian Scriptures command us to love others as we love ourselves. But what if we do not love ourself? Then loneliness becomes especially painful. Using the image of the inner world as a house reveals the connections between loneliness and solitude. In the inner house, there are many rooms and a range of inhabitants. We people our home with good and bad memories; it is furnished with consoling strengths and frustrating weaknesses. Among its many inhabitants are some vulnerable boarders, too —disappointments, guilts, and regrets.

Some days we find ourselves home alone. The silence of this aloneness invites us to take a long look at ourself. Do we like this peculiar person we meet? The experience can be troublesome: we suddenly see a part of ourself that we had successfully avoided. Perhaps we detect a lingering shame we carry concerning our body. We may encounter a painful sense of guilt, uncover the memory of some unforgiven injury. Confronted with this unwelcome guest, what are we to do?

We are tempted to flee. We busy ourselves with more work or turn up the radio or pour another drink. Anything to avoid this painful recognition! But our aloneness presents another possibility: we could face this wounded part of ourself. Gradually, as we become more comfortable with our pain or guilt, we learn to welcome this disowned member of our household.

Doing this, we transform loneliness into solitude. In solitude our aloneness does not panic or punish us. We are at home with the different members of our household. Our home is not a fairy tale abode, filled with illusions. Instead, we have welcomed home some of the regrets and limitations that are part of our life. We no longer need to hide from these mellow companions of our history.

When solitude transforms our loneliness, we can befriend even absence. If we are uncomfortable with the inhabitants of our heart, we will have a difficult time with absence. Any absence —of friends or work or entertainment—will come as an enemy, opening space into which sad or guilty memories flood. Solitude helps us befriend absence. More comfortable with quiet, we treasure time apart. Emptiness becomes a place for all kinds of important activities. The absence that accompanies the death of a friend invites us to accept the loss and begin to build a new presence in our memory. In absence we have the opportunity to feel both gratitude and hope. This empty space gives us the time to be grateful for the people and values that have blessed our life, even as an absence of customary activity impels us to look forward to new relationships in the future.

Anyone who prays regularly must befriend absence, because

some days God's absence is louder than our prayer. But if we have become familiar with absence, God's sometime silence does not discourage us. We remember God's presence in our past and we look forward in hope to God's return. In the time between, we can tolerate the stillness.

Learning from Loneliness

Loneliness invites us to purify our expectations, letting go of those that no longer fit. But for loneliness to serve us, we must learn to both anticipate and appreciate it. We anticipate loneliness by accepting it as an ordinary part of life. This emotion is not an automatic sign of our deficiency, nor is it always terrible and debilitating. It is simply loneliness.

Anticipation also alerts us to the physical demands of loneliness. Part of the mature response to loneliness is to respect these demands and to be good to ourself. This does not mean that we overeat or drink to excess or go on a sexual binge. Being good to ourself can mean that we spend time in activities we enjoy; that we pleasure ourself with a warm bath or comforting massage; that we prepare a special meal; that we write to an understanding friend. In this feasting, we balance the unavoidable fasting that loneliness brings.

We can learn to appreciate loneliness as a potential ally. Loneliness can teach us better ways to be close—ways more appropriate to who we really are, more suited to the people in our lives, more expressive of our own deepest values, more rewarding for us and for our partners.

We appreciate loneliness when we read it properly. Loneliness tells us that our relationships are not working. This painful emotion prods us to look at our life and ask, "Where is this distress pointing? Do I demand more from other people than is realistic? Do I believe that other people should take away all my doubts or fears? Do I expect to always be understood and totally accepted?"

Loneliness urges us to action. Confronted by a relationship in pain, we ask, "What steps do I need to take to develop more satisfying ties between us? Do I need to confront a disagreement that frightens both of us?" Moved by this strong emotion, we expand our range of effective behavior: learning skills of self-disclosure and empathy; finding the courage to face conflict more assertively.

Erik Erikson has spent his life studying those developmental crises "that make patients of us all" and, thus, instruct us in patience. Genuine patience has little to do with passivity or self-pity. A hardier resource, patience steadies us to pay attention to our passion and our pain. The virtue of patience readies us to tolerate our distress long enough to discern its message. At one time or another, the emotion of loneliness makes patients of us all. As good patients, we accept this feeling as an ally of our affections.

REFLECTIVE EXERCISE

Different relationships bless us with different benefits. Consider the range and richness of your own relationships. Begin by listing the persons who belong in the following categories in your own life:

My immediate family and other kin with whom I share life in an ongoing way.

Those who are "like family" for me, people I know I can count on.

Mentors and teachers, who give me support and trustworthy advice.

My intimate friends, who know me well and nourish me with their love and support.

My social companions—people with whom I share leisure time, folks with whom I can enjoy myself and have a good time.

Those whom I care for—my clients, my children—who show me that I am needed and appreciated.

Colleagues who recognize my competence and acknowledge my contribution to projects that go beyond myself.

The groups or communities in which I experience a sense of shared values, the conviction that I "belong."

After you have spent time with these different relationships in your own life, consider these questions:

In which areas of my life are my relationships most fulfilling right now? Take time to savor these relationships and give thanks for the people who enrich your life in these ways.

Where is loneliness most real for me these days, signaling a relationship that is not giving the benefits I need to thrive?

What should be my response? Is my loneliness a call for patience? For purification? For action?

What sources of support are available to me, to help me in my response?

ADDITIONAL RESOURCES

In *Alone in America: The Search for Companionship* (Faber & Faber, 1986), Louise Bernikow identifies stresses in American society that undermine connectedness and offers examples of practical steps that can be taken to reestablish bonds of community and companionship. Robert S. Weiss provides a comprehensive analysis of difficulties in interpersonal attachment in *Loneliness: The Experience of Emotional and Social Isolation* (MIT Press, 1973). John C. Woodward and Janel Queen discuss experiences of loneliness throughout the stages of life; see *The Solitude of Loneliness* (Lexington Books, 1988).

In *Kiss Sleeping Beauty Good-bye* (Harper & Row, 1988), Madonna Kolbenschlag examines the cultural myths and social expectations that often leave women particularly vulnerable to loneliness. Eugene Kennedy reflects on the poignant experience of loneliness in *Loneliness and Everyday Problems* (Image Books/ Doubleday, 1983); see also Paula Ripple's strong and compassionate discussion in *Walking with Loneliness* (Ave Maria Press, 1982).

Sebastian Moore's *The Inner Loneliness* (Crossroad Books, 1982) is a provocative theological consideration of the loneliness of the human condition and the spirituality of an adequate response. In *Beyond Loneliness: A Practical Christian Response* (Twenty-Third Publications, 1986), Edward Wakin and Sean Cooney see loneliness as an important route to self-understanding and identify strategies to assist the reader to explore its personal significance. Robert Neale, in *Loneliness, Solitude and Companionship* (Westminster Press, 1984), examines the essential connections among these three aspects of mature relationships.

Clark E. Moustakas' *Loneliness* (Prentice-Hall, 1961), a now-classic meditation on the links between loneliness and love, has been reprinted many times since its first appearance; see especially his consideration of "The Value of Loneliness." We discuss loneliness and solitude, in the context of an asceticism of self-intimacy, in Chapter 8 of *Seasons of Strength: New Visions of Adult Christian Maturing* (Image Books/Doubleday, 1986).

17.

The Shape of Compassion

> While he was still a long way off, his father
> saw him and was moved with compassion.
> He ran to the boy, embraced him and
> kissed him tenderly. (Luke 15:20)

Jesus tells the story of a wayward son returning to the father he has sorely wronged. The homecoming takes a surprising turn. His father does not respond in anger or hold back until he has received an apology. He seems uninterested in pointing out the error of his son's ways to ensure he has learned his lesson. Instead he rushes out to meet his son, rejoicing in his return. Sensing the boy's humiliation and despair, the father's only concern is to welcome him home. He treats him as an honored guest and plans a great celebration.

This is what God is like, Jesus tells us. God acts toward us not as judge but as *abba*, an extravagantly loving parent. Our care for one another must show the same abundant concern. What God asks of us is not sacrifice but mercy. The lives of the godly will be marked not by the conspicuous good deeds of the righteous, but by the humble compassion of those who respond to the needs of the world.

A Passionate Attachment

Compassion is an experience of intimacy. Ordinarily we think of compassion as commiseration: feeling the suffering of another person. But compassion has a more expansive meaning. With this emotion we enter into all the passions of another—both delight and sorrow, joy and anger. By the bridge of imagination we cross over into another world of feeling. Like empathy, compassion gives us an uncanny capacity to participate in another's inner world, without being engulfed by or fused with that person. We experience with others the excitement of their success; we taste the sorrow that fills another's life. This extraordinary strength, which makes mutuality possible, enables us to enter another's life without intruding on her privacy or manipulating his emotions for our own purposes.

The arousal of compassion includes all the ways that our heart goes out to others. Nature, too, can call forth our compassionate response. Sitting silently on a shore we are drawn slowly into the mood of the breaking waves. Gradually our worry is replaced by another set of feelings. Such compelling awareness of our union with nature and its unhurried rhythms is part of compassion. We share an experience that does not originate in us.

Standing by a polluted stream we feel another emotion, one closer to the ordinary meaning of compassion. Contemplating this damaged resource, we experience regret and sorrow, tinged with a sense of responsibility. Polluting this river dirties our own life. Even if we do not live near the stream, we share its life and its ruin. This mood of regret stirs us to act, to do something to reverse this destruction.

Compassion has special poignancy when it links us to a person in distress. We are drawn to others in their injury and sorrow. The Latin word *misericordia* explains our compassion—we have a heart for those in misery.

But compassion has another dynamic that invites our special

attention. Identifying us with another's loss or pain, compassion makes us vulnerable, puts us at risk. When we are drawn toward an ill person or even a wounded animal, we expose ourselves to their trouble; we come close to something that could harm us; we approach something that could affect our safety. If we could avoid noticing other people's distress, our life would be easier. But compassion opens us to the pain of the world, undermining our security.

This passion challenges the boundaries and barriers that make for a tidy social existence. Ensconced within the firm borders of our ethnic and sexual identity, we need not worry about the problems of others. Race, class, culture separate "us" from "them" and urge us to mind our own business and stay out of other people's affairs. But compassion transgresses these boundaries. We feel the anguish of the battered wife, and we sense the distress of those in prison. Suddenly, the hunger of the famine-stricken, the disorientation of the mentally ill, the frustration of the political outcast become experiences that are not alien. This is dangerous business. Such an arousal may cause us to wonder about the barriers that separate us. Thus, compassion becomes the beginning of justice.

A well-known story in the Hebrew Scriptures exposes the risky dynamic of compassion. The colorful account of King Solomon's wisdom in deciding to which woman a newborn baby belonged (I Kings 3:16–28) is less about the king's wisdom than about a woman's compassion.

Two pregnant women share the same household. Shortly after each delivers a child, one mother rolls over in her sleep, smothering her own baby. Awaking to find her child dead, she exchanges the infants, so that she now holds the surviving child as her own. But she does not fool the other woman, and a fight ensues over the child who is alive. Finally the women plead their case before the sage king. He brings an abrupt and startling verdict: let the child be divided, with each woman having half!

At this the woman who was the mother of the living child addressed the king, for she burned with compassion for her son. "If it please you, my lord," she said, "let them give her the child; only do not let them think of killing it!"

The wise king can now give his real judgment: "Give the child to the first woman," he said, "and do not kill him. She is his mother."

This vivid story describes the inner workings of compassion. A woman is "stirred in her bowels"—the Hebrew word for compassion means, literally, a wrenching feeling in the gut. This visceral arousal responds to a *hidden kinship*: the woman recognizes her own child, though she cannot prove that the infant is hers. King Solomon did not know the child's real kin until the woman's compassion taught him. Compassion leads us to recognize a relationship even with those who are not, on first glance, our relatives. This emotion reminds us of a kinship that we can easily miss.

In her compassion the woman is put at risk. She faces not only her vulnerability before a powerful judge but the possible loss of her child. In the midst of this risky situation we see her compassion leading her to act; she begs the king to give the child away! Her arousal and action bring forth fruit—her child is both spared and returned to her. The woman's compassion makes possible the king's wisdom.

Compassion fails when we allow it to become simply a *private sentiment*. A powerful emotion, compassion is a social instinct that links us to others in feeling and action. By isolating the arousal from effective action we privatize it. Then compassion degenerates into sentimentality. Our emotions are stirred but lead us nowhere. Our tears do not overflow into action; our feelings do not impel us to change anything. They remain stranded in the privacy of our heart. After a good cry, perhaps, we get on with our life. Thus, the rich virtue of compassion flounders in sentiment.

A second way that compassion fails is in pity, which often has about it the taint of condescension. Here our heart goes out in concern for others but in going out, we go down. From a position of moral superiority we "descend" to feel sorry for the less fortunate. Reaching down with pity toward these "lowly" folk, we emphasize and reinforce the differences between us. In Fritz Perl's words, we care for those who are not "our own serious rivals."

Pity does not heal the gap between people, but accentuates it. Our charity and our seeming compassion remind us of our advantage and defend our superiority. We take pity and show mercy to others in a context of no risk. The essential element of compassion—vulnerability—is curiously absent. We help others without identifying with them. Such pity is, at best, compassion compromised.

Learning to Be Kind

Compassion, at first glance, appears to be mostly about intimacy. But this strength also has much to do with justice. Compassionate actions link us in solidarity with those in difficult social straits. These actions help us see through the barriers that separate and isolate us from one another. In crossing these boundaries, compassion opens us to a previously hidden kinship. Compassion reveals the other as our neighbor. Compassion teaches us to be kind.

We can, of course, be kind only to our own kind. We are not kin to aliens or strangers. Many of us have learned to see most other people as foreigners and outsiders. Before compassion can be ignited in our hearts, we need to find a new way of seeing. Often we first have to act "as if" those who are different—an Asian family in the neighborhood, a woman colleague at work, a member of the parish who is developmentally disabled—are, in truth, our kind. When we repeatedly act this way, we perform a kind of magic: these people begin to look like "one of us"; their passions seem very similar to our own. We come to recognize a disguised kinship. Such an insight is an exercise in compassion and is the beginning of justice.

The connections between compassion and kinship become clear in the parable of the Good Samaritan (Luke 10:30–37). A man of Israel lies wounded on the roadside, a victim of highway robbery. Two of his own kind—a priest and a Levite—come upon the stricken man but pass him by. They recognize no kinship with him. He is an inconvenience, a tragic case perhaps, but none of their affair. A third traveler approaches. He belongs to a tribe despised by the Jews; he is a Samaritan, an outsider, an enemy. The foreigner responds with compassion. Moved by the wounded man's plight, the stranger interrupts his journey. He dresses the man's wounds, takes him to an inn, and pays for his care. Ethnic hatred, national rivalry, a heritage of mutual suspicion are set aside in the face of this person's need.

Jesus offered this parable in answer to the question "Who is my neighbor?" He is asked a question about his own kind: "Who has a right to my resources and a claim on my care?" He responds by showing us how a neighbor acts and inviting us to do likewise.

The story Jesus tells is filled with paradox: Where we expect to see group solidarity in action, we find only indifference. Where hostility would not surprise us, we find genuine concern. In the actions of this outsider we see what constitutes kinship. Only he "was moved with compassion when he saw him." Our neighbor, then, is the person in need. Our kind are not just those linked to us by ties of blood or belief. Our kind are all those whose pain and hope we dare open ourselves to share. Compassion creates kinship. To answer the question "Who is my neighbor?" this parable responds: You can become a neighbor by letting yourself be moved to action by another's plight.

More than a surge of sympathy, compassion moves us toward actions that heal. The generosity that stirs us to act toward others as our own kind can set off uncomfortable reflections. Recognizing another's plight, we may come to question how this suffering happened. Compassion may not stop at the level of individual affection and charity. Like empathy, compassion can become a revolutionary emotion. Its arousal can lead us to question social structures and cultural habits that institutionalize injustice and disguise human solidarity. The compassionate recognition of disorder in society can move us to "a blessed rage for order."

The social virtue of compassion places us in a new relationship with the world itself. Theologian Matthew Fox explores this compelling sense of interdependence in *A Spirituality Named Compassion*. According to Fox, this strength and gift allow us to see the interconnectedness of all things, for "compassion is a way of being at home in the universe." This emotion impels us to action. Fox continues: "Compassion is our kinship with the universe and the universe's maker; it is the action we take because of that kinship."

Jesus' life was emphatically about compassion. He made friends of many who seemed aliens: the foreign woman at the well, the tax collector hated by his peers, women of questionable reputation. As he found so many unlikely persons to be his own kind, Jesus continued that special vision of the world that was Israel's heritage. This legacy teaches us that the orphan and the widow are not outcasts, but family; that foreigners and enemies are, finally, part of our community. Jesus called this fragile but persistent vision the kingdom of God. The Christian virtue of compassion impels us to reshape our world according to this vision.

Compassion and Sexuality

We might think that compassion and sexuality would be friends, since both are passionate responses that link us with other people. But, in fact, a fear of sexuality often limits our compassion. Every community—religious and ethnic—develops rules about sexual conduct. The groups we belong to instruct us on the importance of marrying our own kind. We are taught the styles of sexual sharing that are acceptable among us. We learn that those who are sexually "different" must be avoided, even feared.

Fear and avoidance have been especially evident in many cultural and religious responses to homosexuality. Thankfully, however, that is beginning to change. In the Christian community today we hear the first recognitions of the kinship between homosexual and heterosexual believers. Traditionally, religious discussions of homosexuality often degenerated into conversations about "them," alien folk whose lives were consumed (it was said) in perverse and promiscuous behavior. These shadowy "others" were most emphatically excluded from our kind. Defensiveness distracted us from a simple truth, profound in its implications: we are the body of Christ and part of our body is lesbian and gay.

Who are the homosexual members of the body of Christ? They are not "them"; they are us. They are our siblings and our children, our friends and our fellow parishioners. They are persons like us, striving to live generous lives of maturing faith. They are the ministers among us—priests, religious, lay—who, knowing themselves to be gay and lesbian, struggle to serve with integrity in a Church that interprets the movement of their hearts as disordered and shameful.

When we listen well to the lives of these members of the community, we learn what should not be such surprising news: the gay or lesbian person is stirred with the same kind of arousals and attractions that move the heterosexual person. These stirrings, quickened by a smile or a gesture, are more than "near occasions of sin." Like the arousals that stimulate our own loving, they are often occasions of grace.

Arousal is the wellspring of sexuality for all of us—heterosexual and homosexual alike. And for all of us these inclinations are filled with both promise and peril. For both gay and straight persons, these arousals are subject to every conceivable perversion, as the human history of selfishness and sexual violence attests. For all of us—heterosexual, lesbian, gay—questions remain of how we will express our affection and respond to erotic arousal. We each face the challenge of finding a lifestyle and forging fidelities that are both adult and Christian.

The underlying experience of arousal is familiar to all of us—heterosexual and homosexual alike. We share a common passion. But gay and lesbian Catholics have been instructed again and again in official Church documents that—for them—erotic arousal is wrong. Quite apart from decisions about fruitful expression and responsible abstinence (decisions that confront every adult), the inclinations of their heart are judged to be perverse. Their feelings, we are told, do not and cannot resonate with the delight of God's creation. Their emotions are not a part of that human surge of affection that rescues us from our solitary journeys. Some arousals, we are instructed, should have no place in the life of a Christian. The only responsible choice is sexual abstinence, as part of a deeper self-denial.

But a change of heart is taking place in the community of faith, even if this transformation is not yet evident in many official statements. We see its fruit in a new compassion among heterosexual and homosexual Christians. Through compassion, we come to know that for a lesbian to feel erotic delight in the presence of another woman is not unnatural. For her this delight is the most natural feeling imaginable. She may deny these feelings and this denial may grow into a habit of self-hatred. Then she embarks on a life that is truly disordered and unfruitful.

Compassion also helps us recognize that a gay man does not *choose* to set aside his "natural, normal attraction" for women so that he can experience another more perverse kind of sexual excitement. The attraction he feels *is* natural and normal for him.

Spontaneous impulses of arousal and affection are the energetic roots of human love. They can move us toward fidelity and support our efforts to be fruitful. This is so whether we are heterosexual, lesbian, or gay. If these stirrings of the human heart are sordid, we are all in deep trouble.

But if our awareness of homosexuality comes only from media accounts of sexual addiction and promiscuity, we may well have difficulty with compassion. The thought of two men being erotically aroused or two women being sexually engaged may disgust or confuse us. These inclinations seem so foreign; we cannot imagine experiencing them in a way that is healthy or holy. But difficulty with compassion may have a more complicated origin. A young heterosexual man in high school or in the military, for example, may have a confusing sexual encounter with another man. This experience, not in accord with his own sexual orientation, may have been influenced by alcohol or other pressures. The memory lingers with him, accompanied by strong feelings of guilt and shame. When he thinks of sexual intimacy between men, he imagines disturbing experiences like the one he had. Unable to enter into someone else's feelings, he instead substitutes his own painful memories. This, of course, is not empathy but projection. Preoccupation with his own distress clouds his vision and defeats compassion.

Community and Compassion

Where do we learn compassion? How does this virtue begin to grow in our life? The answer to both questions is, of course, in Christian community. In prayer groups and ministry networks, in base communities and other small group settings, believing people experience community in practical and profound ways. As our lives intersect in these gatherings of faith, we come to know each other more deeply. And we begin to learn about each other's enduring hopes and lingering wounds. Sharing these experiences of grace and failure, we participate in one another's passion. We touch lives so different from our own but, in their fragility and faith, so similar.

For many heterosexual Christians compassion takes root when we share the faith journey of a gay friend or lesbian colleague. In this sharing we learn that their attractions and delights are very much like our own: we know the same excitement at the possibility of love and the same terror that devotion might not endure. The lesbian couple in our prayer group hopes to find fidelity and fruitfulness in love, as do the rest of us. The priest who is gay struggles to mature in his sexuality, just as the priest does who is heterosexual. All of us know that holiness does not lie in a denial of our sexuality, but in a discipline that is closer to befriending.

Compassion protects us from equating fruitfulness with biological fertility. A homosexual couple's inability to bear children is sometimes taken as a sure sign that their love is selfish. Our daily experiences in the community of faith tell us something quite different. Here we meet single adults and childless couples whose lives are profoundly fruitful. And, sadly, we sometimes meet married persons with many children but little generosity, whose lives seem sterile and self-centered. In the Christian community, too, we can meet gay and lesbian couples who are deeply generous, whose shared love bears fruit for them and for the world.

But we can avoid these gifts of community. Sexuality can remain a taboo topic, to be discussed—if at all—only within the established guidelines. "I don't know any homosexuals," we insist, oblivious to the sisters and brothers who daily intersect our well-defended lives.

In the practical interplay of Christian community, we learn

the shape of one another's hopes and passions. As we speak the truth to one another we recognize that, in our sexuality as in so much else, we are more alike than we are different. Then a conviction grows among us that homosexual arousal is not unnatural or unholy; it is part of the gift of creation, a sign of God's delight in our bodies. This emerging sense of the faithful does not ignore the responsibility we all share to fashion faithful and fruitful ways to express our love. But it does acknowledge that, in any credible discussion of the shape of Christian sexuality, we must honor the seasoned experience of mature homosexuals.

Through compassion we learn that we are more alike than different, whether woman or man, Hispanic or Anglo, heterosexual or homosexual. To our Christian identity what matters most is not sexual orientation or ethnic origin or gender. What marks us as followers of Jesus is our behavior. From the first century onward Christians provoked the response "See how they love one another!" The fruitfulness of this love is recognized in its respect, generosity, and fidelity. Today the Churches struggle to have their stance toward Christian homosexuals shaped by such compassion.

REFLECTIVE EXERCISE

Reflect for a moment on your own experience of compassion. Recall a recent concrete example, a particular event or exchange in which you were moved—physically, emotionally, intellectually —by another's plight. Spend time bringing the experience to life again: the setting, the reality of the other person, your own thoughts and feelings and behavior. Perhaps take some notes for yourself. Then turn to these questions:

How were the demands of compassion real for you in this instance? Did you feel vulnerable? What was at risk for you here? What invitations for change did the experience hold?

Can you trace the connections between emotion and action

here? Did your compassion find expression? What attitudes were part of your concern? What actions expressed your care?

As you reflect now, what is the most striking feature in this experience of compassion? What affected you most at that time? What seems most significant as you think of it today?

ADDITIONAL RESOURCES

For an excellent study of compassion and its implications for our sexual, psychological and social lives, see Matthew Fox's *A Spirituality Named Compassion* (Winston Press, 1979). Henri Nouwen, Donald McNeill, and Douglas Morrison provide a Christian meditation on compassion and social justice in *Compassion* (Image Books/Doubleday, 1982). Joan Puls expands the reflection in *A Spirituality of Compassion* (Twenty-Third Publications, 1988). South African theologian Albert Nolan discusses compassion as the central experience in the life of Jesus in *Jesus Before Christianity* (Orbis Books, 1978). Elizabeth Janeway explores empathy as a revolutionary power in her *Powers of the Weak* (Knopf, 1980), pp. 154 and following.

In *Gay, Straight, and In Between* (Johns Hopkins University Press, 1988), John Money presents a comprehensive discussion of the findings of current medical and psychological research concerning homosexuality. Vincent Genovesi provides a careful review of recent Catholic moral thinking on homosexuality in *In Pursuit of Love* (Michael Glazier, 1987); see Chapter 7. For a brief, compassionate look at this question, see Edward Vacek's "A Christian Homosexuality?" in *Commonweal* (December 5, 1980), pp. 681–84. In *Another Kind of Love* (Knoll, 1988), Richard Woods calls for creative pastoral responses toward gay and lesbian members of the community of faith.

In *A Faith of One's Own* (Crossing Press, 1986), Barbara Zanotti brings together the moving testimony of Catholic lesbians as they explore the connections between faith and sexuality.

John McNeill's now classic *The Church and the Homosexual* (Beacon Press, 1988) has recently been reissued. For a comprehensive consideration of the theological and pastoral issues involved, see *A Challenge to Love: Gay and Lesbian Catholics in the Church* (Crossroad Books, 1983), edited by Robert Nugent.

18.

Gratitude—A Necessary Feast

I have been tutoring Dolores for about six months. Mostly we work on her English assignments. Often, of course, we will talk about her hopes for college and what kind of career she might pursue after that. It's a delight to watch the world open up for her! I think she is finally beginning to believe that she has more talent than she had previously suspected.

Last Wednesday, walking home from a tutoring session, I was surprised by a powerful memory: Suddenly I was in seventh grade again. My teacher, Sister Mary Rose, was encouraging me to spend more time with my writing. I could remember her leaning over my desk. What a taskmaster she was! No deviation in grammar or spelling ever slipped by without comment. I felt again, with a pleasant shock, that aura of affection and strength that she carried.

The sounds of traffic brought me back from my daydreaming —but not completely. I realized for the first time how Sister Mary Rose was touching Dolores through me. I felt *connected* to them both in a new and exciting way.

Memory is the natural habitat of gratitude. We recall the gifts we have received, and we give thanks. We savor our connections with those who have cared for and protected and encouraged us. Sociologist Georg Simmel has described gratitude as "a kind of moral memory of mankind that binds together those who have exchanged gifts." Gratitude is an arousal of intimacy that keeps community alive.

Gratitude stands at the heart of the religious vision of Jews and Christians. Our worship is an expression of gratitude: we give thanks for creation and for all God's gifts. At the feasts of Passover and Easter we thank God for delivering our ancestors from slavery and for instilling in us the promise of freedom. The most significant liturgical action of the Christian community is Eucharist—thanksgiving. In this final chapter we will explore this passionate, affective bond we call gratitude.

A World of Gifts

In his wonderful book *The Gift*, Lewis Hyde examines the social experience of gratitude. We will draw on his discussion as we return to two concerns that have been central to this book: how eros links us to our past and our future and how sexuality and Christian spirituality are connected.

Hyde begins by distinguishing a market economy from a gift economy. In a market economy we struggle to accumulate, to earn profit, and to save. A very different force is at play in a gift economy: we are more interested in giving and in letting go of what we have. In place of profit we look for fruit. A market economy depends on scarcity: the luxury car and Rolex watch lose their value if many others have them. A gift economy depends on abundance: gifts shared are multiplied and not spent; affections given away are not lost. The exchange of goods and commodities builds a business; the exchange of gifts creates a community. In every culture these economies overlap and complement each other, but their very different energies can teach us about both sexuality and spirituality.

The peculiar nature of a gift, Hyde reminds us, is that it must

be continually given away: "It is kept alive by its constant donation." As we receive gifts—such as our own life, our talents,
deepening love—we must hand them on. To hoard our gifts or
to take them out of circulation is to defeat the gift economy. We
do this when we see our own life as our private affair: we forget
where our life comes from and we plan to enjoy it by ourself. As
we become absorbed in our rights and privileges, we forget to be
either grateful or generous.

The constant movement of gifts, what Hyde calls "a gift exchange," links us with both our past and our future. Grateful for
gifts received, we learn to give: we become generous. Thus, we
create a world where a Christian spirituality can flourish.

According to Hyde, the gift economy is an *erotic* exchange.
Gifts are erotic in at least three ways. First, gifts set off a dynamic
of attraction and union—the concerns of eros. We want to give
gifts to those to whom we are close. And when we exchange
gifts, we draw closer to one another. Second, the giving of a gift
elicits emotions, while the purchase of market goods is ideally
done coolly, without emotion. When we give gifts, gratitude and
generosity forge an emotional bond between us. This is the realm
of eros. Third, gifts are erotic because in losing them the giver is
satisfied, not emptied. When we let go of a gift—of love or
knowledge or talent—we are not diminished, but expanded. Giving does not bring about scarcity, but the realization that we live
amid abundance. Any kind of generosity reminds us of the lesson of eros: we have more than enough love to go around; we
need not hoard our allowance of friends; we can afford to share
the good gifts of the world. Christians recognize here the religious vision of a creation overflowing with gifts that move us to
both gratitude and generosity.

The Good Gift

Not all the things we are given come as true gifts. If the good gift
sets us free, we also become aware of other exchanges. Some

kinds of giving bind us in an indebtedness that cripples us; others entrap us in a demeaning dependency. In each our soul is shriveled rather than expanded.

A false gift carries a hidden price. Accepting the donation, we find ourselves obligated to the giver. Sometimes the gift comes as a "reward." Only later do we see that the reward is meant to be an incentive, urging us to become partner to someone else's plans. What is given comes not from generosity but out of a desire to control.

Gift giving can be perverted in ways that turn gratitude into servitude. The seemingly harmless aspiration of parents or teachers that those in their care will "make them proud" often ends in injury to all parties. A young person labors valiantly to please, to be worthy of the gifts received. In this setting, gratitude is measured in meeting someone else's expectations. The receiver of such a gift finds herself saying, "If I am really grateful, I will do what they want. I will make them proud of me!"

A good gift is "a yoke that is sweet and a burden that is light." It is given not to extract our dependence or even to elicit gratitude. Freely given, a good gift sets us free. A true gift sets the recipient free from false guilt. Without any hidden hooks, it does not bind us to the giver's hopes for us. The genuine gift, let go by the giver, becomes truly *ours*. We remember where the gift comes from, but this memory does not enslave us or inhibit our preparing to hand on the gift.

The good gift also sets us free from fear. A gift economy teaches us the mysterious and inexhaustible wealth of gifts in the world. We learn that we have an endless potential to make new life and to perform acts of charity and generosity. Most mysterious of all, we find that giving gifts does not deplete us. When we give away a gift, we are not diminished. But this extraordinary economy of giving is always threatened by another economy which argues that the other's gain is our loss. In such a world we have to cling to what we have. We need to hoard and defend our goods and gifts. If we give anything, we must receive adequate compensation. In this economy, fear acts like a fierce watchdog. Keenly aware of scarcity and the perils of supply and demand, we keep checking our larder or our bank account. A genuine gift reminds us of a different vision. The gospel judgment that "perfect love casts out fear" is amplified: the good gift casts out fear.

A genuine gift rescues us from loneliness. This mood of isolation often occurs when we wrench ourselves away from a bond that felt like bondage. We broke away from a dependency on a parent, a friend, or a lover, because the relationship was erected on false gifts. Now we are free, but alone. Having severed ourself from such stifling links, we ask, "How do we form new bonds? What if all human connections are bondage? What if all gifts end by enslaving us?"

The good gift shows us another style of bonding. Because the generous giver lets go of the gift, we are free of compensation and restitution. We are free, but still bound—in gratitude. But this is a bonding of delight rather than constraint. And our delight turns us in two directions. We rush back to the giver with freely offered gratitude; we give thanks to God and to others who have cared for us. And we turn to the future to give gifts in the same way. The generosity we have experienced wants to be reproduced. We are not obliged to become gift givers ourself, but the vision of sharing attracts and invites us. These kinds of gifts teach us to be generous. And in our generosity we forge new and fruitful links with others.

A Community of the Generous

Being grateful lifts us out of ourselves. Gratitude locates us where we belong, on the path of generosity that leads from the previous generation to the next. We recognize that we dwell in a community of giving. We can experience a new intimacy with both our benefactors and our beneficiaries.

A community of gifts can become a gathering place for the

generous. A group that lives under contract must be concerned about rules of exchange and the binding structures of constraint. However, the community of the generous lives by covenant, the free and responsible bestowal of gifts. The world of contracts teaches us the important lessons of duty and obligation. But in the world of covenant we learn to trace the connections between gratitude and generosity.

Gratitude invites us to a constant conversion. The interdependence of a vital community reminds us that we are not the owners of our abilities or our ideals. Our hold on these parts of our life is more mysterious than that of possession and control. We are stewards of gifts received, not owners. The best gifts cannot become private possessions, because the gift must always move in order to be shared. The labor of gratitude reminds us that, in Hyde's words, "our gifts are not fully ours until they have been given away." This insight is the heart of generosity.

Gratitude binds us to the gift and to its giver—a parent or friend or God. The goal of gratitude is not to fully repay the debt, since this is impossible. What would be an appropriate price to pay for the gift of our life? How would we determine the fair market price for our good health or the going rate of an abiding friendship? Gratitude instead awakens us to the graciousness of the giver and prepares us to be similarly generous. Being grateful moves us to do more than give thanks; we are eager to hand on the gift we have received. The ultimate act of gratitude is generosity.

Here eros and Christian spirituality embrace. Both teach us about a world of gifts to which we are heirs. Both instruct us in the labor of gratitude and the virtue of generosity. Both induct us into a community of gift givers: an assembly of passionate and responsible adults whose lives witness to the truth that, to echo Meister Eckhart, "the fruitfulness of a gift is the only gratitude for the gift."

The Gifts of Sexuality

Many discussions of sexuality focus on imperatives and prohibitions: things we ought to do and actions we must avoid. But for Christians the first and final word must be gratitude. Christians celebrate sexuality as one of our greatest gifts. In this concluding thanksgiving we will recall four dynamics of sexuality that merit another word of gratitude: passion, commitment, faithfulness, and fruitfulness.

PASSION

We are, first of all, grateful for our arousals. We are thankful for the gift of passion. Philosopher Martin Heidegger reminds us that our passions tune us into the world. Deprived of them, we fall out of touch with life. The energy of our anger urges us to confront injustice; the force of our fear warns us of important dangers; our arousals of affection lure us in the direction of friends and lovers.

Our passions unsettle us, but they are necessary disturbances. They link us, vitally, to other persons and important values. Their energy may confuse us, but we cannot do without them.

The importance of this gift of arousal becomes painfully apparent in its absence. At some time we may enter a period of boredom or depression. No person attracts our attention; no values excite us; no conviction ignites us. Passion has been drained from our life. In a time like this we yearn to be aroused. In our solitude, we await the return of passion.

When we fall in love, we learn more about the gift of passion. Before falling in love, we may have been bewildered and even ashamed of our sexual arousal. We did not know what to do about it. And we may have learned that sexual passion is sinful. Now, with this loving partner, we begin to learn about its goodness. In the coming years through the discipline of eros we will learn the range and limits of our shared passion. We will learn about failure and vulnerability, about communion and delight. And we will learn about fasting from and feasting on this fruitful arousal. And hopefully, in all this we may come to recognize our passion as a gift from God.

COMMITMENT

Christians are also grateful for the commitments to which our arousals lead. The special gift of passion is that it moves us toward other people: it entices us to draw near to others, to espouse an important cause, to extend a willing hand. Then another gift is called for: the ability to leap, to commit ourself to this person or value. This risky movement is a response to arousal; in commitment we become responsible. Commitment moves beyond the immediacy of passion into the future realm of promises. As we saw in Chapter 4, the gamble of a commitment is that it leads us beyond the present. In a commitment we promise ourselves for the future—a time that escapes our control. And we know that commitment does not operate like a factory warranty. A commitment is less a guarantee than a pledge. In a commitment we hold ourself accountable to do *whatever is necessary* to realize this promise. We are building a stable place where our passion can grow and bear fruit. In these promises of love, eros begins its lessons in generosity.

We see the strength of this gift in its absence. A person is attracted to many different people. He likes each of them, but can choose no one as a partner. Each is somehow lacking, not quite right for him. Or a person is drawn toward several service organizations. They all have appealing values and admirable members. But each has problems and drawbacks. She finds she can give herself to none of them. Such persons remain detached. At different times they become excited by new ideas or aroused by new companions. But passion never leads to commitment. Finally the person is left alone. Pained by its absence, we give thanks for the gracious appearance of commitment in our lives.

FAITHFULNESS

Aroused by affection we are foolhardy enough to make promises. To our surprise we find that we are hardy enough to keep them. This is the third cause for our gratitude: the ability to be faithful. The high energy of romance propels us into commitments of love and work. As romance matures, we face the challenge of fidelity: learning how to keep our promises. On the journey of a maturing friendship or marriage we stumble over our conflicts and failures. With frustrating regularity, we let each other down. But we also learn to forgive and to accept forgiveness. We begin again. We are introduced to the fine art of compromise. We gradually shed the illusions and expectations that were necessary at the beginning of the journey but that have now become burdensome. If we are fortunate, we come to know better the real person—particular and peculiar—with whom we pledged our future.

The biggest discovery about fidelity is its flexibility. We have committed ourself to a person who keeps growing and changing. We are trying to be faithful not so much to another individual as to a shared journey, a journey pursued on a moving planet. Agility becomes the requisite for such fidelity. Christians come to expect this flexibility when they realize that their own life, their vocation, is not a single, unambiguous call ("Follow this career; marry this person!"), but a lifelong conversation with God. We continue to be revealed to ourself; we keep finding out who we are and who we might become. Fidelity is not found in a rigid adherence to a single message. Fidelity is achieved within an ongoing conversation.

Traveling together in a mutual commitment, each of us is also keeping conversation with God. Our lives build a network of commitments with overlapping fidelities. We catch a painful glimpse of this complexity when a commitment fails. Not every promise survives. A man finds himself in a religious congregation that is stagnating, unable to adapt to new challenges in the Church. After much prayer and counsel he leaves this group to whom he had pledged his life. A woman faces a marriage that is growing more abusive and violent. With her children she determines to leave this life commitment. For each of these people an important journey ends but another faithfulness endures. In the midst of failure and disappointment, their life conversation with God and their commitment to their own integrity survives.

In these shaky transitions, Christian care has often faltered. Theology has at times given in to the temptation to identify the life commitment of a marriage with a person's faithfulness to God. The failure of one seems to include the failure of the other; then a community feels justified in shunning the divorced as faithless sinners. Looking more closely we see many divorced persons, purified by their loss, growing stronger and more faithful to God. We start to see how promises can end while faithfulness endures. The genuine failure of fidelity occurs when a person can keep no promises. Neither friends nor children nor God can hold their attention as they move from one short-lived enthusiasm to another. Aware of the failure of such a life we give thanks for the fragile gift of our faithfulness.

FRUITFULNESS

Finally we are grateful that love proves to be so fruitful. When we fall in love, we taste its first fruits. Our sexual passion had previously been so self-centered—all its energy seemed focused on ourselves. Suddenly, in the blossoming of love, we are delivered from this self-absorption. Passion finds a partner and, in this discovery, becomes a gift. We know the delight of pleasuring another person. Hesitantly we allow ourself to receive the gift of pleasure.

These first fruits of intimacy spill over into other gifts. As friendship deepens, we undergo a surprising healing. Perhaps old wounds made us suspicious, leading us to interpret every advance as manipulative; perhaps an innate shyness paralyzed us whenever we came close to others. Now another person's affection loosens our heart and robs us of the excuses that protected our lonely privacy. As we are healed, we are revealed. A friend or lover shows us to ourself. We thought we knew ourself but much lay hidden still: strengths we could not trust; fears we would not acknowledge. The fruitful passion of love gently uncovers these parts of ourself. We are exposed by love, and we are not ashamed.

The special magic of love is, of course, that it makes more of itself. "Making love" we make more life—between us and beyond us. When our love generates new life in children, we are astonished and grateful. This is more than our doing! At first, we may see this new life as a "reproduction"—a new version of us. Then we learn the mellow lesson of fruitfulness: this "reproduction" is very different from us, a separate person with new dreams and yet-unheard-of plans. Our child is a gift of God to the world; our role has been to help this happen.

The labor of gratitude, as Lewis Hyde said so well, is generosity. Our thankfulness is transformed into generous action. Gifted, we learn to give gifts; grateful, we grow generous. And generosity's final gift is letting go—of friends who have to leave and of children who must grow up. The gift must keep on giving. We cannot package it or protect it from the future. If we are fully blessed, we come to accept this mystery. Even as we let go of our own life we are grateful. The final word is thanks.

REFLECTIVE EXERCISE

We have all received gifts that free us and gifts that bind us. In this exercise we invite you to recall an important example of each of these gifts.

Remember, first, a gift that became a heavy burden in your life. Recall the gift and its giver. How did you begin to recognize its hidden obligation? What was the feeling that accompanied that realization? How did you deal with this gift?

Now recall a gift that came to you with no strings attached. Who was the giver of this gift? What feelings were aroused in you by the giving? Did this gift hold any surprises? How did you experience gratitude? How did you express it? Can you trace the ways that this good gift has made you generous?

ADDITIONAL RESOURCES

Lewis Hyde presents a wonderful and detailed exploration of giving and gratitude in *The Gift* (Vintage, 1983). In *Guilt and Gratitude* (Greenwood Press, 1982), John Amato examines the intriguing dynamics that link these two passions. For further discussion of gratitude, see Gilbert Meilaender's *The Theory and Practice of Virtue* (Notre Dame University Press, 1984) and Georg Simmel's "Faithfulness and Gratitude," in *The Sociology of Georg Simmel* (Free Press, 1950), especially pp. 379–95.

BIBLIOGRAPHY

Abbott, Walter M., ed. *The Documents of Vatican II.* New York: America Press, 1966.

Adler, Alfred. *Co-operation Between the Sexes.* Edited and translated by Heinz and Rowena Asbacher. New York: Norton, 1978.

"Affectivity and Sexuality." *Studies in the Spirituality of Jesuits* X: 2–3 (March–May 1978).

Amato, John. *Guilt and Gratitude.* Westport, Conn.: Greenwood Press, 1982.

Anzia, Joan Meyer, and Mary G. Durkin. *Marital Intimacy: A Catholic Perspective.* Chicago: Loyola University Press, 1982.

Aquinas, Thomas. *Summa Contra Gentiles.* Translated by Vernon J. Bourke and Charles J. O'Neill. Notre Dame, Ind.: Notre Dame Press, 1975.

Augustine of Hippo. *The Confessions.* Edited and translated by John K. Ryan. Garden City: N.Y. Image Books/Doubleday, 1960.

Balducelli, Roger. "The Apostolic Origins of Clerical Continence: A Critical Appraisal of a New Book." *Theological Studies* 43 (1982): 693–705.

Bankson, Marjory Zoet. *Seasons of Friendship: Naomi and Ruth as a Pattern.* San Diego: Luramedia, 1987.

Baruch, Grace, Rosalind Barnett, and Caryl Rivers. *Life Prints: New Patterns of Love and Work for Today's Women.* New York: New American Library, 1983.

Bernard, Jesse. *The Future of Marriage.* New Haven: Yale University Press, 1982.

Bernikow, Louise. *Alone in America: The Search for Companionship.* New York: Faber & Faber, 1986.

Brown, Peter. *Augustine of Hippo.* Los Angeles: University of California Press, 1967.

Butler, Robert N., and Myrna L. Lewis. *Love and Sex After Forty: A Guide for Men and Women for Their Mid and Late Years.* New York: Harper & Row, 1986.

Cahill, Lisa Sowle. *Between the Sexes: Foundations for a Christian Ethics of Sexuality.* New York: Paulist Press, 1985.

Callam, Daniel. "Clerical Continence in the Fourth Century: Three Papal Decretals." *Theological Studies* 41 (1980): 3–50.

Campbell, Susan M. *Beyond the Power Struggle.* San Luis Obispo, Calif.: Impact Books, 1984.

———. *The Couple's Journey: Intimacy as a Path to Wholeness.* San Luis Obispo, Calif.: Impact Books, 1980.

Cancian, Francesca M. *Love in America: Gender and Self-development.* New York: Cambridge University Press, 1987.

Carnes, Patrick. *Out of the Shadows: Understanding Sexual Addiction.* Minneapolis: CompCare Publishers, 1983.

Carr, Anne. *Transforming Grace: Christian Tradition and Women's Experience.* San Francisco: Harper & Row, 1986.

Chodorow, Nancy. *The Reproduction of Mothering: Psychoanalysis and the Sociology of Gender.* Berkeley: University of California Press, 1978.

Coates, Jennifer. *Men, Women and Language.* White Plains, N.Y.: Longman, 1986.

Colwill, Nina. *The New Partnership: Women and Men in Organizations.* Chicago: Mayfield, 1982.

Conn, Joann Wolski, ed. *Women's Spirituality: Resources for Christian Development.* New York: Paulist Press, 1987.

Covington, Stephanie, and Liana Beckett. *Leaving the Enchanted Forest: The Path from Relationship Addiction.* San Francisco: Harper & Row, 1988.

Cowan, Michael. "Sons and Lovers in a Patriarchical Predicament," *Journal of Pastoral Counseling* XXII (1987): 46–64.

Crossan, John Dominic. *Cliffs of Fall.* New York: Seabury Press, 1980.

———. *In Parables: The Challenge of the Historical Jesus.* San Francisco: Harper & Row, 1973.

Curran, Charles. *Themes in Fundamental Moral Theology.* Notre Dame, Ind.: University of Notre Dame Press, 1977.

Dominian, Jack. *The Capacity to Love.* New York: Paulist Press, 1985.

———. *Marriage, Faith and Love.* New York: Crossroad Books, 1982.

Donnelly, Doris. *Putting Forgiveness into Practice.* 5th ed. Nashville: Abingdon Press, 1986.

Driver, Tom F. "Speaking from the Body." In *Theology and Body,* edited by John Y. Fenton. Philadelphia: Westminster Press, 1974, pp. 100–26.

Durkin, Mary G. *Feast of Love: Pope John Paul II on Human Intimacy.* Chicago: Loyola University Press, 1984.

———. *Guidelines for Contemporary Catholics: Sexuality.* Chicago: Thomas More Press, 1987.

Egan, Gerard. *The Skilled Helper.* 3d ed. Monterey, Calif.: Brooks/Cole, 1985.

———. *You and Me: Skills of Communicating and Relating to Others.* Monterey, Calif.: Brooks/Cole, 1977.

Eichenbaum, Luise, and Susie Orbach. *Between Women: Love, Envy, and Competition in Women's Friendships.* New York: Viking, 1987.

———. *Understanding Women.* New York: Basic Books, 1983.

Erikson, Erik. *Childhood and Society.* 2d ed. New York: Norton, 1963.

———. *Insight and Responsibility.* New York: Norton, 1964.

———. *The Life Cycle Completed: A Review.* New York: Norton, 1982.

———. *Toys and Reasons.* New York: Norton, 1977.

———, Joan M. Erikson, and Helen Q. Kivnick. *Vital Involvement in Old Age.* New York: Norton, 1986.

Farley, Margaret. *Personal Commitment: Beginning, Keeping, Changing.* San Francisco: Harper & Row, 1986.

Faul, John, and David Augsburger. *Beyond Assertiveness.* Waco, Tex. Word Books, 1980.

Fausto-Sterling, Anne. *Myths of Gender: Biological Theories About Women and Men.* New York: Basic Books, 1985.

Ferder, Fran. *Words Made Flesh: Scripture, Psychology and Human Communication.* Notre Dame, Ind.: Ave Maria Press, 1986.

Filene, Peter G. *Him/Her/Self: Sex Roles in Modern America.* 2d ed. Baltimore: Johns Hopkins University Press, 1986.

Fink, Peter E., ed. *Reconciliation.* Collegeville, Minn.: Liturgical Press, 1987.

Fiske, Marjorie, and Lawrence Weiss. "Intimacy and Crises in Adulthood." In *Counseling Adults,* edited by Nancy K. Schlossberg and Alan D. Entine. Monterey, Calif.: Brooks/Cole, 1977, pp. 19–33.

Fox, Matthew. *Original Blessing.* Santa Fe: Bear and Company, 1983.

————. *A Spirituality Named Compassion.* Minneapolis: Winston Press, 1979.

Gaylin, Willard. *Feelings: Our Vital Signs.* New York: Ballantine, 1979.

————. *Rediscovering Love.* New York: Viking, 1987.

Genovesi, Vincent. *In Pursuit of Love: Catholic Morality and Human Sexuality.* Wilmington, Del.: Michael Glazier, 1987.

Gilligan, Carol. *In a Different Voice.* Cambridge, Mass.: Harvard University Press, 1982.

Goergen, Donald. *The Sexual Celibate.* New York: Seabury Press, 1974.

Greeley, Andrew. *Sexual Intimacy.* Chicago: Thomas More Press, 1982.

Harrison, Beverly Wildund. *Making the Connections—Essays in Feminist Social Ethics.* Edited by Carol S. Robb. Boston: Beacon Press, 1985.

Haughey, John C. *The Faith that Does Justice.* New York: Paulist Press, 1977.

————. *The Holy Use of Money.* Garden City, N.Y.: Doubleday, 1986.

Haughton, Rosemary. "The Meaning of Marriage in Women's New Consciousness." In *Commitment to Partnership,* edited by Willian Roberts. New York: Paulist Press, 1987, pp. 141–54.

Helldorfer, Martin, ed. *Sexuality and Brotherhood.* Lockport, Ill.: Christian Brothers National Office, 1977.

Heller, Jim, John Reid, and Mary Savoie. *The Gospel Call to Collaborative Ministry.* Mesa, Ariz.: National Association for Lay Ministry, 1987.

Henchal, Michael J., ed. *Repentance and Reconciliation in the Church.* Collegeville, Minn.: Liturgical Press, 1987.

Huddleston, Mary Anne. *Celibate Loving.* New York: Paulist Press, 1984.

Hyde, Lewis. *The Gift: Imagination and the Erotic Life of Property.* New York: Vintage Books, 1983.

Illich, Ivan. *Gender.* New York: Pantheon, 1982.

Israel, Martin. *Living Alone.* New York: Crossroad Books, 1983.

Janeway, Elizabeth. *Powers of the Weak.* New York: Knopf, 1980.

Josselson, Ruthellen. *Finding Herself: Pathways to Identity Development in Women.* San Francisco: Jossey-Bass, 1987.

Juergensmeyer, Mark. *Fighting Fair.* San Francisco: Harper & Row, 1986.

Keane, Philip. *Sexual Morality: A Catholic Perspective.* New York: Paulist Press, 1978.

Keen, Sam. *The Passionate Life.* San Francisco: Harper & Row, 1983.

Kelsey, Martin and Barbara Kelsey. *Sacrament of Sexuality: The Spirituality and Psychology of Sex.* Warwick, N.Y.: Amity House, 1986.

Kennedy, Eugene. *Free to Be Human.* Garden City, N.Y.: Image Books/ Doubleday, 1987.

―――. *Loneliness and Everyday Problems.* Garden City, N.Y.: Image Books/Doubleday, 1983.

―――. *On Being a Friend.* New York: Ballantine, 1982.

―――. *Sexual Counseling: A Practical Guide for Non-professional Counselors.* New York: Continuum Books, 1980.

―――. *A Time for Love.* Garden City, N.Y.: Image Books/Doubleday, 1987.

Kohn, Alfie. *No Contest: The Case Against Competition.* New York: Houghton Mifflin, 1986.

Kolbenschlag, Madonna. *Kiss Sleeping Beauty Good-bye.* New ed. San Francisco: Harper & Row, 1988.

Landgraf, John R. *Creative Singlehood and Pastoral Care.* Philadelphia: Fortress Press, 1982.

Lawyer, John W., and Neil H. Katz. *Communication Skills for Ministry.* Dubuque: Kendall/Hunt, 1983.

Lee, Bernard. "The Appetite of God." In *Religious Experience and Process Theology,* edited by Harry Cargas and Bernard Lee. New York: Paulist Press, 1976, pp. 369–84.

―――, and Michael A. Cowan. *Dangerous Memories: House Churches and Our American Story.* Kansas City: Sheed & Ward, 1986.

Leonard, Cargan, and Matthew Melko. *Singles: Myths and Realities.* New York: Sage Publications, 1982.

Lewis, C. S. *The Four Loves.* New York: Harcourt Brace Jovanovich, 1960.

McCary, James. *Human Sexuality.* 3d ed. New York: Van Nostrand, 1978.

McNamara, Jo Ann. *A New Song: Celibate Women in the First Three Christian Centuries.* New York: Hawthorne Press, 1983.

McNeill, John J. *The Church and the Homosexual*. 3d ed. Boston: Beacon Press, 1988.

Mace, David. *A Male Grief: Notes on Pornography and Addiction*. Minneapolis: Milkweed Editions, 1987.

May, Rollo. *Love and Will*. New York: Norton, 1969.

Meilaender, Gilbert. *The Theory and Practice of Virtue*. Notre Dame, Ind.: Notre Dame Press, 1984.

Miles, Margaret. *Fullness of Life*. Philadelphia: Westminster Press, 1981.

Miller, Jean Baker. *Toward a New Psychology of Women*. 2d ed. Boston: Beacon Press, 1987.

Miller, Stuart. *Men and Friendship*. Boston: Houghton Mifflin, 1983.

Money, John. *Gay, Straight, and In Between*. Baltimore: Johns Hopkins University Press, 1988.

————. *Love and Love Sickness*. Baltimore: Johns Hopkins University Press, 1980.

Montague, Ashley. *Touching: The Human Significance of Skin*. 2d ed. San Francisco: Harper & Row, 1978.

Moore, Sebastian. *The Inner Loneliness*. New York: Crossroad Books, 1982.

Moustakas, Clark E. *Loneliness*. Englewood Cliffs, N.J.: Prentice-Hall, 1984.

Murphy, Roland. "Song of Songs." In *The Jerome Biblical Commentary*. Englewood Cliffs, N.J.: Prentice-Hall, 1968, p. 506.

Neale, Robert E. *Loneliness, Solitude, and Companionship*. Philadelphia: Westminster Press, 1984.

Nelson, James B. *Between Two Gardens: Reflections on Sexuality and Religious Experience*. New York: Pilgrim Press, 1983.

————. *Embodiment: An Approach to Sexuality and Christian Theology*. Minneapolis: Augsburg, 1978.

————. *The Intimate Connection: Male Sexuality and Masculine Spirituality*. Philadelphia: Westminster Press, 1988.

————. "Reuniting Sexuality and Spirituality." *The Christian Century*, February 25, 1987, pp. 187–90.

Newman, John Cardinal. *On Consulting the Faithful in Matters of Doctrine*. New York: Sheed & Ward, 1961.

Nicholson, John. *Men and Women: How Different Are They?* New York: Oxford University Press, 1984.

Nolan, Albert. *Jesus Before Christianity.* Maryknoll, N.Y.: Orbis Books, 1978.

Noonan, John. *Contraception.* Enlarged ed. Cambridge, Mass.: Harvard University Press, 1986.

Nouwen, Henri J. M. *Clowning in Rome.* Garden City, N.Y.: Image Books/Doubleday, 1979.

————, Donald McNeill, and Douglas Morrison. *Compassion.* Garden City, N.Y.: Image Books/Doubleday, 1982.

Nugent, Robert, ed. *A Challenge to Love: Gay and Lesbian Catholics in the Church.* New York: Crossroad Books, 1983.

Ohanneson, Joan. *And They Felt No Shame: Christians Reclaim Their Sexuality.* Minneapolis: Winston Press, 1983.

Osiek, Carolyn. "Relation of Charism to Rights and Duties in the New Testament Church." In *Official Ministry in a New Age,* edited by James Provost. Washington, D.C.: Canon Law Society of America, 1981, pp. 41–59.

Ozick, Cynthia. "Ruth." In *Congregation,* edited by David Rosenberg. New York: Harcourt Brace Jovanovich, 1987, pp. 361–82.

Payne, Dorothy. *Singleness.* Philadelphia: Westminster Press, 1983.

Perkins, Pheme. *Love Commands in the New Testament.* New York: Paulist Press, 1982.

Pierce, Carol, with Bill Page. *A Male/Female Continuum: Paths to Colleagueship.* Lanconia, N.H.: New Dynamics Publications, 1986.

Pope, Marvin. *Commentary on the Song of Songs.* Anchor Bible Series. Garden City, N.Y.: Doubleday, 1977.

Puls, Joan. *A Spirituality of Compassion.* Mystic, Conn.: Twenty-Third Publications, 1988.

Raymond, Janice G. *A Passion for Friends: Toward a Philosophy of Female Affection.* Boston: Beacon Press, 1986.

Renshaw, Domeena. "A Modern View of Ancient Taboos—Masturbation, Oral and Anal Sex." *Consultant,* September 1981, pp. 207–12.

Ripple, Paula. *Called to Be Friends.* Notre Dame, Ind.: Ave Maria Press, 1980.

————. *The Pain and the Possibility.* Notre Dame, Ind.: Ave Maria Press, 1982.

————. *Walking with Loneliness.* Notre Dame, Ind.: Ave Maria Press, 1982.

Rubin, Lillian. *Intimate Strangers: Men and Women Together.* New York: Harper & Row, 1983.

————. *Just Friends.* New York: Harper & Row, 1985.

Ruether, Rosemary Radford. *Sexism and God-Talk.* Boston: Beacon Press, 1983.

Russell, Letty M. *The Future of Partnership.* Philadelphia: Westminster Press, 1979.

————. *Growth in Partnership.* Philadelphia: Westminster Press, 1981.

Ryan, Thomas. *Fasting Rediscovered.* New York: Paulist Press, 1981.

Scanzoni, Letha Dawson. *Sexuality.* Philadelphia: Westminster Press, 1984.

Scarf, Maggie. *Intimate Partners: Patterns in Love and Marriage.* New York: Random House, 1987.

Schaef, Anne Wilson. *Co-Dependence: Misunderstood, Mistreated.* San Francisco: Harper & Row, 1986.

Schillebeeckx, Edward. *Ministry.* New York: Crossroad Books, 1981.

Schneider, Carl. *Shame, Exposure and Privacy.* Boston: Beacon Press, 1977.

Schneiders, Sandra. *New Wineskins.* New York: Paulist Press, 1986.

Shelton, Robert. *Loving Relationships.* Elgin, Ill.: Brethren Press, 1987.

Simmel, Georg. *The Sociology of Georg Simmel.* New York: Free Press, 1950.

Smedes, Lewis B. *Caring and Commitment.* San Francisco: Harper & Row, 1987.

Solomon, Robert. *The Passions.* Notre Dame, Ind.: Notre Dame Press, 1983.

Tavris, Carol, and Carole Wade. *The Longest War: Sex Differences in Perspective.* 2d ed. New York: Harcourt Brace Jovanovich, 1984.

Trible, Phyllis. "Depatriarchalizing in Biblical Interpretation." *Journal of the American Academy of Religion* 41 (1973): 30–48.

————. *God and the Rhetoric of Sexuality.* Philadelphia: Fortress Press, 1978.

Tyrrell, Bernard. *Christotherapy.* New York: Paulist Press, 1975.

Tyrrell, Thomas J. *Urgent Longings.* Whitinsville, Mass.: Affirmation Books, 1980.

Ulanov, Ann. *The Feminine in Jungian Psychology and in Christian Theology.* Evanston: Northwestern University Press, 1971.

Vacek, Edward. "A Christian Homosexuality?" *Commonweal,* December 5, 1980, pp. 681–84.

Vaillant, George. *Adaptation to Life.* Boston: Little, Brown, 1977.

Von Rad, Gerhard. *Genesis: A Commentary.* Philadelphia: Westminster Press, 1961.

Wakin, Edward, and Sean Cooney. *Beyond Loneliness: A Practical Christian Response.* Mystic, Conn.: Twenty-Third Publications, 1986.

Weeks, Jeffrey. *Sexuality and Its Discontents.* Boston: Routledge & Kegan Paul, 1985.

Wegscheider, Sharon. *Another Chance: Hope and Health for the Alcoholic Family.* Palo Alto, Calif.: Science and Behavior Books, 1981.

Weiss, Lawrence, and Marjorie Fiske Lowenthal. *Four Stages in Life.* San Francisco: Jossey-Bass, 1975.

Weiss, Robert. *Loneliness: The Experience of Emotional and Social Isolation.* Boston: MIT Press, 1973.

Wesley, Dick. *Morality and Its Beyond.* Mystic, Conn.: Twenty-Third Publications, 1984.

———. *A Theology of Presence: The Search for Meaning in the American Catholic Experience.* Mystic, Conn.: Twenty-Third Publications, 1988.

Whitehead, Evelyn Eaton, and James D. Whitehead. *Christian Life Patterns.* Garden City, N.Y.: Image Books/Doubleday, 1982.

———. *Community of Faith: Strategies for Developing Christian Communities.* San Francisco: Harper & Row, 1982.

———. *Marrying Well: Stages on the Journey of Christian Marriage.* Garden City, N.Y.: Image Books/Doubleday, 1984.

———. "Women and Men: Partnership in Ministry." Videotape with workbook. Chicago: National Federation of Priests' Councils, 1988.

Whitehead, James D. "The Practical Play of Theology." In *Formation and Reflection: The Promise of Practical Theology,* edited by Lewis

Mudge and James Poling. Philadelphia: Fortress Press, 1987, pp. 36–54.

————, and Evelyn Eaton Whitehead. *Seasons of Strength: New Visions of Adult Christian Maturing.* Garden City, N.Y.: Image Books/Doubleday, 1986.

Whitfield, Charles. *Alcoholism, Other Drug Problems, Other Attachments, and Spirituality.* Baltimore: The Resource Group, 1985.

Winnicott, D. W. *Playing and Reality.* New York: Basic Books, 1971.

Wood, John. *What Are You Afraid Of?* Englewood Cliffs, N.J.: Prentice-Hall, 1976.

Woods, Richard. *Another Kind of Love.* Rev. ed. Ft. Wayne, Ind.: Knoll, 1988.

Woodward, John C., with Janel Queen. *The Solitude of Loneliness.* Lexington, Mass.: Lexington Books, 1988.

Young, James J. *Divorcing, Believing, Belonging.* New York: Paulist Press, 1984.

Zanotti, Barbara, ed. *A Faith of One's Own.* Trumansburg, N.Y.: Crossing Press, 1986.

INDEX

EVELYN EATON WHITEHEAD is a developmental psychologist with a doctorate from the University of Chicago. She writes and lectures on questions of adult development and aging, leadership development, and collaboration in ministry.

JAMES D. WHITEHEAD is a pastoral theologian and historian of religion. He holds a doctorate from Harvard University, with a concentration in Chinese religions. His professional interests include issues of contemporary spirituality, pastoral leadership, and theological method in ministry.

The Whiteheads are authors of *Christian Life Patterns, Marrying Well, Seasons of Strength, Method in Ministry, Community of Faith,* and *The Emerging Laity.* Through Whitehead Associates, they have since 1978 served as consultants in education and ministry in the United States and elsewhere. They are members of the associate faculty of the Institute of Pastoral Studies at Loyola University in Chicago. They make their home in South Bend, Indiana.